(continued from front flap)

They offer new observations and raise questions that will be of interest to anyone interested in the study of law, government, administration, social structure, or American civilization.

About the Author

WILLIAM M. EVAN has degrees from the Universities of Pennsylvania and Nebraska and received a Ph.D. from Cornell University. He has taught sociology at Princeton University (1954-1956) and Columbia University (1956-1959). He has contributed articles to major journals in several fields and is coeditor (with Quincy Wright and Morton Deutsch) of *How to Prevent World War III*. Since 1959 he has been Research Sociologist at the Bell Telephone Laboratories.

Law

and Sociology

CONTRIBUTORS

Alfred W. Blumrosen
School of Law, Rutgers—The State University

Harry C. Bredemeier
Douglass College, Rutgers—The State University

Thomas A. Cowan
School of Law, Rutgers—The State University

William M. Evan
School of Industrial Management,
Massachusetts Institute of Technology

Talcott Parsons
Department of Social Relations,
Harvard University

David Riesman
Department of Social Relations,
Harvard University

Fred L. Strodtbeck
Department of Sociology, University of Chicago

Hans Zeisel
School of Law, University of Chicago

LAW AND
SOCIOLOGY

EXPLORATORY ESSAYS

Edited by *William M. Evan*

with a foreword by *LEHAN K. TUNKS*

The Free Press of Glencoe

TO THOMAS A. COWAN

Foreword

Some concept of ordering human affairs by means of law seems to have been a part of almost every society of which we have records. While law has always dealt with conflicts and imperatives over the widest scale of human affairs, those concerned with the administration of the law—the legal profession —in the English-speaking countries tended to regard it during the nineteenth and early twentieth centuries as a self-contained discipline whose rules, procedures, doctrines, and methods were to be applied to the other nonlegal "facts" of civilization. This tendency to consider law as a self-sufficient discipline has been breaking down in our century. Increasingly, law—particularly as it emerges from legislatures and administrative agencies and as it concerns the profession—involves specialized forms of knowledge hitherto not mastered by the law student, practitioner, or legal scholar. This knowledge is embraced increasingly within the concept of what it is that the profession is concerned with. It is not thought to be outside the ambit of the profession, nor is it considered a part of the nonlegal "facts" to which law as a self-sufficient discipline may be applied.

The growing demands on law to contribute to the preservation of world peace and to the alleviation of the growing pains of the world community of nations, perhaps more than any other development, make the adequacy of the frame of reference of the discipline a matter of public concern. For, unless law is viewed in a way to permit it optimum effectiveness in the task it has with respect to the social order, our society will be forgoing—at a time when effective tools are desperately needed—what has in the past proved to be an effective tool.

It was because of some awareness of the potential challenges in store for law and the legal profession that the Rutgers University Law School organized a seminar in 1956 to stimulate new and more successful thinking on ways of bridging the chasm between law and social science, with particular attention to sociology.

In this volume of essays are represented some groping but provocative efforts to accomplish this goal. Not all of the essays were in fact presented at the seminar, but all are closely linked in spirit to this endeavor. If this book stimulates renewed interdisciplinary interest in the legal and sociological fraternities, our conference will have more than fulfilled its expectations.

LEHAN K. TUNKS
Dean

School of Law
Rutgers—The State University
Newark, New Jersey
June, 1961

Acknowledgments

This book would never have come into being without the assistance of many persons and organizations. I wish first to thank Dean Lehan K. Tunks for his enthusiastic support of the proposal that the Rutgers Law School sponsor a seminar on "Sociology and the Law." A special debt of gratitude is due to Professor John W. Riley, Jr., then Chairman of the Department of Sociology of Rutgers University, for ably chairing this seminar. To the Rutgers University Research Council, thanks are also due for a grant that made it possible to organize this seminar.

Of inestimable value was the aid of the Russell Sage Foundation, which awarded a grant to Professor Alfred W. Blumrosen of the School of Law and to Professor Harry C. Bredemeier of the Department of Sociology, both of Rutgers University, for collaborative research in law and sociology. The interest and participation in the seminar of Dr. Donald Young, President of the Russell Sage Foundation, were invaluable.

I am especially grateful to Professor Alfred W. Blumrosen for his generous help in seeing the book through to publication. And last, but by no means least, is a personal debt of gratitude to Professor Thomas A. Cowan, of the Rutgers Law School, who not only conceived the idea for this seminar but also inspired me and others to explore the knotty and significant problems of the relation between law and sociology.

W. M. E.

CONTENTS

xi

Law

and Sociology

William M. Evan

Introduction

Some Approaches to the
Sociology of Law

For over a decade there has been a renewal of interest in the sociology of law, in Europe as well as in the United States.[1] Legal scholars and sociologists appear to be engaging to an increasing extent in some form of collaborative effort. The present collection of essays may be viewed as part of this trend.

In examining the contributions to this book the editor dis-

1. See, for example, Hans Zeisel, "Sociology of Law, 1945–55," in Hans L. Zetterberg, ed., *Sociology in the United States of America: A Trend Report* (Paris: UNESCO, 1956), pp. 56–59; *Annales de la Faculté de Droit et des Sciences politiques et économiques de Strasbourg, Methode sociologique et Droit* (Paris: Librairie Dalloz, 1958); Julius Cohen, Reginald A. H. Robson, and Alan Bates, *Parental Authority: The Community and the Law* (New Brunswick, N.J., Rutgers University Press, 1958); Philip Selznick, "The Sociology of Law," in Robert K. Merton, Leonard Broom, and Leonard S. Cottrell, Jr., eds., *Sociology Today: Problems and Prospects* (New York: Basic Books, Inc., 1959), pp. 115–127; Torstein Eckhoff, "Sociology of Law in Scandinavia," in Folke Schmidt, ed., *Scandinavian Studies in Law*, vol. IV (Stockholm: Almqvist and Wiksell, 1960), pp. 29–58.

cerned five distinct approaches to the sociology of law, which may be designated as role analysis, organizational analysis, normative analysis, institutional analysis, and methodological analysis.[2]

Role Analysis

A role-analysis approach to the sociology of law focuses on "legal statuses," that is, on the various types of personnel performing recurrent functions of legal systems. In literate societies these statuses include, among others, judges, lawyers, legislators, administrators, policemen, and jurors. It would seem that for the sociologist with relatively little knowledge of the technicalities of legal systems this approach to law is most hospitable. This is particularly true of sociologists interested in the sociology of occupations. With the exception of the juror, who performs a transitory function not involving an occupation in the legal system, all other statuses mentioned are a source of livelihood for the incumbents. Hence they lend themselves to the study of an array of sociological questions on recruitment, socialization, colleague relationships, codes of ethics, and so on. Nevertheless, relatively few sociological studies have thus far been conducted concerning the legal profession or any of the other legal statuses in the United States or in any other literate society.[3]

David Riesman's essay in this book is an illuminating example of the role-analysis approach. In recruitment, training, and type of colleague relationships the lawyer—at least in the

---

2. For further elaboration of these approaches to the sociology of law and related questions, see William M. Evan, *Sociology and the Field of Law*, forthcoming.

3. See, for example, Jerome E. Carlin, *Lawyers on Their Own* (New Brunswick, N.J.,: Rutgers University Press, 1962); Hubert J. O'Gorman, *Lawyers and Matrimonial Cases* (Columbia University: Doctoral Dissertation, 1961). Two noteworthy studies in progress are: Erwin O. Smigel, *The Wall Street Lawyer;* and Jerome E. Carlin, *The Metropolitan Law Office.*

United States—contrasts sharply with the sociologist. The adversary method of trial pervades the training process and the relationship between the law student and his professors. This encourages an independent and aggressive orientation on the part of the law student. In contrast, the training process of graduate students in sociology tends to generate a feeling of intellectual dependence and submissiveness. This is conducive to a different ethos in each field: intellectual confidence in law and intellectual diffidence in sociology.

Apart from implicitly suggesting problems for research on the socialization of law students, Riesman argues persuasively for a sociology-of-occupations approach to law. In fact, he contends that at the present stage of development of sociology this is virtually the only fruitful research strategy.

In the essay by Parsons the legal profession is viewed as a mechanism of social control. Charged with upholding a complex, ambiguous, and changing legal tradition, the legal profession is simultaneously subjected to pressures of conflicting parties and interest groups. The lawyer stands between "public authority and its norms and the private individual or group whose conduct or intentions may or may not be in accord with the law" (p. 66). The consequent strains in the lawyer's role, as in other roles, engender various types of deviant behavior such as expediency—principally in the form of succumbing to financial temptations, excessive legal "formalism," and "sentimental" exaggerations of the claims of clients. As in the case of the doctor vis-à-vis the patient in a psychotherapeutic relationship, so the lawyer in his relations with clients, Parsons points out, can encourage or discourage deviant behavior.

Still conspicuously lacking in the role-analysis approach to the sociology of law is an effort to relate an analysis of "legal statuses" to the normative and organizational components of legal institutions. In this respect Weber's analysis of the relationship between type of legal training and degree of codification in law still stands as a pioneering effort.[4]

---

4. Max Rheinstein, ed., *Max Weber on Law in Economy and Society* (Cambridge: Harvard University Press, 1954), pp. 198–223, 271 ff.

Organizational Analysis

That every legal system has recourse to some organizational structures in discharging its functions is quite evident. The nature of the organizational structures of courts, legislatures, administrative agencies, and enforcement agencies helps determine the kinds of legal norms that develop, the type of interpretation and enforcement of norms, and, in short, the impact of legal norms on people's behavior.

The organizational-analysis approach is illustrated in the essay by Evan on the legal structure of public and private organizations. Attention is drawn to analogous structures and functions in public and private legal systems, which, in turn, point to potential interrelationships among them and to their consequences for the growth and transformation of law.

The interplay between changes in legal doctrines and changes in organizational structure is analyzed by Blumrosen in an essay on labor law. As trade unions have grown more powerful in comparison with employers, their legal status has changed from that of a criminal conspiracy in the early nineteenth century to that of a legally equal party in collective bargaining relations in the twentieth century.

Blumrosen's analysis points to the impact of different organizational structures on labor law. The courts, in fashioning common law with respect to the employment relationship, were prone to restrict the right of workers to organize into trade unions; legislatures, on the other hand, more responsive to the pressures from labor, slowly moved in the direction of institutionalizing the right of union organization.

Strodtbeck's essay presents an argument for collaborative research on the jury. Drawing on three studies of the Chicago Jury Project,[5] Strodtbeck illustrates some of the problems of

---

5. See, for example, the following publications based on the jury study at the University of Chicago: Hans Zeisel, Harry Kalven, Jr., and Bernard Buchholz, *Delay in the Court* (Boston: Little, Brown and Co., 1959); Fred L. Strodtbeck, "Sex Role Differentiation in Jury Deliberations," *So-*

such research. If the jury is viewed as an organizational subunit of the structure of the court, these studies, and possibly others stemming from this Project, may be interpreted in terms of the impact of extraorganizational statuses and values on the behavior of individuals in such social structures.

Normative Analysis

A normative-analysis approach to the sociology of law may sound very familiar to the legal scholar, but what we designate as "normative analysis" must not be confused with the traditional "doctrinal" analysis of the legal scholar or with the philosophical sense of an assertion of a value judgment. This approach entails an analysis of legal norms in relation to their underlying values and to the social units or status groupings that are the objects of legal norms.[6] In sociological terms, two levels of analysis are involved: the analysis of some facet of the "culture" of a society and the analysis of some facet of the "social organization" of a society.

With the aid of this approach it would in principle appear possible to discover how legal norms are reinterpreted and transformed over time. Such an analysis requires, at the very least, an inquiry into (a) changes in the hierarchy of values in a society as reflected in the legal system and (b) changes in power and prestige of the social units or statuses affected by the legal norms. As these two types of changes occur, we would expect "legal personnel"—whether judges, legislators, or others—to reevaluate and restructure legal norms.

Blumrosen's essay on labor law is a highly instructive demonstration of the potentialities of normative analysis for the sociology of law. Throughout much of the history of labor law in the United States the value rationale of court decisions was

---

ciometry, vol. XIX (March, 1956), pp. 3–11; Fred L. Strodtbeck, Rita M. James, and Charles Hawkins, "Social Status in Jury Deliberations," *American Sociological Review,* vol. 22 (December, 1957), pp. 713–719.

6. Cf. William M. Evan, "Value Conflicts in the Law of Evidence," *American Behavioral Scientist,* vol. 4 (November, 1960), pp. 23–26.

in terms of individualism as expressed in the doctrine of freedom of contract. The competing values of equality and pluralism
occupied a position subordinate to that of individualism; hence
freedom of association was accorded less importance than freedom of contract. With the growth of trade unionism there has
been a gradual increase in the power and prestige of workers.
This change in status of workers vis-à-vis employers was regis-
tered in the legal system through the enactment of legislation
institutionalizing the right of workers to organize for collective
bargaining, thus elevating the values underlying freedom of
association above those underlying freedom of contract. As the
right to organize collectively is established, it, in turn, leads to
conflicts of interest between the trade union and its members,
on the one hand, and the trade union and the "public," on the
other. These conflicts, as discerned by judges, officials of
administrative agencies, and labor arbitrators, result in a subsequent delimitation of the rights of trade unions. Blumrosen's
analysis of the process whereby "rights" and "interests" come
into conflict has implications for empirical research and provides the raw materials for the development of theoretical
propositions about the nature of conflict in general and conflict in labor-management relations in particular.

Institutional Analysis

As an institution of society, law regulates social interaction,
thus minimizing overt and covert conflict. In order to perform
this function a legal system, according to Parsons, must solve
four problems: legitimation of rules, interpretation of rules,
application of sanctions, and determination of jurisdiction. How
it does so is largely a function of its relation to other institutions of society. The analysis of the manner in which a legal
system solves these problems, we suggest, may provide a fruitful basis for the comparative study of legal systems.

A crucial problem posed by this mode of analysis is the
relation between one institution and any other institution
within the social structure of a society. Law is a unique type

of institution in that its complex of norms and organizational structures cross-cuts all other institutions in a society. The degree to which the structure of law is a function of any one institution or combination of institutions, on the one hand, and an instrument of change in other institutions, on the other hand, is still inadequately understood.[7]

Bredemeier explores a facet of this problem of institutional interrelationships with the aid of Parsons' scheme of four functional processes in a social system: adaptation, goal attainment, pattern maintenance, and integration. He modifies Parsons' scheme in several respects, especially in identifying integrative processes with law. Defining the function of law as the "orderly resolution of conflicts," Bredemeier traces interchanges of "inputs" and "outputs" between the legal system—in particular the court system—and each of the other three systems, the adaptive or economic system, the goal-attainment or political system, and the pattern-maintenance or socialization system. Bredemeier's analysis of problems of institutional interrelationships with respect to law deserves much further attention from those interested in this field.

Methodological Analysis

A methodological approach to the sociology of law appears to be of particular interest to lawyers and legal scholars, some of whom believe that in the present state of sociology they can profit most from the research techniques used in that field, rather than from substantive analysis. This interest is reflected partly in the Chicago Jury Project, whose various techniques included survey analysis and experimentation.

In his essay Zeisel considers the potential usefulness of the "tool chest" of the sociologist for the study of law. Taking the logic of the laboratory experiment as a model for research

7. See, for example, Yehezkel Dror, "Law and Social Change," *Tulane Law Review*, vol. 33 (June, 1959), pp. 787–802; Adam Podgórecki, "Law and Social Engineering," *Human Organization*, 1962 (in press); William M. Evan, "Law as an Instrument of Social Change," *Estudios de Sociologia*, 1962 (in press).

design, he presents four studies from the Chicago Jury Project, each of which utilized experimental procedures, statistical analysis of documentary data, or survey analysis.

Strodtbeck's essay also emphasizes the advantages of using experimental procedures to simulate real-life processes of a judicial nature. A great deal more can be done to simulate in the laboratory various features of legal processes and legal structures.[8]

These two essays are methodological in that they concern the logic or technology of inquiry. Another and quite different meaning of methodology is the metalogic of inquiry. Cowan in his essay attempts to combine the two meanings of methodology. With respect to the first, he draws the sociologist's attention to the lawyer's art of cross-examination as a possible useful research technique. As to the metalogical meaning of methodology, Cowan questions the tacit assumption of scientific method of classifying rather than individuating phenomena. He doubts that this is an adequate logic for the handling of problems of decision-making in law, which he views as a "system for organizing and systematizing feeling-judgments" rather than truth-judgments. He thus suggests that the sociologist examine value decisions in the judicial process in light of the need for a "logic of the future" capable of individuating objects and not merely classifying them.

Future Research

Each of the five approaches discussed above, explicitly or implicitly articulated by the authors, holds promise for research. They do not by any means exhaust all those possible in a field whose boundaries have yet to be drawn. Underlying them are two dimensions of analysis: comparative and historical. Each of the five approaches may suggest research in either comparative

---

8. Cf. Morris Zelditch, Jr., and William M. Evan, "Simulated Bureaucracies: A Methodological Analysis," in Harold Guetzkow, ed., *Simulation in Social Science—Readings* (Englewood Cliffs, N.J.: Prentice-Hall, 1962), pp. 48–60.

or historical terms, or both. Nor should it be presumed from our discussion that all the approaches discussed are of equal potential significance for the development of the sociology of law. Although it is possible to argue *a priori* the relative advantages of a particular approach or strategy, only empirical research can establish which approach or approaches will "pay off" from either a theoretical or a practical point of view.

In our discussion of some alternative approaches to the sociology of law, we have deliberately eschewed a formal definition of the field; given the amorphous state of this research area such an effort would be premature. This should not preclude a consideration of the merits of the research approaches discussed above, nor the undertaking of research they suggest.

In this interdisciplinary field, as in any other, at least three basic questions remain to be answered:[9]

1. What empirical data being accumulated in law could be illuminated by sociological concepts, and vice versa?

2. What concepts and hypotheses developed in law open up new problems and stimulate research in sociology, and vice versa?

3. Can the two disciplines bring their respective theoretical frameworks to bear on the investigation of the same empirical problems?

With respect to the first question, the empirical data being accumulated in sociology are enormously varied. Some of them could probably be illuminated by concepts existing in law, provided those concepts were clearly delineated and possibly "codified" for research purposes. For example, some use has been made of the concept or doctrine of "due process of law" in analyzing interstatus relations in formal organizations.[10]

---

9. These questions are partly modeled after Komarovsky's cogent analysis of modes of potentially fruitful interdisciplinary cooperation. See Mirra Komarovsky, ed., *Common Frontiers of the Social Sciences* (New York: The Free Press, 1957), pp. 22–28.

10. See, for example, Philip Selznick, *op. cit.*, pp. 122–124; Howard M. Vollmer, *Employee Rights and the Employment Relationship* (Berkeley: University of California Press, 1960), pp. 85–140; and the following articles by William M. Evan: "Power, Bargaining and Law: A Preliminary Analysis of Labor Arbitration Cases," *Social Problems*, vol. 6 (Summer, 1959), pp. 4–15; "Organization Man and Due Process of Law," *American Sociological*

When we consider the question of the nature of the empirical data being accumulated in law, it becomes understandable why sociologists have made so little effort to utilize these data; the data accumulated in law, at least in literate societies, are very difficult to transform to the uses of social science. They consist largely of cases at the trial court and appellate levels, various records of legislative and administrative actions, and judicial and administrative statistics. Some of these materials pose many problems of transformation into some quantitative form, notwithstanding the availability of content analysis procedures.

The second question, whether the concepts and hypotheses of one field can stimulate research in the other, again points up the difficulties of interdisciplinary research. The sociologist's answer might be that such concepts as role-set, role conflict, institutionalization of norms, socialization, and formal organization may suggest questions about the legal system. But it is not at all clear what the legal scholar's answer would be. To the sociologist at least, one possibly fruitful answer appears to have been given some years ago by Hohfeld in his scheme of "jural correlatives."[11] Would the legal scholar say that such legal concepts as *stare decisis,* judicial review, or contributory and comparative negligence are useful in generating interdisciplinary research?

It appears that legal scholars would have to re-examine, possibly together with sociologists, the welter of concepts or categories in law to stimulate interest in interdisciplinary research. To a sociologist, as to any scientist, a concept is a means of coordinating some phenomenon with an element of a body of theory. The legal scholar, again possibly in collaboration with the sociologist, would have to select concepts of critical signifi-

Review, vol. 26 (August, 1961), pp. 540–547; "Conflict and the Emergence of Norms: The 'Springdale' Case," *Human Organization,* vol. 19 (Winter, 1960–1961), pp. 172–173; "Due Process of Law in Military and Industrial Organizations," *Administrative Science Quarterly* (September, 1962, in press).

11. Wesley N. Hohfeld, *Fundamental Legal Conceptions* (New Haven: Yale University Press, 1923), pp. 23–114. For an effort to use Hohfeld's categories, see E. Adamson Hoebel, *The Law of Primitive Man* (Cambridge, Mass.: Harvard University Press, 1954), pp. 46–63.

cance to a theory or theories of law that might fit in with concepts and propositions in sociological theory.

Concerning the third question, whether the theoretical frameworks of law and sociology can be brought to bear on the investigation of the same empirical problems, there are few studies that have achieved this form of interdisciplinary integration. There is no doubt, however, that some problems of interest to the practicing lawyer and legal scholar might also be of interest, though from a different standpoint, to the sociologist. A case in point is the problem of delay in the courts. This problem is of considerable practical interest to legal scholars; to sociologists it may be of interest as a special case of a general problem of organizational functioning or possibly as an indicator of the value system and social structure of a society.[12]

When the three questions discussed above are answered in such detail as to provide guideposts for research, we will have witnessed notable progress in this field.[13] If it is true, as Henry De Wolf Smyth says, that the great scientific discoveries of the present era have been in borderline fields,[14] then future explorations in the sociology of law, possibly along the lines suggested by the approaches discussed above, may prove to be rewarding.

---

12. Zeisel, Kalven, Buchholz, *op. cit.*; Maurice Rosenberg and Michael I. Soverin, "Delay and the Dynamics of Personal Injury Litigation," *Columbia Law Review,* vol. 59 (December, 1959), pp. 1116–1170; A. Leo Levin and Edward A. Wooley, *Dispatch and Delay: A Field Study of Judicial Administration in Pennsylvania* (Philadelphia: Institute of Legal Research, The Law School, University of Pennsylvania, 1961).

13. Although we have considered the problems of the sociology of law in terms of *interdisciplinary* research, it is possible that a *multidisciplinary* approach may prove necessary and most fruitful. Thus, instead of integrating law and sociology, it may be necessary to integrate law with, for example, sociology, anthropology, and history.

14. Henry De Wolf Smyth, "The Nature of Research," *University: A Princeton Magazine,* no. 6 (Fall, 1960), pp. 4–8.

David Riesman

Law and Sociology

Recruitment, Training,
and Colleagueship

The different patterns of recruitment into law and into sociology and the different experiences of students and practitioners in both milieus are critical factors bearing on the relation between the two fields.[1]

I cannot here delineate the immense variety of academic
climates but will confine my comparisons to the leading law
schools and graduate schools, respectively, and even within this
group to a small minority of "national" schools. Non-lawyer
readers should realize that the differences among law schools

Work on the problems discussed in this article has been facilitated by
a grant of the Carnegie Corporation for studies of higher education and
has also benefited from discussion at a Conference on Higher Education,
sponsored by Carnegie, at Princeton in April, 1957. See Earl J. McGrath,
ed., *The Carnegie Conference on Higher Education* (New York: Carnegie
Corporation, 1958), pp. 98–112.

1. Publication of my Rutgers lecture in the *Stanford Law Review*,
vol. 9 (1957), pp. 643–683, has garnered helpful criticisms, which I have
sought to take account of in this revised and expanded version.

are enormously wider than those among medical schools, or even, in all probability, those among graduate schools of arts and sciences. That is, the gap is huge that separates the few, mainly Ivy League, law schools, that funnel their best graduates into leading firms and government offices, and the poorer (often proprietary) night schools that upgrade immigrants' children into white-collar work (though it should be added that this may often involve "legwork" such as bill collecting or ambulance chasing). In between there are private law schools that aim to be national, though they draw on a largely local clientele (for example, University of Pennsylvania, University of Buffalo); and state university law schools, some of which (for example, Michigan) are more "national" in purpose and market than others that dominate their locale (for example, the University of Washington).

As legal education at the state university level improves and becomes more professional (with law professors increasingly taking graduate work in law at Harvard or Columbia), there is a pull towards "nationalization," which is also reflected in the upgrading of the law reviews. But the parochial pull in the other direction remains powerful, tied up as it is with the social mobility of disadvantaged groups, with the power of the local bar over bar examinations and admissions, and with the parochialism built into state decisions and courthouse folkways. A study by Carlin, *Lawyers on Their Own,* indicates that the overwhelming majority of practicing lawyers in Chicago are small entrepreneurs, practicing virtually on their own, and helping other small entrepreneurs (or small people who have trouble or a claim) through the interstices of the lower courts and lower bureaucracies, private and public; large affairs are concentrated in the hands of a relatively small group of lawyers, primarily the seven or eight per cent in the thirty-five largest firms that include fifteen or more lawyers, as well as a handful of lawyers practicing alone or in small firms or as house counsel in large corporations.[2] To repeat: I am not talking about the

2. See Jerome E. Carlin, *Lawyers on Their Own* (New Brunswick, N.J.: Rutgers University Press, 1962). Carlin's data also indicate the relatively modest origins of the great majority of these lawyers—frequently from immigrant families of limited education.

vast majority of lawyers nor the schools they attended (no doubt, a few of the nonprofessional lone practitioners went to leading law schools, but did not go on from there in the approved pathways). And even among the schools attended by the minority, there are still great differences: thus, Harvard, Yale, Chicago, and Columbia Law Schools all have somewhat different clienteles, markets, and forms of being "national." Of necessity, in generalizing about these schools and their products, I shall overgeneralize.

My concern here, however, is less with legal education as a whole than with the law schools as a possible place for sociological work, and with the law professors in such schools as possible colleagues in interdisciplinary teaching and research. Furthermore, I shall have very little to contribute in this paper to the sociological study of the legal corpus or of major legal institutions. Sociology in its present phase can grapple with a profession or occupation; and, with its anthropological and social-psychological allies, it can seek to embrace a whole culture (if not too big); it can study stratification—and the way this shows up in jury deliberations or in the social mobility of lawyers. But, so far as I can see, sociology is not now prepared to embrace the legal order within its own categories in terms sufficiently detailed and concrete to shed new illumination. There is not only a certain intellectual impenetrability about the law, reflecting and resulting from the achievements of generations of jurists; there is an even more important factual impenetrability resulting from the sheer overwhelming and opaque bulk of data that must be mastered to link the empirical with the interpretive or the ideal-typical. And in the law, and even in its manifold branches, there is nothing so lucid, so condensed, so truly theoretical, as classical price theory in economics. Law (or what Karl Llewellyn called "law-stuff") is everywhere in its impact; it is almost everywhere in such forms as judicialization and the use of precedent; and men trained in law (or at least graduates of law schools) can be found in many obviously significant social roles. No "pure theory of law" has won anything like universal assent, or even awareness, from students of law and jurisprudence; nor do we have an adequate

Sociologists have often operated with an image of lawyers as men concerned with sanctions, with the enforcement of rules. This all too uncomplicated definition must make the law-man restive. For, as already indicated, the law-trained person is likely to be found almost anywhere in the American social structure. Precisely because the commitment of going to law school and the socialization that ensues for those who do go is less thoroughgoing than medical education imposes, and because, moreover, no Flexner Report has limited the numbers who can get a legal education,[6] the law remains par excellence the career open to talent. Librarian of Congress, President of Chrysler, Secretary of State, and at less exalted levels insurance executive, realtor, publisher—almost any managerial, commercial, or nonspecialized intellectual job you can think of—are within the reach of the law-trained man.[7] It is arguable that this escalator that the law provides is at least as important as a function of legal training as the functions more frequently discussed; arguable that the criminal law, or the sanctioning, legitimation, and interpreting functions, which Talcott Parsons among others has discussed, have no greater impact on the social order than this function of keeping open the channels of mobility for the

---

work done at the bottom of the ladder—whether palpating a patient or trying a case—is somehow more real than the work entered, without apprenticeship, at the top of the ladder where the grass never grows. Involved, too, is American "thingmanship" and subtle anti-intellectualism. And this means that youngsters in a rapidly changing society enter callings such as the law under the spell of an obsolescing image of the work done in them. And, as the callings themselves pass the point of no return, the captives in them may tend to feel displaced.

6. There *was* such a report—the Redlich Report of 1914. But legal education has been an inexpensive moneymaker. Without laboratories, large classes can be managed, often brilliantly. And, as suggested at the outset, the law school world at large, with its support in the practicing and legislating bar, still clings to its night and proprietary schools and its often parochial standards of performance.

7. In principle, one could imagine more relevant training for each of these careers—just as Freud, in my opinion rightly, envisaged more relevant training than medicine for the practice of psychoanalysis. For historical reasons, law school has visibly, in this country as abroad, remained the royal road. (However, it is my impression and that of other observers that many young men are perhaps somewhat less eager than heretofore to travel on a royal road—and, as indicated in the following footnote, other roads are now providing competition.)

boy who can talk, who is not too narrowly self-defined—who is a kind of roving fullback of American society and can and does go anywhere.[8]

The Self-Confirming Myth
of Legal Education

Is there anything the law schools do to facilitate this, or is it a purely accidental connection? I have elsewhere described the so-called legal mind, as selected and turned out by the best national law schools, as the nonlegalistic mind: the mind that has learned skepticism of abstractions and yet at-homeness with them.[9] The atmosphere of such schools, moreover, may help narrow the range of curiosity for some of the more humanistically oriented, but, unlike what sometimes happens in graduate school to social scientists, law students do not become more stupid and more cowed than they were as undergraduates. Or perhaps I should qualify this, bearing in mind the loss of curiosity and breadth of perspective that one often finds as students "progress" from their first to their final years in law school, especially if they are gifted but neither make the law review nor get involved in legal aid work. I should say instead that law students may get more stupid in the sense of a constricted *Weltanschauung,* more ready prey to a fundamental complacency; but at the same time they are apt to gain in confidence and craftsmanship.

This is a somewhat different process from that at work in comparable graduate schools, at least in the social science de-

---

8. There are other competitive roads that, arguably, have a better chance in the future than law. There are the more technical roads, for example, economics or psychology, engineering or city planning, perhaps more adaptable intellectually in an age of automation; there are the still less technical roads, such as public relations.

9. See David Riesman, "Toward an Anthropological Science of Law and the Legal Profession," *American Journal of Sociology,* vol. 57, pp. 121–135 (1951), reprinted in *Individualism Reconsidered* (New York: The Free Press, 1954), pp. 440–466.

partments. Students in the latter emerge often less confident than they entered, less "promising." Just as they seldom get their doctoral degree within a regulation three or four years, but remain instead in an amorphous zone of delayed maturity; so they sometimes (unlike most law students) reach for an identity by incorporating a professor's definition of what they "are," while being subjected to his personal view of the "field" in grading, in thesis supervision, and orals.[10] In contrast, law students do not to the same extent find their identity as lawyers by "incorporating" their professors, who may or may not qualify as practitioners as well as teachers; and the system under which the law students operate is far more impersonal. People *do* get through law school in three years; there is very little of the protracted uncertainty of much graduate study, or of the umbilical clinging to one's teachers that failure to finish a thesis permits. This happens, in part, because law professors, whether full-time or part-time, are more worldly and better paid than most social scientists; they are intelligent, but rarely intellectual; student devotion is nice, but they have alternative ways of "spending" their affects, and relatively little need constantly to prove the validity of their profession or their specialty through the shining eyes of indoctrinated students. The validity of their profession is only marginally in question: its success is historically solid and daily attested in the market place of American careers. Although, to be sure, sensitive lawyers and law professors suffer because of some popular disesteem for lawyers (though Supreme Court justices stood at the very top, even above physicians and physicists, in the National Opinion Research Center poll of the relative standing of occupations), and because they realize that some of this disesteem is deserved, it

---

10. Of course, this puts in a bleak way an apprenticeship that can be, and sometimes is, a relationship in which there is learning and discipline on both sides. And it ignores the many schools where laxity and laissez faire are more serious problems than subjection and fanaticism. The position stated above is based both on personal observation and on the report of the committee of graduate deans (working under the auspices of the Fund for the Advancement of Education) chaired by M. E. Hobbs and including Jacques Barzun, Peter Elder, and A. R. Gordon. Cf., for example, Jacques Barzun, *Graduate Student Study at Columbia* (extracts from the Dean's Report) (New York: Columbia University Press, 1957).

seldom shakes their belief in the legal career as such, but rather
reinforces their belief in a variant model of it, such as the
Brandeis-at-the-bar model, or the small-town independent lawyer model, or that of the crusading government lawyer.

Intellectual craftsmanship in the law, moreover, is a fairly
visible and surprisingly unidimensional thing, so that law professors (with whatever unconscious injustices) can evaluate
each other's competence rather readily, as mathematicians are
said to be able to do, or organic chemists. Only an occasional
heretic who tries something new creates problems for this system of ranking—and, just as Picasso might for once draw like
Ingres to show he could do it, so such a legal scholar can often
take a turn at the conventional games to maintain his professional standing. One has to be "real gone" to be read out of
the fold, as Hohfeld was for some during his lifetime, and as
perhaps Myres McDougal of Yale is now for anti-Lasswellians.

These comforts, as compared with the much more polemical
situation in some branches of the social and humanistic sciences,
seem to me among the reasons that law professors, although
they, like all teachers, can be wounded by their students, often,
when they seek disciples, do so with twinkling eye and chastened
zeal. There is a readier dialectical give-and-take in most good
law schools than I have observed in graduate schools of arts
and sciences at the same or comparable universities: the law
student is encouraged, in part of course by forensic tradition,
to talk back to his professors, even in huge classes, with a verve
and lack of fear of what might happen to him that one seldom
finds in graduate school.[11]

If law is esoteric to the layman—without having to fight for
its mystique, as psychology and sociology sometimes feel they
must—it is not kept esoteric vis-à-vis the student who, after a
year, can become a law review editor, which involves sometimes editing his professors (even reviewing their casebooks, the
only "books" the professors are apt to "write") or taking issue
with them in student notes and comments on recent decisions.
There are some 150 law reviews, often subsidized by the school
as part of its public relations work or as due its image of itself,

---

11. The Harvard School of Business Administration encourages a similar
freedom, in large classes and small. Here, too, the case method reigns.

and of course often also guided by the faculty. But there is, so far as I know, nothing comparable to this development in the graduate schools, despite the frequently lesser professionalization of the latter (or perhaps because of this). Although several interesting ventures have appeared lately (for example, among sociology students at Berkeley and anthropology students at Chicago), graduate students do not run the social science (or humanities) periodicals and lack the confident impetus this involves. Law-review and other law students more than compensate for the lacunae of their teachers by educating each other. And although this happens also in graduate school, it is less firmly institutionalized.[12]

The appearance of objectivity in law-school grading—and recall again that I am speaking here of the leading national schools—is part of one of the most remarkable self-confirming prophecies in vocational choice and selection. A young man who does "well" at law school in terms of its frequently numerical grading system is (barring an aggressively unfortunate personality) ticketed for life as a first-class passenger on the escalator for talent. Nicholas Kelley, not a naive man, writes some revealing things on this score.

A man . . . who wishes to prepare himself for corporation law will get himself into the best law school that will take him and will exercise all his powers to graduate as high as he can. Studying law in a good law school is stimulating, interesting and competitive. The marks that a good law school in this country gives are almost an unfailingly accurate grading of analytical power of mind and power to express it. Coming well through this testing and selecting process marks a man as valuable and promising for a wide variety of work even though he does not stay in the law.[13]

12. Understandably, I find this contrast a source of sorrow. Whereas as a law teacher I was aware that my students "knew" ever so much better than I what the law was like, and hence rejected their faculty's innovations with Philistine abandon, as a sociology teacher I find students coming with little extra-academic sense of the field, and almost too ready to accept professorial models of life within it. However, I have the impression that contemporary law students are somewhat less Philistine and considerably less hostile to the social sciences than they were when I was a law teacher—part of a secular development in our educational system as a whole.

13. The *Harvard Crimson, A Guide to Career Opportunities* (1956), p. 78.

This is so thoroughly believed by victims as well as victors in the system that I have seen men of outstanding undergraduate attainment, Rhodes scholars and junior Phi Betes, let mediocre grades in law school convince them that they were mediocre men. In contrast, the law-review men went into the office of Kelley, Drye, Newhall and Maginnes and the other big corporate firms and had their chance to meet Chrysler Corporation executives, as Nicholas Kelley did, and thus to gain experience and connections that could later be used to prove that law school marks are infallible. Naturally, the confidence that comes of believing this—believing that one got one's start through ability and not looks or luck (confidence that in other versions has been part of the dynamism of the self-made man)—is purchased at the cost of others' being robbed of confidence.[14]

14. There is the more subtle cost for some of those who do well that they might have enjoyed doing something else even better; among their congeries of gifts, they prize what others prize and can seemingly measure. At the same time, since the law opens such a variety of doors, subsidiary or second-choice careers are available to many law-trained men who discover their hidden or suppressed talents after graduation.

A thoughtful law-review editor, Robert A. Anthony of Stanford, wrote me the following comments on these matters in a letter:

"As to law review experience, there is in my mind no doubting its worth as a training beyond classroom learning. On the other hand, there is no doubting the arbitrariness of judging men for after-life largely by the historical fact of their having done law review work (itself a reflection of first-year grades). Granting that law reviews are worth their cost, can the arbitrary status given by nonassociation with them be avoided? I don't see how. Even if there is money for a second-string intramural law review, as at NYU, the distinction will remain. The prestige of the first string is self-perpetuating. Is there any test to select law review men less arbitrarily than by first-year grades? Again, it's hard to see how. Any other method would probably involve a gamut of more open competition and politicking which would heighten the abrasiveness of law-school life and put a premium on hateful sorts of aggressive self-assertion. . . . Perhaps as a phenomenon over time, the status created by law review participation is shaking down a bit. Perhaps the profession has lived with non-law-review men long enough to appreciate the fact that some are as good as law review men. Surely there are plenty of solid non-law-review members of my class whose dignity and work quality has been maintained without a disruption of confidence. They are a good example for their less confident but equally endowed colleagues. Through the influence of such persons, both in law school and after, a dignity commensurate with ability should be attainable for the whole group of competent non-review men. The balance might quietly be redressed over time, without necessarily

Sociologists through the
Legal Looking Glass

This confidence, as I shall try to show shortly, presents certain threats to interdisciplinary work involving lawyers. But before turning to this, I want to round out my comments on mutually coercive images by indicating that the lawmen have similarly hampering images of the social scientist. For instance, not many law professors realize the variety of intellectual pursuits that go under the label "anthropologist": human biology, archaeology, "primitive" cultures, modern nations, industrial enterprises and other reaches of applied anthropology, linguistics, and so on. There may be a sense in which some of these men are not "real" anthropologists: maybe they have to be "kings" of an Indian tribe, "their" tribe, to so consider themselves. But "the" anthropologist concerned with contemporary legal institutions (rather than with African legal forms) is likely to have his tribeship well behind him, and not to fit neatly into the law professor's simplified definition.

So, too, with sociologists, a group which today comprises a rapidly changing configuration of concerns. Sociologists used to come into contact with lawyers primarily in a mutual pursuit of relatively powerless and underprivileged groups: immigrants, criminals, juvenile delinquents, the insane, the generally disorganized. This was when sociology had as its clients the fringes of society to which the more vested academic interests had not laid claim, the way economists lay claim to the economy, political scientists to the state, and historians to all these things when dead. Today, as my preceding remarks have illustrated, sociologists are apt to take lawyers themselves for "clients" in the sense of an interest in studying the profession, its training, and its day-

taking the form of an anti-intellectual revolt against the plutocracy of the law review elite. I suppose it all boils down to a matter of whether the non-review men can (as I think they can) pierce the transparency of the grading system enough to keep the quiet confidence that will best aid their success. . . ."

to-day life. Just as the anthropologists no longer stay put with
their preliterates, the sociologists no longer concentrate on il-
literates but lay claim to the highly literate and influential sectors
of society. They are no more willing to stay in place in a mobile
America than the lawyers are—though, unlike the lawyers, they
make only an intellectual's, but seldom a consultant's, livelihood
from other people's jurisdictional disputes.

Sociologists in a Legal Setting

In a law school or other legal environment sociologists and
their intellectual allies are, of course, newcomers, and they often
seek to behave in a way that will impress the lawyers. One can
observe analogous tendencies when social scientists work in a
medical environment and come up against psychiatrists and
others who have acquired prestige and authority from having
been tested in medical school (whatever may be the derogation
they feel at not being "real doctors," as indicated above).

An aspect of the famous jury-recording case at the University
of Chicago Law School furnishes an illustration. It is my impression that, in part, that situation arose because of some lawyers'
desire to show their "hardheaded" colleagues of the legal profession that a study of experimental small groups, not legally
called juries, was actually a study of juries. Lawyers and law
professors, in my observation, are very apt to be scornful of the
findings of social science. This is an offshoot of a professional
self-image of omnicompetence based in some degree on the
self-confirming tendencies mentioned above. It is also a reflection of the lawyer's wish to maintain a pattern of practice and
teaching in which he can play by ear.[15] Science threatens this—

15. I have wondered whether this pattern has any connection with the
English source of our law, for England is the country where the amateur
is still an influential model, and it is bad form to be too clever, too far-
sighted, too technical. While our graduate schools are built on the German
academic model, our law schools may reflect British values in somewhat
greater measure, at least in this respect.

I think many students of the common-law tradition would agree that
judicial amateurism is enshrined by the case-to-case workings of the

just as the coming of automation and the enormous demands for planning threaten the similar play-it-by-ear tendencies of old-fashioned business executives. Thus the lawyers were ready as professional skeptics to discount findings on juries—and the easiest way to do this was to say "they are not 'real' juries" (we are back again by another route at the intransigent "realism" of the lawyers' self-image). With some reluctance, the Chicago group was led into this trap of playing the other fellow's game.[16] But, on the whole, sociologists are not going to win by meeting the lawyer's presumed standards and momentarily impressing him. For the latter can always fall back on the clinching phrase —how often have I heard it used in interdisciplinary talk, "I don't know anything about it, but . . ."—a phrase that is always a preface to an ex cathedra opinion, as arrogant and impervious to "scientific method" as you please.

However inconvenient and irritating this arrogance may be —an arrogance akin to that of the man who has "met a payroll" —we should not forget its positive side, its value for the lawyer in opening many careers to him, as we have seen, and even for us in providing an occasionally useful corrective for inflated claims. But, speaking for myself, I must say that the atmosphere

---

common law; thus, it is well known that many judges resent (quite apart from content) the strait jacket that codes and legislation seek to impose on their wish to maintain an easy (or, invidiously, a "muddling through") fluidity in selecting which precedents in the armory of case-law to follow. The resistance most courts have displayed, until quite recently, to accepting sample surveys as evidence of public opinion (whether in libel cases, trademark cases, motions for change of venue, or other situations where an estimate of public opinion is relevant) would seem to me part of the same constellation of attitudes. (Some social scientists lay such matters to "lag"—a term that always seems to me the beginning of inquiry, not the end of wisdom; in any case, judges and lawyers in America have been fabulously inventive, for example, in the field of corporation finance, dragging the rest of society along.)

16. There may sometimes be unintended advantages to social science in doing this. Thus, Julius Cohen, Reginald Robson, and Alan Bates at the University of Nebraska Law School conducted interviews throughout the state on popular conceptions of justice in adoptions and like cases; they engaged their respondents in strikingly argumentative and dialectical interviews, rather than the usual nondirective sort—not because they were being at the moment experimental in interviewing technique but in order to meet anticipated objections from lawyers that all they had gotten were off-the-cuff and ill-considered opinions.

of a law school is too abrasive, too cocky, to make for an easy colleagueship on matters where the social scientist is apt to feel grave self-doubt—notably, at the frontiers of intellectual work. If one is jogging along an already laid-out track—as one can so readily do in many fields of psychology—it is one thing, but if one is exploring rather new areas, with all the misgivings to which pioneering intellectual work is prone, then to meet constantly the really quite amiable needling of the skeptical lawman may be tiresome. A certain amount of cultism, even occultism, I am suggesting, is an almost necessary part of new intellectual enterprise, and although, like any other morale-building efforts, this can go too far and become an end in itself, it is part of the protection that uncertain activity demands.

Correspondingly, it is up to the lawyer-critic to make some effort to understand the terms and categories of the newer social sciences, with due sympathy for these problems of protection of novelty; of course, once the novelty wears off, what was once faddist language is either abandoned or becomes part of staple intellectual discourse and hence no longer recognizably exotic (this is what has happened to many terms and concepts in law and economics). By the same token law professors can sometimes serve social science in the role of amateur yet serious and reasonably acculturated critics.[17]

Many law professors have little understanding of this because they can live their whole lives as apparently active but intellectually passive feeders on the pulp of advance sheets daily turned out by the West Publishing Company, coupled with the superb index system that the legal profession has developed for itself.[18] The law professor can, like a book reviewer, depend on

17. Willard Hurst of the University of Wisconsin Law School has made this point in correspondence. A good example is the careful examination by Walter J. Blum and Harry Kalven, Jr., of the University of Chicago Law School, of Samuel Stouffer's *Communism, Conformity, and Civil Liberties* (New York: Doubleday, 1955). They treat the Stouffer study as an exemplar of general methodological problems in public opinion research. Walter J. Blum and Harry Kalven, Jr., "The Art of Opinion Research: A Lawyer's Appraisal of an Emerging Science," 24 *University of Chicago Law Review* 1 (1956).

18. Professor Albert Ehrenzweig reminds me that the indexing system presents the legal profession with many unsolved problems that would

a steady supply, without the need many social scientists have to create their own data; he can say wherein this case is like that case, and not like some other case, and he, like his students, can take an endless delight in showing how the court "forgot" to take these and these things into account. Since judges (as the Blaustein and Porter book, *The American Lawyer*, shows) are less well educated than the average of the practicing and teaching bar, there is never any deficit of judicial limitations to be pointed out. This work of the law professor is so pleasant and so lacking in risk, and on the whole so well regarded if done in a craftsmanlike way, that it is a real sacrifice, a labor of love, for a law professor to get deeply involved in interdisciplinary ex-

---

profit from sociological inquiry; for the decision by an indexer as to what a case is "about" may bury or mislocate its implications, as in any unimaginative system of semantics or filing. As the flood of published case law continues, only sloppily mopped up by restatements, texts, and annotations, those who would make sense of the law may be overwhelmed by the keys, the labels, intended to keep track of the material. Of course, United States Supreme Court decisions don't get "lost" this way: the justices themselves, their law clerks, and the bar and professoriate who follow these decisions find them manageable in scope and amount. And in the past a few voracious or imperialistic masters sought to keep track of cases in a single area of private law, as Wigmore did for evidence and Williston for contracts. But as "the literature" expands to include many intermediate courts of appeal and even of first instance, such heroic efforts at subsumemanship no longer suffice. It would be interesting to know how law students, trained towards coherence through mastery of selected cases, cope on graduation with the semiliterate products of the benches in their home jurisdictions—perhaps "play it by ear" may be an outcome of this encounter also.

There are other perspectives, however, in which the torrent of advance sheets would appear to be advantageous for legal education, if not for legal practice. For example, the fact that new decisions constantly impend is a kind of reminder of mortality to theoreticians: their concepts are apt to be "good for this trip only," and elaborate effort at the restatement of the law, even by the willful and ingenious, has definite limits. Other intellectual enterprises have methods for postponing the reckoning with discomforting data (this sometimes gives them time to mature without being too much swayed by present trends and the hegemony of the hour), but a decision by a leading court can always surprise the law professor and hence teach him something. And the student can find in a new decision support for his earlier skepticism of his teachers' generalizations. Indeed, some of the often bracing intellectual climate of the best law schools is reflected in the fact that the law is not presented as something given, merely to be learned; too much discovery in other fields is presented to students as frozen metaphors and dead "results."

ploration, since this means relinquishment of that sanctuary.[19]

The law students, as a whole, feel even less free to take social science too seriously, for they are still seeking sanctuary. A teacher who reminds them too much of an undergraduate social science instructor may threaten the still unformed crust of vocationalism. Even those students who will, on graduation or thereafter, not practice law in anything like the forms taken for granted in law school may want to try on the mask, the identity, of the "real lawyer" before modifying or exchanging it. A social scientist who comes bearing techniques—for example, for selecting juries by a rough SES (socioeconomic status) index or for interviewing witnesses with greater psychological acumen—may be well received by a minority of students, but only if he doesn't try to interest them in fundamental theoretical or methodological matters. Thus, the sociologist teaching in a law school, like one teaching in an engineering school, will tend to be forced into the role of salesman for his stuff (though he may have at the same time a certain freedom from some of the professional pressures he would face in a graduate school). And his success will in some measure depend on the attitudes towards him of his law professor colleagues—attitudes that the students, for reasons just indicated, will quickly pick up and magnify.

In this situation, the readiest accommodation of the sociologist in a law school setting is probably in terms of an unequivocal policy orientation, a direct concern with the potential relevance of social science for solving problems as lawyers see and present them, as against a more academic concern with theoretical understanding of legal processes. At its lowest level, social science provides new gimmicks to be used in advocacy. I believe this to be the function of the "Brandeis brief," an allegedly impartial but actually polemical use of documentation (largely economic) to overwhelm or provide new rationalizations for judges.[20] At

---

19. And, as my former colleague Anselm Strauss has pointed out to me, teaching law is only one of many avenues for the law graduate: not only does it select to begin with a small, more or less scholarly minority, but it continues to do so as the other alternatives (for example, practice, government service, the judiciary) remain alive.

20. Professor Paul A. Freund of Harvard Law School has pointed out to me that the Brandeis brief was originally designed to show that an

a less forensic level, there is no doubt that a concern for policy often provides a common motivation for lawmen and social scientists. Yet the use of this concern as the principal lever for interdisciplinary projects frequently leads to the choice of a relatively unexamined standard policy topic from the law to be treated by a no less standard method from the social sciences. As Dean Edward H. Levi of the University of Chicago Law School has observed, this puts the social scientist in the role of an intellectual subcontractor, limits the extent to which he can influence law professors' thinking about what topics they might study and what categories they might discover, and hence minimizes his impact on legal education and the atmosphere in which law students develop. Although much useful work gets done this way, it is my belief that the most demanding and most potentially fruitful work requires a joint decision both on topic and method: a redefinition of the "problem" as presented by the lawyer and of the "method" as owned by the social scientist.

This is perhaps not so hard as it seems because, underlying the genuine concern for policy, there is a mutual but usually unavowed curiosity—an interest in knowledge for its own sake. The sociologists who came before the Rutgers Seminar on Law and Sociology in general assumed that the law professors are *that* interested in the traditional problems of the law: in the problems of social control, or of better legal aid, or of more humane or sensible treatment of insanity, and so on. The law professors tended to accept such ascriptions of motive, partly out of politeness, partly because the stated motives are part of the configuration, partly because, for reasons already indicated, well-understood and hence "realistic" motives seem truer than less palpable ones. Actually, I doubt whether most of the law professors at a seminar like this one would stay around if they were not intrigued intellectually—if they were not eager to see what kinds of birds sociologists are!

Let me recur to the medical field for an illustration. When

impressive body of opinion could be mustered to support the judgment of a legislature against constitutional attack; its aim was to resist the "play-it-by-ear" tendency of cavalier judges, but not to set itself up as a scientific arbiter beyond that.

medical authorities turn to sociologists and anthropologists, it is surely in part because they want to run a more effective hospital or group health plan, or to bring better medical care to urban immigrants from the Southern hills or Puerto Rican villages. But, having talked to a few of the doctors who have been leaders in extending invitations to social scientists, I am inclined to think that the joint concern for welfare is not the whole story on either side. The doctors come as one alternative to getting psychoanalyzed, or taking a trip to Europe or Japan: they are interested, and they want to see what we have to say. And I know that some of the sociologists go because they are curious about doctors: curious, and even sometimes quite hostile to the forms medical arrogance takes (we are all arrogant in our different ways, much as nations are), and envious of the glamour and prestige of the medical profession with its unbeatable combination of service, individualism, guild feeling, and science. These transactions tend to be covered over, just as in the case of the law, by talk exclusively of "problem-solving," "policy-orientation," or "basic research." I think we could be more creative in our meetings, and could more readily begin to invent topics and methods in the grooves of neither field, if we felt freer to recognize our fuller panoply of motives.

Sociologists, of course, have motives, too; for some of us an aggressive lack of interest in policy problems occurred during our socialization in graduate school, since our teachers grew up in the generation when sociology was striving to become "scientific," to free itself from association with socialism, social work, and other good causes. Many have observed how the sons of ministers substituted Science for God, the search for truth for the search for salvation or reform.[21] Thus, when a law professor

---

21. For fuller discussion, cf. my paper, "Some Observations on Social Science Research," *Antioch Review*, vol. 11 (1951), pp. 259–278; reprinted in *Individualism Reconsidered*, pp. 467–483.

An unpublished study, "Occupational Commitment of Graduate Sociology Students," done by Charles R. Wright of the Bureau of Applied Social Research, indicates that many students retained their personal definitions of the field, in terms of broad and philosophical concerns, in the face of a contrary emphasis on methodology insisted upon by the graduate faculty

comes to a sociologist because he is worried about the unequal
distribution of justice, and regards legal aid work as a drop in
the bucket, the latter's preoccupation with methodology and
lack of reformist concern may surprise him and send him back
to his own devices.

Differences in Legal and Sociological Styles

We may put this in terms of the different forms worldliness
takes among sociologists and among law professors. The more
sophisticated the former are, the more likely they are to be
scornful of "do-good" activities (as professionals, if not as citizens). Yet, precisely in part because they eschew such activities,
they often remain sheltered academicians in comparison with
even the full-time law professors who bring the swish of practice, of affairs, into the atmosphere of a law school.[22] In a medical
school, the arts of practice are carried in with the bodies of
patients, emphasizing the split between the research-minded
and science-minded temper of the professors in the preclinical
years, and the practical and often business-getting arts emphasized by the Cadillacs if not the comments of the part-time
men in the later clinical years. In the leading law schools, where
only the Legal Aid Society, less prestigeful than the law review,
has clients, and where the best students prefer to serve as clerks
to judges when they graduate and thus continue for another
year or so a law-review kind of existence, this split exists more
within individual faculty members than between the men who

(and encouraged, I might add, by available job opportunities). Wright
speculates as to why professionalization does not always take, and notes
that many who resist it drift off into other fields without taking their
degrees.

22. To be sure, to some of the even more sheltered humanists on the
faculty of arts and sciences, sociologists may appear to be extremely worldly
men, a cliché's throw from Madison Avenue or the CIA or immersion in
factory life or popular culture.

teach in different years or even different courses. Recall that I
am speaking of the major national schools, whose students en-
visage themselves, in the model case, as entering a large firm
and hence a setting where their first "clients" are fellow lawyers
rather than customers picked up off the street—a setting, that is,
where they can remain somewhat impersonal and objective and
not have to bend all efforts towards getting and retaining individual lay clients.[23]

The aroma of practical affairs is imported into such schools
partly by men who have had bursts of practice, especially in
the government, and partly by a sort of inside-dopesterism characteristic of the major law schools in which the factions of the
Supreme Court (or, sometimes in addition, the United States
Courts of Appeals) are refracted among the faculty who have
been law clerks to judges or who know them personally or at
least share a common culture. (It is this, *inter alia,* that makes
the teaching of constitutional law in a law school so different
from its characteristic teaching by political scientists, who are
apt to take doctrine more seriously.) Moreover, a law school
faculty is constantly engaged in consulting, so that, for example,
Karl Llewellyn, one of the law teachers who was an eminent
intellectual and not only a very intelligent man, led another
existence as a Commissioner on Uniform State Laws, meeting
with bankers and manufacturers in efforts to unify commercial
codes. Likewise, Herbert Wechsler, another intellectual, has
been active on many consultative fronts, as in aiding the Depart-

---

23. The briefs written in these firms are, like the anonymous law review note, usually colleaguial enterprises; their audience (and that of many
documents, such as SEC registration statements) is primarily a legally
trained official; moreover, the ties of large corporations to their law firms
do not suffer from instability comparable to that of advertising agency accounts, allowing the law firm to maintain a certain professional dignity in
its relation to corporate clients (and, on occasion, to exploit them).

In contrast, the small-time lawyer practicing on his own often must aim
to impress his client rather than his adversary; and, like the doctor in general practice, he may worry about his desk-side manner and his ability to
deliver the goods quickly and visibly. The student who expects to become
such a lawyer may find his professors often much too "impractical" and
"highfalutin'," and he may worry more about how to pass the bar examination (a routine left to cram schools by the leading university law schools)
than about not knowing enough law when out in practice.

ment of Justice in drafting rules of criminal procedure and as Reporter of the Model Penal Code. Thus, even the more theoretically oriented among a law faculty are seldom theorists pure and simple.

The aroma of practice, moreover, is strengthened by the programmatic success of the movement of "legal realism" over the last generation. Realism in the law, like naturalism in the novel or behaviorism in psychology, is a convention, an artifice like any other theoretical approach; it highlights certain features of the legal process and underplays others. It leads in the classroom to an insistent emphasis on "what did the court really do?"—to an emphasis on the factual substratum rather than on the metaphysical "superstructure." (It is thus adaptable to American home-grown pragmatic Marxism or to Freudianism or to any other reductionist theory.) In the main, this movement has purged law schools of much that was dogmatic, legalistic in the pejorative sense, and ritualistic. But the victory—now taken for granted among the younger men and hence scarcely to be called a movement any more—has done nothing to repair the divorce between the law school and the other graduate schools. Since the better law schools (and this is to their credit) do not enforce a prelegal undergraduate curriculum (though a good many prelaw students do major in political science or economics), and since most law school courses emphasize casework and an ideology of empiricism, one can graduate from law school without having ever read any major abstract or theoretical works in the social sciences—neither Plato nor Max Weber nor Durkheim nor Marx.[24]

In comparison with a law school, a medical school is a far more complex enterprise: it treats patients; it aims at serious research; some of its teachers are scientists with Ph.D.'s, for instance, in physiology. Although occasional law professors draft bills or codes, law school is primarily oriented to teaching and

---

24. Conversely, the enthusiasm with which some first-year law students take to their studies is frequently the result of a reaction against "impracticality" and seeming lack of relevance or concreteness in their undergraduate courses: the case-method attracts them by its plunge into a filtered documentary detail, and by its characteristic insistence (muted through growing epistemological sophistication) that it is factual and untheoretical.

to conserving and ordering the corpus of the law; ordinarily, what is called legal research is similar to the critical work done in some of the humanities: a tracing of influences, an appreciation of (judicial) styles, a critique of (judicial or legislative) work, or an anthologizing of cases (casebooks, however, are becoming more complex, garlanded as the cases are with references to materials that are increasingly drawn from outside the case-law). In fact, some of the relatively casual quality of law schools, on the faculty side, in contrast to the greater intellectual tension in comparable graduate schools, may be due to the fact that research and "productivity" do not have the same primacy. Men can become professors in major law schools without any publications (other than their student work on the law review); and they can lead a life as capable teachers and consultants (for example, as arbitrators) with very little writing, none of it "research," or at any rate none of it regarded as a contribution to cumulative scientific endeavor. There is seldom anyone around a law school (unless it be a social scientist on a temporary project) who brings another model of the scholarly career than this —anyone with a degree other than an LL.B.[25] Legal history, where it is taught as a separate subject and not as part of every subject, is almost invariably taught by law-trained men—who, with the lawyer's gift of omnicompetence I have discussed earlier, may have in fact become excellent historiographers but rarely have much contact with the members of the history faculty in the graduate school.[26] The principal beachhead of science that

25. There are some law librarians who have been trained in librarianship but lack a law degree; however, given the culture of law schools as I have described it, plus the complex filing and indexing tasks of the law, it is not surprising that most librarians in large schools do have an LL.B. Good M.D.'s are scarce and need to be conserved for major medical tasks; good LL.B.'s are more plentiful, hence available for paralegal work.

26. Mark Howe teaching law to Harvard undergraduates is a hopeful exception. Harold Berman also teaches law to Harvard undergraduates— and to social scientists as well. And Willard Hurst at the University of Wisconsin Law School has long made common cause with social scientists. But, so far as I can discover, these devoted men have few successors among the younger generations of law professors.

Since presenting this paper at Rutgers I have had the opportunity to examine Harold J. Berman's *On the Teaching of Law in the Liberal Arts Curriculum* (Brooklyn: Foundation Press, 1956), a report of a conference

may be considered an established exception is the presence of economists at the Chicago Law School and formerly at Yale. Economics, in its law school versions, is a "hard" science, no less proud of its achievements than the law itself, and many of its disciples are far more rationalistic than most well-trained lawyers. Moreover, as implied earlier, economics possesses a resounding theoretical structure as inhospitable to most inter-disciplinary work with "softer" and "newer" social sciences as the law has hitherto been. Some varieties of economics have proved practically useful in tax and especially in antitrust work.

It seems to me that it is, in part, just because full-time law professors have one foot in academia and because a few law schools have, with economics and occasionally government or planning, one foot in the social sciences, that further steps are so difficult. Many industrialists today, not to speak of mer-chandisers and advertising men, are far more committed to ap-plied social research than most law schools are, whereas the law schools, in Lasswell's phrase, have restricted social science by partial incorporation. "I don't know anything about it, but. . . ." This really means, "I do know a little."

I have indicated how hard it is to interest law students in knowledge for its own sake, and that this intellectual allergy exists even among those many law students at the better schools who were humanistically inclined as undergraduates, for these often feel "we're in the army now," and hence are threatened by reminders of not wholly rejected concerns and curiosities. More-over, since many law professors teaching first-year courses make it their business to root out ethical and other un-Holmesian ap-proaches to law, the not-yet-solidified vocationalism of these students is given powerful faculty support.[27] Hence, the "show-me" attitude of much of the law faculty toward the newer social sciences is as nothing in comparison with the drive in the stu-

---

at Harvard Law School; this volume develops many of the problems of law as a humanistic subject that are implicit in the foregoing.

27. In fact, as with most narrow vocationalism, the sacrifices made on behalf of future practice are largely unnecessary, since the changing society with its changing career patterns makes much that is learned (including the seeming toughness of first-year attitudes) obsolete in the later lives of many graduates.

dents to initiate themselves as completely as possible, burying self-doubts and alternative hankerings, in an unequivocally legal atmosphere. Conceivably, this drive is enhanced, as compared with earlier student generations, by the relative evaporation of political commitment[28] and by the momentum of the desire of the young to anticipate the future by early marriage, early career choice, early settling down.

In the past ten years I have had a number of sociology students come to consult me about their decision to go to law school. Since I made the opposite switch, they are worried lest it turn out that I discovered something unwholesome about the law that they ought take into account. (I have told many of them, I might note, that if they will but keep their sociological eye, they can help cultivate the borderland between law and social science, since men with double training will increasingly be given opportunities in interdisciplinary seminars!) Almost invariably, in discussing their reasons for changing, these students have said that sociology is somehow not "real," whereas law unquestionably is. Sociology is a goal or an attitude in the minds of men; law exists *out there*. In my opinion, they exaggerate the difference. Men worried lest what they are doing not be real are not inevitably going to find a less ambiguous identity in the law. But it remains true, I think, that the atmosphere of a law school, especially among the students, is far more monolithic in its belief in the reality of its activities than is the atmosphere of a sociology department, where competing definitions of what sociology "is," combined with the fact that parents and laymen generally have not the vaguest idea what it is, often gives chronic disquietude to the better students, for whom total immersion in such subfields as criminology or demography is not a complete answer.

The "play-it-by-ear" approach of the lawman is part of the lawyer's relentless and in some ways admirable individualism, which is all the more striking because, in practicing law, he must

---

28. I do not refer here, of course, to the law students who are going to enter politics as part of their career plan, for example, by running for district attorney or joining the Young Republicans, for this is not the kind of more idealistic political commitment relevant to an interest in the social sciences.

so often counter the willful individualism of his clients. In spite of what I have said earlier about colleaguial work on briefs and memoranda, even a huge "law factory" has a more individualistic air than most corporate bureaucracies do—or, indeed, than most large hospitals do. The very universalism of the emphasis on grades, on performance, that one finds in law school tends to carry over into the big offices, at least in the junior ranks that are not responsible for getting or retaining business. Likewise, though a pair of law professors may coauthor an article or put together a casebook, a law school resists intellectual teamwork much as do men in the humanities, and sociologists are sometimes looked down upon for their presumed addiction to it. Moreover, the law professor, seeking to maintain the interest of large classes in an active dialectic, tends to cultivate his gifts as a showman—hence, as an individualist—rather more than do most teachers in the other graduate schools.

This Tocquevillian sort of individualism has been self-renewing in America, where its wastes and hazards, its egocentricities and eccentricities, appear to be justified by immense natural resources and where the mercantilist past has long been buried under the ideology of free enterprise. Moreover, the lawyer's individualism bears a paradoxical relation to the common-law tradition: that tradition seems in many ways irrational, out of tune with modern times and the scientific temper, yet it protects the lawyer's effort to maintain objectivity and distance from contending factions in public and private affairs; it gives him a foundation from which to move towards empiricism and objectivity. Working in a case-by-case, ad hoc fashion, the lawyer gains the ability (often warped, to be sure, in cases involving labor unions, real or alleged Communists, and so on) to resist the claims of fashion and fanaticism. The lawyer, much like the engineer or the businessman, prides himself on his directness and rationality; he tends to resist what he regards as the message of determinism—whether in his own buried psyche or in the society—in much work of the social scientist, and he also regards this work as oblique and indirect, not getting to the point. The lawyer does not regard society as the product of vast, impersonal, though conceivably comprehensible, forces; the universalism referred to above is more an insistence on equality and performance than an explicit ideology.

And, as already indicated, the lawyer is simply not impressed by the claims of the social scientist, any more than he is impressed by the plausible client's tale that may turn out not to be true; this skepticism is indeed an aspect of his individualism. (In this connection, who will deny that behavioral science, as a new, booming field, "made in America," has attracted many vulgar boosters, defensively boastful in the face of attack from the threatened, the snobbish, and the skeptical?)

Moreover, the lawyer's "play-it-by-ear" tendency supports the wish most of us have, as adults, that we will not have to learn anything really new. I recall talking to a thoughtful practitioner who wanted to know what I thought of the new journal, *Behavioral Science,* and the work of such model-builders as Herbert Simon, Jacob Marschak, and Anatol Rapoport. He really wanted to be told that I thought it was all the bunk, that it was not the wave of the future, and that he did not "have" to pay attention to it.[29] The eagerness of quite a few law professors to convince themselves that sociologists have nothing to say, that their vaunted methods are the imposing cover over the unimpressive hunches, occasionally has similar sources.[30] Naturally, the intramural arguments among sociologists can then be used, if caught wind of, to dismiss the whole affair.

One source of these arguments could, I think, be somewhat assuaged by training sociology students in the art of easy movement from one metaphorical or semantic scheme to another. I have, for instance, seen sociologists operating in a medical school who would insist on using a Parsonian frame of reference, or just as vehemently a non-Parsonian frame, clinging, with a defiance that would be admirable in a better cause, to the inessentials as well as the real contributions of the scheme. I think that, for the foreseeable future, sociologists need to learn to be

---

29. Cf., for comments on judicial resistance to medical experts, Hans Zeisel, "The New York Expert Testimony Project: Some Reflections on Legal Experiments," 8 *Stanford Law Review* 730 (1956).

30. I do not mean to suggest here that the sources of an idea are relevant one way or the other for determining the soundness of an idea. It may well be that the law professors are right.

friendly mediators among metaphors, never doubting that metaphors matter, but doubting whether they matter as much as the master's disciples aver. Yet, once we recognize that metaphorical schemes serve many social scientists as a magical penumbra, guarding against uncertainty (as in Malinowski's theory of magic), we cannot be too hopeful of fostering among students a more detached attitude toward such schemes and a greater willingness to move with linguistic ease and flexible freedom among them. Furthermore, we must also recognize that a certain amount of terminological solipsism has accompanied some of the most truly innovative work, as in psychoanalysis, as well as some of the unfruitful work. Such solipsism may serve to protect tentative gropings from too ready incorporation into the main body of accepted views, and psychoanalysis is an example of a movement that needed in its early stages to be protected from the overwhelming leveling power of common sense. Indeed, common sense, as we have already seen, frequently characterizes the law professor's impermeable defense against sociological or psychological experimentalism.

Some readers may wonder why I have talked about the opacity or rigidity of some sociological systems and not about the Anglo-American folderol of legalism that so many great writers have satirized. One personal reason may be that I have never found legal jargon as forbidding as it sounds. With a legal dictionary and some guidance on procedural points, any literate person can read Supreme Court opinions, and many do so; and legal documents, with their attempt to foresee a variety of contingencies (for example, all possible orders of deaths in a family or partnership), seem to me easier to follow than many mathematical or philosophical arguments. But a more important reason for not emphasizing the impenetrability of legal discourse is that generations of law reformers since Bentham have done a great deal to put the law and its forms into basic English; moreover, the better law schools on which I have been concentrating in these remarks have been fighting ritualism and semantic silliness with marked success. The briefs produced in the major Wall Street and government law offices are models of clarity, marching with military precision to the points made,

and using citations of previous authority with the finesse of a
mutually understood shorthand, rather than as uninterpreted
obfuscation. No wonder many judges crib from these briefs in
"writing" their opinions. Indeed, the sense for style and elegance
of form common among the best practitioners and professors is
understandable in a generation nurtured on the opinions of
Holmes, Cardozo, and Learned Hand, and taught to admire the
simplicity and lack of pretense of some of the great state court
judges of the last century. The best law reviews are schools for
condensed yet comprehensible writing far more than are the
learned periodicals in other fields.

Correspondingly, once the law professor makes up his mind
to it, he will have little more difficulty in understanding work
in the less mathematical parts of social science than in other
feats of "translation" that may come his professional way—as
when he must master accountancy to grapple with tax problems,
or technical matters in connection with patent law, or theories
of oligopoly in antitrust law. A lawyer is, after all, supposed to
be able to understand the problems of any client and to "talk
his language." If he is prepared to give the time, his confidence
will go a long way to level obstacles. Furthermore, he has little
in terms of status at stake to block his learning in these areas,
for his legal colleagues (as I found in my own case), not being
in the main intellectuals, have less pride of system than intellectuals often possess, and the individualism of law schools means
that a law professor who meets his classroom obligations can
undertake almost any scholarly enterprise and count on a kindly
if not always comprehending audience. True, a law professor
who uses sociological jargon will meet with kidding, just as the
sociologist himself will, and, if he forces his views, he will encounter resistances of the sort I have sought to portray. But the
kidding will be unmalicious and he will have nothing to lose
but his diet of advance sheets. Thus, I believe that generally the
barriers of terminological nationalism are greater within the
social sciences than between them and the fraternity of law
professors.

Interpersonal or Interdisciplinary?

I was asked at Rutgers, as again during the Harvard Social Science Research Council Seminar on Law and Social Relations, for suggestions as to topics that lawyers and sociologists might jointly pursue. I felt able to say more about how not to choose a topic than about such choice in the abstract, for I insisted that people worked best at what interested them, and that one had to be flexible in interdisciplinary work in using the talents and interests the local setting provided. I added that I was unsympathetic to command performances based on some map of the gaps in social science integration or some judgment of a constituency as to what was important, for I had faith that if scholars are not entirely alienated from their culture, and not wholly constrained away from a vivid curiosity by their disciplines, they will be interested in what is important, and what is important will be interesting to them.

I think I can recognize some of the limitations of this position, as of theories of progressive education generally. Interest often follows rather than precedes effort, and sociologists, too, have their forms of playing by ear: as Professor Fred L. Strodtbeck has pointed out to me, our guild may prefer to pursue familiar problems of motivation and socialization rather than less familiar problems of structure and substance. And when I examine the work done by scholars in universities in comparison with applied work done in answer to some client's need, I cannot argue that the track of the discipline produces in general more seminal research than the quest of an answer to an extra-academic problem. Only a very rare person will be an intellectual self-starter.[31] And even he needs to start somewhere (just as

31. Some problems probably cannot be studied at all without a client's invitation. But in the law, issues of entrée would seem to be surmountable by careful planning, in part because for a variety of reasons lawyers are far less self-protective as a guild than, for instance, doctors are. Professor Erwin O. Smigel of the Department of Sociology of New York University has found that even busy Wall Street lawyers will respond to long and

Freud started with patients who raised questions no one had
been able to answer); a client's question can often be that
"somewhere." Nevertheless, I think that really significant work
must build its own track, one marginal both to the genres of the
sociology of the professions and to the stock of problems the
legal profession will bring to a seminar.

In my own talk at the Rutgers seminar I drew on studies that
some participants undoubtedly thought frivolous. One study, by
a graduate student in human development, dealt with law students' luncheon conversation and its object was to ascertain
how the group socializes its members in the legal culture in
their leisure time. (What he actually found, with one such group,
is that they scarcely ever talked "law," but rather what I might
term "office gossip," that is, the personalities and idiosyncracies
of the faculty, the students, and judges and other legal lumi-
naries; also about TV personalities and other handy human
fodder.)[32] I also mentioned Dan Lortie's study of practicing
lawyers five years out of law school, in terms of their career
alternatives, their judgment on their education, and the relation
of their experiences to their earlier ideals of the life of the law.
And I drew on published material, such as the Blaustein and
Porter volume,[33] to shed light on the factors leading students

---

searching interviews (indeed they would *only* respond to searching interviews that gave them an opportunity to confide in an understanding and
disinterested outsider). Likewise, Dan C. Lortie and Jerome Carlin have
been able to go over records and life histories with lawyers in Chicago. [See
Dan C. Lortie, *The Striving Young Lawyer: A Study of Early Career Differentiation in the Chicago Bar* (Unpublished Doctoral Dissertation, Department of Sociology, University of Chicago, 1958).] Courtrooms and
cases, of course, are open to all. Members of the Jury Project at the University of Chicago Law School have found it possible to talk to judges as
to how they would decide cases, and to trial lawyers about their tactics.
Sociologists have not been around lawyers enough to wear out their wel-
come.

32. Cf. Kenneth Feigenbaum, *The Limited Hour: Situational Study of
Sociable Interaction* (Unpublished Master's Thesis, Committee on Human
Development, University of Chicago, 1958).

33. Albert P. Blaustein and Charles O. Porter, *The American Lawyer*
(Chicago: University of Chicago Press, 1954), pp. 187–188. They indicate that 12 per cent of law students decide on law before age fifteen, and
13 per cent after twenty-five. Thirty per cent of them have lawyer relatives, and 45 per cent have some interest in future political activity when

to select law as a career. The image of the lawyer that the students appear to have when they turn up at law school seems to be framed—I go on very little evidence—by college campus politics, debating teams, and friends and relatives who tell a youngster that he will make a good lawyer (and who have perhaps business to throw his way when he does). In upper-class families, as Charles McArthur noted in longitudinal studies of prep school boys at Harvard,[34] the law sometimes comes close to being one ascribed career among very narrow alternatives. In ethnic families, in contrast, it is a form of mobility both for the individual and, through its ethnic "mouthpieces," for the group.[35] And not only the "mouthpiece," of course, but a symbolic figure, as the Italian judge rivals the Italian mayor as a sign to the Irish to make way for a new urban hegemony.

In the field of medicine we know (particularly from the studies by Hall)[36] that an able doctor of ethnic background sometimes can choose between the security of a practice within the ethnic community and its hospitals and the risks of the wider, ordinarily Protestant, medical world; he may try for the latter and, failing, be unable to fall back upon his alienated ethnic connections. The wider medical world usually has the attraction of higher

they are in law school. Compare with this the relatively late decision of students to do graduate work in the social sciences. See Elbridge Sibley, *The Recruitment, Selection, and Training of Social Scientists* (New York: Social Science Research Council, 1948), pp. 17–21.

Since writing the foregoing, I have profited from Wagner Thielens, Jr., "Some Comparisons of Entrants to Medical and Law School," in Robert K. Merton, George Reader, and Patricia L. Kendall, eds., *The Student-Physician: Introductory Studies in the Sociology of Medical Education* (Cambridge, Mass.: Harvard University Press, 1957), pp. 131–52.

34. Charles McArthur and Lucia Beth Stevens, "The Validation of Expressed Interests as Compared with Inventoried Interests: A Fourteen-Year Follow-up,'" *Journal of Applied Psychology,* vol. 39 (1955), p. 184.

35. When recently an Indian came from one of the reservations to study anthropology at the University of Chicago, it was perhaps evidence that this native minority had "arrived" and no longer needed to send all its articulate men into law to fight for the rights of the tribe. Perhaps it also showed that anthropology had "arrived," and competes with the law as a way of fighting the battles of the underprivileged!

36. Oswald Hall, *Informal Organization of Medical Practice: Case Study of a Profession* (Unpublished Doctoral Dissertation, University of Chicago Department of Sociology, 1944).

standards, as well as higher prestige, and medical school may reshape a young man's aims toward an ideal of practice resembling that of his teachers in the big university hospitals. Likewise, the "national" law schools, while turning out many who will end up in a parochial orbit, set a model of performance before the alert students and, in addition, bestow prestige on certain fields of public and corporate law as fields in which these high standards may be obeyed. Surely, one reason for the distaste with which the graduate of a major law school regards the criminal law and trial practice generally (not, of course, antitrust and like trials) is because these areas cannot be recreated in the law-school image.[37] Corporate law, on the other hand, and many fields of appellate litigation, can be so created and recreated; for the finespun artifices of the legal imagination on which our corporate (and tax) structures rest rise far above the intellectual slums where, in the big cities, a largely ethnic bar carries on the Anglo-Saxon rites of trial by jury and "contaminates" the legal ideal with the demagogic practice.

So far as I am aware, not much is known about the way in which law students see these alternatives and choose among them, let alone what the contingencies are of their later careers. Recently, Dr. Osler Peterson of the Rockefeller Foundation made

---

37. In my brief exposure to trial practice, as a briefcase-carrying aide at Lyne, Woodworth and Evarts, I quickly found how little of my book-learning was relevant. In studying the law of evidence in law school we had spent most of our time on the fabulous elaborations of the hearsay rule, which forbids, so it says, the introduction of hearsay testimony save in exceptional circumstances. In many trials I attended, it appeared that practically everything that went to the jury *was* hearsay "legally" admissible under none of the exceptions to the rule. In preparing trial briefs, I had begun by assuming that much of this testimony would be excluded. But I soon found that judges did not like to be deprived of hearing evidence that might be relevant, and that counsel, as previously stated, liked, along with judges, to "play by ear," and resented any attempt to alter the live-and-let-live rules of the game as played in the courts in and around Boston. Even where a statute explicitly ruled out certain kinds of evidence, I found judges allowing it in "provisionally" and making clear their resentment of statutory curbs on looseness of presentation. To be sure, we could have appealed, but in most of these cases, where amounts involved were small and lower-court discretion large, my seniors sagely fought to win the jury and feared offending them by seeming to act like a brain-trust, limiting what they would be allowed to hear.

a study of general practice in North Carolina, visiting doctors and observing them in their day-to-day work. He and his colleagues were shocked by the low order of performance they discovered, and also by finding that standings in medical school made no difference in the low level to which the doctors sank. (In my own surmise, the high-ranking students who ended up in small-town general practice may have felt a kind of destructive despair at their unanticipated fate, while the low-ranking students rose somewhat on discovering that, after all, they could be of some use.) These doctors lacked either clients or colleagues to keep them on their toes (it must be added that they apparently practiced an even poorer grade of medicine than had been taught the old-timers; they declined with the years, rather than remaining on a plateau). Would a study of the general practice of law find so depressing a story? Or does the occasional competition through the possibility of litigation act as a brake against the most abysmal sloppiness—at least where there is a chance that a "gentlemen's agreement" to cover for each other might be broken, as always seems more likely in the less guild-controlled legal profession than in medicine? Indeed, is the cynicism of the practicing lawyer less than that of the isolated doctor because his ideals were never so high, nor his training so exigent?[38] And because in most cases it is "only money" and not life that is involved? How many intelligently critical clients and demanding problems does a practicing lawyer need to keep mentally and morally awake?

Likewise, as a student of the dialectic between work and leisure, I expressed in the seminar at Rutgers an interest in the relations between a lawyer's life in and outside the law. Does the latter reflect, refresh, or reinforce the former? In the Auchincloss novels, the able and domineering lawyer is pictured as the

---

38. In two fine novels, James Gould Cozzens has concerned himself with the ideals of the two professions, as practiced in small communities. See *The Last Adam* (medicine) and *The Just and the Unjust* (law). The novels of Louis Auchincloss brilliantly portray the ethical temper of large downtown office lawyers; see, for instance, his discussion of the problem of partnership loyalty (akin to that found in advertising agencies) in *A Law for the Lion*, and his sensitivity to ethnic and social-class differences in *The Great World and Timothy Colt*.

unempathic spouse. Certainly, the older tradition of the big
offices was fiercely work-minded, and men enjoyed (while com-
plaining about) the all-male atmosphere of night work as if
they were in the Foreign Legion. Utter absorption was regarded
as both essential for one's career and a test of one's manhood.
Today, even the lawyer has been influenced by the leisure revolution and the ideals of suburban *Gemeinschaft* and family life.
Just as the Armed Services have difficulty in enforcing the ardu-
ousness of training routines, so with full employment the big
offices can no longer afford to drive the young recruits with
savage intensity; the "man in the gray flannel suit," fonder of
his wife than of his work, now brings the pressure of his marginal
utility to bear on the old Cravath firm. The study of law students'
luncheon sociability I mentioned earlier first struck me as evidence that the students were relaxing at lunch from the rigors
of their work, but I later doubted this and felt that law school
itself was no longer quite the arduous quest that Nicholas Kelley
speaks of; conceivably, the rate-buster or eager beaver may be
under slight pressure even there. But we would need many
diaries of law students as they go through their careers, and
many studies of law schools such as Robert K. Merton and his
associates and Everett C. Hughes and his are now making of
medical schools, before we could begin to understand these
changes.

    This "interpersonal" approach to lawyers, as against an "in-
stitutional" approach to the law, led to what I regard as very
clarifying criticisms from both law professors and sociologists
at Rutgers—and again at Harvard.[39] Robert Rodes, now at Notre

---

    39. Herbert Spiro, a political scientist at Harvard, suggested that my
interest in motivation and interpersonal relations was very "American," as
compared with a Continental concern for institutional forms. And he felt
that my frankness about the psychological sources of cooperation and competition among the disciplines put a tactless demand on the nonsociologists
to be equally frank or to seem stuffy. He and others regarded the "personality and culture" approach with a distaste akin to that felt by British
"structural" anthropologists. This and allied approaches, especially perhaps
when brought home from the preliterate field, or from the clinic, do in my
opinion raise serious problems for all participants, and not merely on the
level of good taste. See my introduction to *Crestwood Heights: A Study
of the Culture of Suburban Life* by John R. Seeley, Alexander Sim, and
E. W. Loosley (New York: Basic Books, Inc., 1956).

Dame Law School, expressed his point of view at the Rutgers seminar in the following manner:

As a lawman, I am predominantly concerned with the law as a particular type of social control. That means that, professionally, I am very much interested in the behavior of other people, just as sociologists are; and this, it has seemed to me, is the fact that makes it promising for sociologists and lawmen to cooperate and pool their knowledge and resources. It also means, however, that *professionally,* the one person in whose behavior I am not interested is myself. The suggestion that sociologists cooperate with lawmen by studying them strikes me as a step away from interdisciplinary cooperation.

If it is useful to sociologists to make the kind of studies you suggest, I would be very happy to cooperate—I'll be glad to help you fellows do your job by submitting myself as a specimen; but I don't see how the things you tell me about myself will help me do my job. I would be interested in the results intellectually; but they are outside my concern so far as my professional role is concerned.

There are, after all, several ways in which the lawman might tell the sociologist about himself, from the frame of reference of the professional lawman. We might consider such questions as whether sociologists, when they interview their subjects, are negligent if they trespass on the subject's privacy. If so, are they sued? What damages are awarded? Do they commit any crime? Are they in contempt of court when they "bug" juries? Does it constitute a legal defense that they are gathering data?

Sociologists might be interested in such analyses, but I don't think they would be professionally interested in them; and if I were to say that that is the only way in which lawyers are interested in sociologists, I think the sociologists would pack up and go home.

It may be that sociology is not yet ready to contribute major insights into law as a particular type of social control. If so, that would be interesting to know and it would be understandable; but the point I want to emphasize is that our major effort should be on the attempt to discover whether or not it is so. It should not—except insofar as sociologists would themselves profit—be on questions that are peripheral to the professional concerns of the lawyer, such as the nature of lunch-table conversations or whether it helps a lawyer in a big corporation to know how to play tennis.

These observations are well taken, and it is no answer to them to comment that Professor Rodes implicitly speaks for an older

tradition—"a government of laws and not of men"—which many
legal realists have sought to debunk. The belief of lawyers, that
something called "the law" exists, has protected many clients
from loss of rights and many counsel from too ready compromise
and self-doubt; it has also been the source of willful stupidity,
even fanaticism. But Professor Rodes' appeal is not merely for
the rejection of gossip and other lowbrow concerns as fundamentally irrelevant: he is not simply setting up the "big power"
world of social controls as more significant than the small power
world of informal controls on the profession. Rather, he is asking, as his colleague Professor Thomas Cowan did in other terms,
for help from sociologists in grasping the channeling of behavior
by the legal structure. He would, I assume, be more interested
in studies of decision-making among corporate executives to see
to what extent the corporate income tax guided their investment and inventory policy than in studies of decision-making
among law students as to whether to enter corporate work or
not. Certainly, Professor Cowan, judging from his comments
and his writings, felt that changes in legal and administrative
constraints offered the social scientist ample opportunities for
studies of change—opportunities that could even be enhanced
by judicious legal experiment.

At this point in the Rutgers discussion several sociologists
made common cause with Professor Rodes. Thus, Paul Massing
raised the question as to what were the really important problems for American society that the legal order presented and
implied that a sociology of the profession was at best a roundabout way to these problems. Likewise, Jackson Toby further
clarified for the group the nature of disciplines as sets of abstractions. He declared:

> The significance of the kinds of observations you have been
> emphasizing, it seems to me, lies in their bearing on the *difficulties*
> of interdisciplinary research. That is to say, the role of the sociologist
> and the role of the lawyer are germane to the interdisciplinary task
> insofar as they create barriers to communication or motivated bases
> for noncooperation. As such, they are important for us to recognize.
> But their importance is not as foci of research; it is rather as *barriers*
> to interdisciplinary cooperation.

In order to find common ground for some kind of interdisciplinary work, we have to look, not at the roles of lawyers or sociologists, but at the disciplines themselves, law and sociology. What we are trying to blend are not people but concepts and theories.

It is true that the *discipline* of sociology does not exhaust the interests of sociologists, nor does the *discipline* of law exhaust the interests of lawyers. There undoubtedly are many kinds of questions in which the lawyer-as-intellectual and the sociologist-as-intellectual could be jointly interested; and they might very well profit immensely from cooperative research on such questions. But they would profit as individuals. The profit would not be to *sociology* or to *law,* unless the focus of activity is a central concern of law and of sociology.

Sociology is one abstraction and law is another. When we keep this clearly in mind, we have the possibility of the blending of the abstractions by incorporation at strategic points of elements from the other field. But the more we focus on concrete persons, lawyers or sociologists, the less chance we have of learning from one another something about the respective abstractions which make each field a *discipline* rather than a congeries of persons engaging in various kinds of activities and defense mechanisms.

In response to these criticisms, another sociologist, Alisa Lourié, sought to interpret my outlook, as well as her own. She observed:

Lawyers and sociologists use different kinds of abstractions. "The law" is a tremendous abstraction; in a sense, "the law" doesn't exist; it is a fiction. The sociologist tends to operate on a lower level of abstraction. He is concerned with what people actually do, with patterns of behavior, of interaction. Law, of course, affects these patterns of behavior; but when the sociologist starts to talk about law, he almost automatically glides over into talking about lawyers and how they act.

"Lawyers and how they act" interests me, as Miss Lourié saw. But I am only one kind of sociologist—and not that kind all the time. I do not share the inverse snobbery that sometimes elevates "facts" and "what people actually do" into a behavioristic distaste for more inclusive concepts. True, at a time when I was less unfamiliar than I am now with European and American jurisprudence, I was depressed by the sterility of much discourse concerning law that seemed to me to take it out of the context of institutions, of lawyers, officials, clients, and other relevant publics and audiences. But, having seen in economics how much the system-builders have contributed in comparison with the institutionalists, I am even more convinced that there are no royal roads to understanding society, and that paths that strike any of us as unpromising may turn out to carry much intellectual traffic. Certainly, I would not agree with Mr. Rodes or with Mr. Toby that there should be a distinction between what sociologists do *professionally* and what they do as *intellectuals* or as individuals curious about their place and that of others in the scheme of things. On the contrary, one of the chief problems of being one of my versions of sociologist (the same holds for some versions of psychiatry) is that one never stops working. For example, when recently on an airplane I chanced to sit next to a lawyer in a large firm who spends nearly all his time as counsel to a major airline, I interviewed him both about his role in helping to rationalize a once-hazardous industry and about his feeling of possible imprisonment with a single— and extremely touchy—client. Did he have more in common with lawyers in general, with airline executives, or with the few people (some of them on the Civil Aeronautics Board) who shared his combination of vantage-points? How free was he, in the event of a conflict with his client, to switch, after a dozen years of specialization, to some other field of law? And how long would the airlines, increasingly routinized, hold his interest? I began by chatting with him, but then felt impelled to reveal my own profession, while aware of the quasi-eavesdropping of what I had done, and the arguable violation of club-car norms. Novelists seem little troubled by the ethics of privacy, whereas thoughtful sociologists are greatly troubled. The latter are concerned lest their questions, even when invited, raise problems that had best be left untouched, and for which they lack any therapeutic magic. Unlike Mr. Rodes, they cannot close the office door and leave their profession behind.

Accordingly, I would not be entirely happy if Mr. Rodes should surrender his defenses and widen his definition of his own job and what might illuminate it. For, as I have already implied in commenting on the lawyer's traditional individualism and as I have emphasized in my article, "Toward an Anthropological Science of Law and the Legal Profession,"[40] the very distaste of many lawyers for knowing "too much" about personality may have certain advantages for the legal order. Tocqueville saw the legal profession in the United States as a link between the common people and the fragmentary elites of wealth and birth, and as a potential aristocracy. And the law in this country, despite elements of populism (as in the jury) and long-run obedience to public opinion, has been for better or worse a means of providing minority constituencies with an effective voice—a pattern sometimes supported today by the very fact that leading members of the bar are inner-directed men, able to defend the rights of clients in the face of public disapproval.

Thus, I know a number of men in the older generation of large law firms whose perennial complaint is that their clients, individual or corporate, have no guts and will not, in litigation or other public forums, take an unpopular stand. Among these lawyers are some whose ferocity toward labor unions was forcibly muted by their clients' insistence that they had to "live with the bastards" even after winning a Labor Board or court case. But there are also some who have been prepared to defend men accused of Communism or other outrageous views—and who have kept looking for harassed professors or suspended civil servants who would have the nerve to incur the publicity of a fight.[41] We know all too well that the law does not defend

---

40. *American Journal of Sociology*, vol. 57 (1951), p. 121.

41. When, as has happened recently in Cleveland, in New Jersey, and elsewhere, lawyers become victims of "guilt by association" with their clients, this vital source of freedom is terrifyingly jeopardized. In fact the freedom has already been jeopardized, judging by the difficulties some men accused of subversion or disloyalty have had in finding counsel—particularly, respectable non-Communist counsel. I have the impression that some former Communists who have been encouraged by their lawyers to plead the Fifth Amendment before congressional committees have had the bad luck to fall in with Communist-controlled counsel because no other members of the bar seemed readily available to them (others, of course, still tied to the Party, would choose such counsel anyway). I need not spell out the sorry consequence, if not for the individual, certainly, for the clarification of issues in the field of civil liberties—the committees, of course, wanted

the voiceless, but, given the moderate immunity of some of the courts to immediate legislative rebuke, the voices of those who have but a small local constituency can be defended.[42] Even while violence flares about them, lawyers for the NAACP can be heard in Southern courts, and the same "aristocratic" strength sustains judges and lawyers, and the many law professors who have actively defended civil liberties, against more subtle pressures to go along. The return to respect for *stare decisis* in a number of law schools reflects on the one hand the wider currents of the "new conservatism" and on the other hand a realization (perhaps most clearly elucidated by Mr. Justice Stone)[43] that judicial obstinacy may serve in the field of civil liberties to hold open the door of the future in a way that it has not

just such counsel to defend the people they harassed. Cf. my article, "The Supreme Court and Its New Critics," *New Republic*, July, 1957, pp. 9–13.

42. A small example from private law may make the amplitude of my point clearer. When a testator died childless in a Midwestern town, he left a moderate fortune for the study of cancer at an Eastern university, and appointed a physician there as his executor. Local relatives questioned his sanity, whipping up xenophobia against the gift's going out of the state. The probate judge, with an election coming up, appointed a local attorney as coexecutor, contrary to the will. A good deal of pressure was brought against the university's counsel to permit this appointment to go through as a sop to local feeling—especially since it is so nearly impossible to impugn the "discretion" of the lower court; state law was cited to this effect. But the out-of-state counsel did not cave in, even when the probate judge's discretion was sustained in an intermediate appeal; they kept insisting that what was clearly an invasion of the testator's prerogative could not be "the law," no matter what more timid people argued. Their anger at finagling and injustice—at "particularism" in Talcott Parsons' terms—sustained them against the risk of further antagonizing the appointed coexecutor and the probate judge by continuing to litigate the latter's decision. Virtue won: the state's supreme court reversed the lower courts by a one-vote margin—and the probate judge was defeated for re-election. I am inclined to think that men more sensitive to public relations would not have carried the fight so far, nor have imagined that they could win it.

43. *United States v. Carolene Products Co.*, 304 U.S. 144, at 152–153, n. 4 (1938). Mr. Justice Stone's point, as I understand it, was that the courts should apply to governmental interferences with civil liberties severer standards—that is, lesser degrees of deference to the so-called legislative judgment—than in due process cases not involving freedoms of similar importance for the health and tone of free discussion; he felt that there is something irreversible about an interference with civil liberties. I think that, were he alive today, he would find much evidence (and too few justices) to support his judgment.

always done in protecting property rights against regulation. Since I see the courts, and the bar that serves and uses them, as a "countervailing power" vis-à-vis parochial coercion, and see them in fact as making insufficiently self-conscious use of this power, I am not entirely happy with developments in our society that would rob the judge and lawyer of their protective insulation against preoccupation with public relations: we still need men who care more for what the books should say than for what people will say.[44]

The Danger of Needing Quick Results from Research

Yet such considerations, relevant as they may be for the recruitment and training of law students and for the understanding of the political and cultural leverage of the bar, do not help us very much in planning joint engagements of sociologists and law professors. In such planning it is important to know what one is up against. In areas such as crime and insanity, where legal processes are at once highly visible and almost surely inadequate, there is a fairly unequivocal invitation

44. To some extent, of course, these problems beset all professions that desire to establish professional distance from lay pressures and controls. Academic freedom, including power to set standards for admission to college, is cut from similar cloth. Correspondingly, there is always the danger that *public* relations will count too little, and *professional* relations too much —as when doctors gang up to curb public health programs (as, in Chicago, against free Salk shots), or when lawyers sell out their clients for fear of offending their brethren or offending a judge before whom they want to live to plead another day. Tension is inevitable here, and the public must remain a countervailing power against the profession, as well as vice versa. C. Wright Mills in *The Power Elite* (p. 289) links the corporation lawyer and the investment banker as go-betweens among the various elites of industry, the military, and the government. Correspondingly, he seems to give the lawyer little independent role but to regard him as a sort of high-class messenger who shares the values of his clients. Many lawyers themselves feel and fear this, and look back to an earlier day of greater independence. Plainly, any study of the role of the corporation lawyer cannot be separated from the question whether he has any impact on his clients, as well as vice versa, and how if at all these interpenetrations are changing.

to the outsider to pitch in. The outsider also has access to appellate cases, especially in the public law fields, and he can be the beneficiary of the generations of law professors who have sought to reduce the chaos of decisions to some sort of order, at best "restating" it or at worst, as already indicated, indexing it under literal-minded headings. Even with respect to these cases, however, new modes of looking at the material, which could invite the attention of sociologists generally, are not easy to come by. For instance, it is possible to read upper-court cases with an eye for style, looking, for instance, for rococo or Edwardian modes of exposition, but this would only be the beginning in an effort to subsume the material under rubrics relevant for the understanding of American institutional life.

And beyond the decisions, and as everyone knows more meaningful for the daily conduct of business and government, is the more impalpable "law-stuff" of office practice. It is understandably easier for an anthropologist to make sense of a primitive legal system because, in the tradition of the one-man expedition, he can relate it to kinship and other structural elements, than for him to make headway with the problems created for the student of American law by its sheer bulk as it occurs in organizations large and small—for only a narrow definition of his task would limit him to the formally declared legal agencies while excluding from view the "law-stuff" that exists wherever judicialization and channeling of dispute go on. This material is frequently buried in files and memories and in commercial and governmental routines.

In this situation, the pioneering work of Underhill Moore, with its enormous input of labor always in danger of bringing forth a mouse, has had few successors; but it is this order of work that I believe to be necessary before the programs implicit in the comments of Messrs. Toby, Rodes, and Massing can even be glimpsed. I have indicated why the track of case-criticism is so commodious and rewarding for legal scholars that lack of an audience among them for other types of work, such as Underhill Moore's, is not surprising.

On the sociological side, too, despite the current boom in the social sciences, most of us are unwilling to do what the physical scientists take for granted, namely, to undertake work that has very little chance of producing positive results, and then to report any negative findings. We are still sufficiently intellectual underdogs to need more "results" per year or per project than are likely to flow from the sort of immersion in day-to-day normative data Underhill Moore attempted. And this is not merely a matter of professional inferiority and misgiving. One should not underestimate the courage it takes to embark on a sea of data whose outlines cannot yet be mapped and through which no currents of ascertained relevance already run. Just as economists prefer to study aggregates or models and not to take the chance of becoming participant-observers in a firm that might turn out at the end of years of work not to be "typical," or to be affected by influences from outside that could not be measured or even ascertained, so similar risks would attend a scholar who took the plunge in an effort to grasp the bearing of legal thinking (or thinking by law-trained men) on the conduct of life. Indeed, such a man would take even greater risks than an economist, for legal practice outside the case-law is probably even more diversified in our society than is business. For the legal subcultures are nurtured by the "tariffs" of state and local boundaries creating parochial idiosyncracies perhaps even greater than those to be found in the subcultures of particular industries. For such work one would need the omnivorousness of an old-fashioned historian who is willing to plow through mountains of documents for an occasional clue, plus that eye for what goes together with what that constitutes the sociologist's imagination.

Talcott Parsons

The Law
and Social Control

From a variety of points of view I think it can be said that law and sociology have an unusually wide area of overlapping interests. But for various reasons the exploration of these interests and the implications of the relationships have not been very adequately pursued. Perhaps the very extent to which sociology is such a young discipline plays a major part in bringing about this situation.

It may be useful to call attention, at the start, to two salient general considerations about the law as seen from a social scientist's point of view. In the first place, law is not a category descriptive of actual concrete behavior but rather concerns patterns, norms, and rules that are applied to the acts and to

This essay was written, first for oral delivery, in the spring of 1956. It has not seemed possible to undertake extensive revision for present purposes. My own thinking on the matter has, however, undergone considerable development since then. This has occurred in particular in connection with a projected general book on American society in collaboration with Dr. Winston White and with the able assistance of Mr. Leon Mayhew. A fairly extensive treatment of the place of the legal system in American society, including the part played in it by the legal profession, will be included in the forthcoming book, to be published by the Free Press.

the roles of persons and to the collectivities of which they are members. Law is an aspect of social structure but one that lies on a particular level, which should be carefully specified. In a certain set of sociological terms I should call it an institutional phenomenon. It deals with normative patterns to which various kinds of sanctions are applied. This is a level that on general sociological grounds it is important to distinguish from that of the concrete structure of collectivities and roles in them.

The second salient characteristic of law is that it is nonspecific with respect to functional content at lower levels. Functional content, understood in the usual sociological senses, refers to such categories as economic, political, and a variety of others. There is law defining the Constitution and political processes within it. There is a law of business and of labor and the relations of business to labor. There is a law of the family, of personal relationships, and a variety of other subjects. Indeed *any* social relationship can be regulated by law, and I think every category of social relationship with which sociologists are concerned is found to be regulated by law in some society somewhere.

It seems justified to infer from these considerations that law should be treated as a generalized mechanism of social control that operates diffusely in virtually all sectors of the society.[1]

Law, of course, is not just a set of abstractly defined rules. It is a set of rules backed by certain types of sanctions, legitimized in certain ways, and applied in certain ways. It is a set of rules that stands in certain quite definite relationships to specific collectivities and the roles of individuals in them. Perhaps we can approach a little closer characterization of the place of law in a society by attempting to analyze some of these relationships, and by showing some of the conditions on which the effectiveness of a system of rules can be held to rest.

---

1. Of course it is better adapted to some problems of social control than to others. It is notorious that the more refined and settled sentiments of individuals cannot be controlled by legal prescription. Nevertheless, it is one of the most highly generalized mechanisms in the whole society. It is located primarily, as I said, on the institutional level. It is not isolated but is one of a family of mechanisms of control. At the end of this discussion I will sketch its relations to one or two others.

The Functions of Law and
Some Structural Implications

Let us suggest that in the larger social perspective the primary function of a legal system is integrative. It serves to mitigate potential elements of conflict and to oil the machinery of social intercourse. It is, indeed, only by adherence to a system of rules that systems of social interaction can function without breaking down into overt or chronic covert conflict.

Normative consistency may be assumed to be one of the most important criteria of effectiveness of a system of law. By this I mean that the rules formulated in the system must ideally not subject the individuals under their jurisdiction to incompatible expectations or obligations—or, more realistically, not too often or too drastically. In the nature of the case, since they act in many different contexts and roles, individuals will be subject to many particularized rules. But the rules must somehow all build up to a single, relatively consistent system.

In this respect we may suggest that there are four major problems that must be solved before such a system of rules can operate determinately to regulate interaction. (Even though the questions are not explicitly put by the actors, an observer analyzing how the system operates must find some solution to each of them.)

The first problem concerns the basis of legitimation of the system of rules. The question is why, in the value or meaning sense, should I conform to the rules, should I fulfill the expectations of the others with whom I interact? What in other words is the *basis* of right? Is it simply that some authority says so without further justification? Is it some religious value, or is it that I and the others have some natural rights that it is wrong to violate? What is the basis of this *legitimation?*

The second problem concerns the *meaning* of the rule for me or some other particular actor in a particular situation in a particular role. In the nature of the case, rules must be formulated in general terms. The general statement may not cover all of the circumstances of the particular situation in which I am placed. Or there may be two or more rules, the implications of which for my action are currently contradictory. Which one applies and in what degree and in what way? What specifically are my obligations in this particular situation or my rights under the law? This is the problem of *interpretation*.

The third basic problem is that of the consequences, favorable or unfavorable, that should follow from conforming to the rules to a greater or lesser degree or from failing to conform. These consequences will vary according to the degrees of nonconformity and according to the circumstances in which, and reasons for which, deviation occurs. Under a system of law, however, the question of whether or not conformity occurs can never be a matter of indifference. This, of course, is the problem of *sanctions*. What sanctions apply and by whom are they applied?

Finally, the fourth problem concerns to whom and under what circumstances a given rule or complex of rules, with its interpretations and sanctions, applies. This is the problem of *jurisdiction*, which has two aspects: (1) What authority has jurisdiction over given persons, acts, and so on in defining and imposing the norms? (2) To which classes of acts, persons, roles, and collectivities does a given set of norms apply?

We may now attempt to say something about the conditions of institutionalizing answers to these questions in a large-scale, highly differentiated society. At the outset I want to suggest that a legal system must not itself be regarded in an analytical sense as a political phenomenon, although it must be closely related to political functions and processes. The two systems are most intimately related with respect to the problems of sanctions and of jurisdiction. Of these, the connection with respect to sanctions is in a sense the more fundamental.

We may speak of the existence of a continuum of sanctions, ranging from pure inducement to sheer and outright coercion. By inducement I mean the offer of advantages as a reward for actions that the inducer wishes his role-partner to perform. By coercion I mean the threat of negative sanctions for nonperformance of the desired course of action. Both inducement and coercion operate in all social relationships. The basis of the relation of law to political organization lies primarily in the fact that at certain points the question must inevitably arise as to the use of physical force or its threat as a means of coercion; that is, a means of assertion of the bindingness of the norm. If physical force is altogether excluded the ultimate coercive sanction is expulsion, as for example in the case of excommunication from a church. In many cases, however, expulsion will not be a sufficiently severe sanction to prevent undesirable action from taking place. And if it is not sufficient, resort must be had to force. Force is, at least in the preventive sense, the ultimate negative sanction.

Thus if rules are taken sufficiently seriously, inevitably the question will sometime be raised of resort to physical sanction in a preventive context. On the other hand, the use of force is perhaps the most serious potential source of disruption of order in social relationships. For this reason in all ordered societies there is at least a qualified monopoly of the more serious uses of physical force. This monopoly is one of the primary characteristics of the political organization, in its more highly developed forms leading up to the state. If, then, it becomes necessary in certain contingencies to use or threaten physical force as a sanction for the enforcement of legal norms, and if the legitimate use of physical force is monopolized in the agency of the state, then the legal system must have an adequate connection with the state in order to use its agencies as the administrators of physical sanctions.

The problem of jurisdiction is obviously closely linked with that of sanctions. One of the main reasons that the jurisdiction of political bodies is territorially defined is precisely the importance of the use of physical force in their functioning. Physical force can be applied only if the individual to whom it is directed can be reached in a physical location at a given time. It is therefore inherently linked to territoriality of jurisdiction. Hence a legal system that relies at certain crucial points on the sanctions of physical force must also be linked to a territorial area of jurisdiction.

A further source of linkage between law and the state requires me to say a word about the imperative of consistency.
On the level of the content of norms as such, this imperative
exerts a strong pressure toward universalism (a trait that is
inherent in systems of law generally). I spoke above of consistency from the point of view of not subjecting the same
individual to contradictory rules. The obverse of this imperative is the recognition that, when a rule has been defined as a
rule, it must be impartially applied to all persons or other
social units that fall within the criteria that define the application of the rule. There are inherent limitations in systematizing
legal systems, that is, in making them consistent, if this criterion
of universalistic application cannot be followed.

In its practical implication this criterion of universalism,
however, connects closely wth territoriality, because it is only
within territorial limits that enforcement of universalistically
defined rules can effectively be carried out. It follows from
these considerations that enforcement agencies in a legal system are generally organs of the state. They carry a special
political character.

Enforcement agencies are, however, ordinarily not the central organs of the state. They are not primarily policy-forming
organs but rather are organs that are put at the service of the
many different interests that are covered by the rules of a
legal system. The fact that even the enforcement agencies are
not primarily political is vividly brought out by their relations
to the courts. In most legal systems what they may do, and
to a considerable degree how they may do it, is defined and
supervised by the courts. Where enforcement agencies gain too
strong a degree of independence of the courts, it may be said
that the legal system itself has been subordinated to political
considerations, a circumstance that does occur in a variety of
cases.

The interpretive and legitimizing functions in law are even
less directly political than are the sanctioning and the jurisdictional functions. First let us take the legitimation function,
which concerns to an important degree the relation and the
distinction between law and ethics.

We may say that, in the deeper sense, the lawyer as such tends to take legitimation for granted. It is not part of his professional function, whether as attorney or as judge, to decide whether the existence of a given rule is morally or politically justified. His function rather concerns its interpretation and application to particular cases. Even where, as under a federal system, there may be certain problems of the conflict of laws, it is the higher legal authority—for example, that of the Constitution—that is the lawyer's primary concern, not the moral legitimation of the Constitution itself. Nevertheless, the legal system must always rest on proper legitimation. This may take forms rather close to the legal process itself, such as the question of enactment by proper procedures by duly authorized bodies. For example, legislatures are responsible to electorates. But in back of proper procedure and due authorization of law-making bodies lies the deeper set of questions of ultimate legitimation.

In the last analysis this always leads in some form or other either to religious questions or to those that are functionally equivalent to religion. Law from this point of view constitutes a focal center of the relations between religion and politics as well as other aspects of a society.

Turning now to "interpretation," it must be noted that here again there are two basic foci of this function. One concerns the integrity of the system of rules itself; it is rule-focused. The other concerns the relation of rules to the individuals and groups and collectivities on whom they impinge. In a legal sense this latter function may be said to be client-focused. Taken together in these two aspects, the interpretive function may be said to be the central function of a legal system.

The first, the rule-focused aspect of the law, is primarily the locus of the judiciary function, particularly at the appellate levels. The second is the focus of the functions of the practicing legal profession. With respect to the judiciary certain sociological facts are saliently conspicuous. Wherever we can speak of a well-institutionalized legal system, the judiciary are expected to enjoy an important measure of independence from the central political authority. Of course, their integration with it must be so close that, for example, practically always judges are appointed by political authority. But usually (unless hold-ing office for specified terms) they enjoy tenure, they are not removable except for cause, and it is considered most improper for political authority to put direct pressure on them in influ-encing their specific decisions. Furthermore, though not a constitutional requirement in the United States it is certainly general practice that judges, the more so the higher in the system, must be lawyers in a professional sense. This is not a function ordinarily open to the ordinary lay citizen.

Furthermore, the judicial function as part of the attorney's function is centered in a special type of social organization: the court. This is an organization that directly institutionalizes the process of arriving at decisions. This is done, of course, through the bringing of cases to the court for adjudication, in the course of which not only are the rights and obligations of individual petitioners settled but the rules themselves are given authoritative interpretations. We might perhaps say that authori-tative interpretation in this sense is perhaps the most important of the judicial functions.

With respect to the legal profession in the sense of the practicing attorney, there is a conspicuous dual character. The attorney is, on the one hand, an officer of the court. As such he bears a certain public responsibility. But at the same time, he is a private adviser to his client, depending on the client for his remuneration and enjoying a privileged confidential relation to the client. This relation between lawyer and client parallels, to an interestingly high degree, that between physician and patient, its confidential character being one of the principal clues to this parallel. It is focused, however, on situations of actual or potential social conflict and the adjudication and smoothing over of these conflicts. It is not primarily person-oriented as the health-care functions are, but rather social relationship-oriented.

Performance of the interpretive function is facilitated, we have said, by such structural devices as "judicial independence" from political pressure, professionalization of the judicial role, and institutionalization of the decision-making process. These general kinds of structural facilities, however, are not sufficient to prevent the interpretive role from being the focus of certain inherent strains; and certain more specific mechanisms are required to check a tendency toward deviant reactions to the strains.

Strains in the Lawyer Role

The severity and difficulty of the problems of conflicts between mutually contradictory statutes is well known to lawyers. Anglo-American law relies heavily on the processes of judicial decision and, through these, the accumulation of precedents. But the problem of maintaining the internal consistency of the precedent system, even to a tolerable degree, is formidable. Furthermore, there must be orientation to the authority of the basic constitutional documents, which naturally means continual reinterpretation of them, and to the positive acts of legislation that are continually being produced.

The problems faced by our legal profession in this respect may be compared with two other types of situations. First, there is an analogy to the professions concerned with the application of scientific knowledge, such as engineering and medicine. In these cases it is a sociologically central fact that the available knowledge is far from adequate to cover the practical needs. Nevertheless, established scientific knowledge does constitute a highly stable point of reference. Hence the "authority" of the relevant professional groups for interpretations can always be referred to such established knowledge. This is, moreover, a basis of reference that is steadily growing in stability. The other type of case is very different, namely, that in which there is a fountainhead of authority beyond which there is no appeal. The Roman Catholic Church is perhaps the most conspicuous large-scale example, though the Soviet Communist Party is in certain respects similar. The essential point is that the "correct doctrine" is assumed not to be dependent on any human will, but to be infallibly specific and definite, with a clearly authorized human agency for its implementation.

As compared with both of these our secular law is considerably looser in its points of reference. The Constitution is considerably less clear-cut than the authoritative canons of the church and even the Supreme Court is less "canonical" than is the papacy. The legal profession, then, has to maintain difficult balances in a tradition that is in itself exceedingly complex, that is applied to very complex and changing conditions, subject to severe pressures from interest groups, authoritatively based only on very general and partly ambiguous documents, and subject to change within considerable limits by the more or less arbitrary and unpredictable "will of the people."

We know from analysis of a great many such situations that the assumption of responsibility for such functions where within considerable limits no clearly "right" answers can be attained is a source of strain. We also know that in relation to such strains tendencies to various types of "deviant" behavior are likely to develop. One of these is probably yielding to expediency, through financial temptations and other pressures from clients. Ideological trends in our society are such that there is almost certainly serious exaggeration in the views of many circles about lawyers on this point, but that the tendency exists to abdicate responsibilities in the service of their own financial "self-interest" or "peace" in the face of severe pressure can scarcely be doubted.

A second type of deviation consists in exaggerated legal "formalism," the tendency to insist on what is conceived to be the "letter" of the law without due regard to a "reasonable" balance of considerations. Legal "technicalities" may of course be, and often are, invoked as tactical weapons in various types of procedures, a point that will be discussed briefly below, but apart from their instrumental use, undoubtedly there is a tendency in many legal quarters to exaggerate the importance of being formally "correct" down to the last detail. In psychological terms, the legal profession probably has at least its share, if not more, of "compulsive personalities" as compared with other occupations. The essential point is that this tendency in the profession is not simply a result of certain types of people "happening" to be lawyers, but grows out of the situation in which lawyers as a group are placed.

The third type of deviant tendency prominent in the law

may be said to be the "sentimental" exaggeration of the substantive claims of clients or other "interests" represented by the
lawyer. Thus corporation lawyers may often become more
lyrical about the rights of "property" than the main tradition
of the law warrants, or labor lawyers about "human rights"
and the like. Or, to take another example, the lawyer who iden-
tifies with an injured client to the extent of fighting very hard
to get for him what, on cooler consideration, look like highly
excessive damages, is guilty of "sentimentality" in this sense.

With the appropriate qualifications for specific features of
its role and situation, the legal profession shares certain fundamental characteristics with the other professions. Its members
are trained in and integrated with a distinctive part of our
cultural tradition, having a fiduciary responsibility for its maintenance, development, and implementation. They are expected,
within limits, to provide a "service" to the public without
regard to immediate self-interest. The lawyer has a position
of independent responsibility, so that he is neither a servant
only of the client, though he represents his interest, nor of *any*
other group—in the lawyer's case, a group embodying public
authority.

Above all, the member of a profession stands *between* two
major aspects of our social structure; in the case of the law,
between public authority and its norms and the private individual or group whose conduct or intentions may or may not
be in accord with the law. In the case of the physician it is
between the worlds of sickness and of health; he himself is
defined as not sick, but he participates more intimately with
the sick than any other category of well person. In the case
of the teacher it is between the world of childhood—or, on advanced levels, of relative "untrainedness"—and the full status
of being trained.

The professions in this sense may, sociologically, be regarded
as what we call "mechanisms of social control." They either,
like the teaching profession, help to "socialize" the young, to
bring them into accord with the expectations of full membership in the society, or like the medical profession they bring
them *back* into accord when they have deviated. The legal

profession may be presumed to do this and two other things: first, to forestall deviance by advising the client in ways that will keep him better in line, and also by "cooling him off"; second, if it comes to a serious case, to implement the procedure by which a socially sanctioned decision about the status of the client is arrived at, for example, the determination of whether he is innocent or guilty of a crime.

Except for the formal determination of innocence or guilt, which has certain special features, analysis has shown that effective performance of these functions depends on whether the role in which they are performed meets certain broad sociological conditions. These have been worked out most clearly in connection with the psychotherapeutic functions of the medical profession. It can, however, be shown that they are of considerably more general significance, applying to "socialization" both in family and in school, to some aspects of religious ritual, and to various other situations. In conclusion I may briefly outline these conditions and indicate how they apply to the legal case.

In the first place, in situations of strain, scope seems to be required for a certain permissiveness for expression of attitudes and sentiments that, in ordinary circumstances, would not be acceptable. If this permissiveness is to operate effectively it must be associated with relief from anxiety. In order to be capable, psychologically, of "getting things off his chest" a person must be assured that, within certain limits, otherwise ordinary or possible negative sanctions will not operate. In general this implies a protected situation. The confidential character of the lawyer's relation to his client provides just such a situation. The client can talk freely, to an understanding and knowledgeable ear, without fear of immediate repercussions. What is relayed beyond this confidential relationship is selected through the screen of the lawyer's judgment.

To some extent the same kind of thing occurs in other phases of the legal process, notably the hearing by judges of some evidence in chambers. It could be a feature of the process of trial itself, and under the most favorable circumstances probably is. This tendency is, however, counteracted by the publicity of trials, which has developed rather special features in the United States on account of certain of the characteristics of our press.

In the case of the law, the situations of strain with which it deals focus to a large extent on conflicts. One of the very important aspects of legal procedure is to provide mechanisms for the "cooling off" of the passions aroused in such situations. Undoubtedly the private attorney does a great deal of this. Like the physician he helps his client to "face reality," to confine his claim to what he has a real chance of making "stand up" in court or in direct negotiation, and to realize and emotionally to accept the fact that the other fellow may have a case too. The element of delay in bringing things to a head, though doubtless often carried too far because of crowding of court calendars and the like, may have a similar function. The important thing here is that a person under strain should have some opportunity for "tension release" that is treated as institutionally legitimate.

Secondly, it is a feature of the types of situation I am thinking of that there is some assurance of "support" or "acceptance" within broader limits than would otherwise be the case. The physician in one sense tends to be particularly "tolerant" of human beings; he does not judge them morally, but tries to "help" them as best he can. Certain features of legal practice also seem to fit into this pattern. Although there are expectations that the attorney will not consciously attempt to "get off" a person he knows to be guilty of a crime, there is on the other hand the presumption that the client is entitled to a "fair trial" not only in the formal sense, but a hearing from his attorney, and any help within the bounds of reason and professional ethics.

The lawyer is not easily shocked in the way the general public may be; he is familiar with the complexities of human living and ready to "give a break" to the person who has become involved in a difficult situation. Perhaps the presumption of innocence, not only as a canon of formal trial procedure but as a deep-seated trend of the ethos of the profession, is the primary focus of this feature of the institution of the law. It

is strikingly symbolized by the fact that, as in the medical profession, payment for the services of lawyers is not on an ordinary "commercial" basis, but on a "sliding scale." There is
a presumption that the lawyer will be willing to help his
client relatively independently of whether it is financially worth
his while in the particular case.

But while the lawyer tends to be both permissive and sup-
portive in his relation with his clients, there is another side to
the picture. He is, after all, schooled in the great tradition of
the law. As a member of a great profession he accepts responsibility for its integrity, and his position in society focuses that
responsibility upon him. His function in relation to clients is
by no means only to "give them what they want" but often to
resist their pressures and get them to realize some of the hard
facts of their situations, not only with reference to what they
can, even with clever legal help, expect to "get away with"
but with reference to what the law will permit them to do. In
this sense, then, the lawyer stands as a kind of buffer between
the illegitimate desires of his clients and the social interest.
Here in a sense he "represents" the law rather than the client.
His tendency under certain circumstances to give way to the
pressures of client interest is one way in which, as noted above,
he can be "deviant." But in this connection he can retreat into
the formalism of the law as a means of resisting these pressures.
From the present point of view the significant point is that *both*
these functions are combined in a particular way in the same
agency.

What I have referred to above as permissiveness and support are relatively "unconditional" in that the lawyer will not
betray his client's confidence or refuse to give him the presumption of innocence while he is hearing his story. But there
is another class of his services that are to be treated as conditional, namely, the specific, positive services he is willing to
provide, especially those performed in public where the lawyer's own reputation may be involved. The negative aspect of
this has just been discussed, the things that the lawyer refuses
to do for his client, but there is also a positive aspect. His legal
competence, his knowledge of situations and of people, his

skill in negotiation, and so on are at the service of his client, but—even after he has taken on the case—not wholly on the client's terms, but to an important degree on his own terms. From a sociological point of view he is "manipulating rewards" in such a way as to have an important effect in influencing the behavior of the client. This influence operates not only through what the client "gets" in the sense of achieving the original goals for which he consulted a lawyer, but through the impact on the client of the lawyer's *attitude*, his expressed or implied approval of this as so legitimate that a lawyer is willing to help him get it, whereas other elements of the client's goals are disapproved and help in getting them is refused.

The upshot of these commonplace considerations is that the sociologist must regard the activities of the legal profession as one of the very important mechanisms by which a relative balance of stability is maintained in a dynamic and rather precariously balanced society. The most significant thing is that a pattern of analysis worked out in an entirely different context, the psychotherapeutic aspect of the role of the physician, turns out to be applicable in this field as well. This is a connection of which I myself was not aware until I attempted to put together some thoughts about the legal profession.

Law and Other Mechanisms of Social Control

Despite these general ways in which lawyers, as professionals, contribute to social control, it is important to note certain crucial differences between law and other control mechanisms. A useful point from which to approach the distinction, and from which to make clear its functional importance, is the set of remarks made above in connection with the functions of legitimation and interpretation.

From the combination of the interpretive function and that of legitimation, we may begin to understand some of the reasons for the emphasis in the law on procedural matters. As Max

Weber put it, "the rationality of law is formal rather than substantive." Certainly one of the basic conceptions in our Anglo-Saxon legal systems is that of due process. Here, of course, it even goes to the point where the question of substantive justice may not be an issue, and injustice may have no legal remedy so long as correct formal procedure has been observed. It may be noted that if pressure becomes strong with reference to either the question of enforcement or the question of legitimation, it may operate against the integrity of the procedural traditions and rules. People who are sufficiently exercised about questions of substantive justice and injustice are often not strong respectors of complicated legal procedure. Similarly, if disobedience to law is sufficiently blatant and scandalous, there may be a demand for direct action that altogether by-passes the rules of procedure.

From this point of view, it may become evident that the prominence of and the integrity of a legal system as a mechanism of social control is partly a function of a certain type of social equilibrium. Law flourishes particularly in a society in which the most fundamental questions of social values are not currently at issue or under agitation. If there is sufficiently acute value conflict, law is likely to go by the board. Similarly it flourishes in a society in which the enforcement problem is not too seriously acute. This is particularly true where there are strong informal forces reinforcing conformity with at least the main lines of the legally institutionalized tradition. In many respects, modern England is a type case of this possibility.

Law, then, as a mechanism of control may be said to stand in a position midway between two other types of mechanisms:

(a) On the one hand, there are two classes of mechanisms that focus primarily on the motivation of the individual: those that operate through the media of mass communication— through the distribution and allocation of information and the concomitant emotional attitudes; and those that operate more privately and subtly in relation to the individual. Though there are many of these latter mechanisms, a particularly conspicuous one in our own society, administered by a sister professional group, is that of therapy. The line of distinction between ques-

tions that can be handled by legal procedure and those that
involve therapy is a particularly important one.

(b) In another direction, the law must be distinguished
from those mechanisms of social control that focus on the solution of fundamental problems of value orientation involving
basic decisions for the system as a whole, rather than regulation
of the relations of the parts to each other. Politics and religion
both operate more in this area, and because of this difference
it is particularly important to distinguish law from politics
and religion.

Finally, it may perhaps be suggested that law has a special
importance in a pluralistic liberal type of society. It has its
strongest place in a society where there are many different
kinds of interests that must be balanced against each other and
that must in some way respect each other. As I have already
noted, in the totalitarian type of society, which is in a great
hurry to settle some fundamental general social conflict or policy,
law tends to go by the board.

Both individually and collectively, law imposes restraints
on precipitate and violent action. I might recall the words with
which the recipients of law degrees are greeted by the President
of Harvard University at every commencement. He says, "You
are now qualified to help administer those wise restraints which
make men free."

Harry C. Bredemeier

Law as an
Integrative Mechanism

It is important to distinguish between two kinds of enterprises relating sociology and law: one is denoted by the phrase "sociology *of* the law," the other by "sociology *in* the law." The first makes "the law" a focus of sociological investigation in the same way that "small groups" and "voting" are foci. The goal here is either to describe the significance of the law for the larger society or to describe its internal processes or both. The second aims to facilitate the law's performance of its functions by adding sociological knowledge to its stock of tools. Clearly, the second aim depends on the first; there can be no sociological knowledge that is useful to the law until there is sociological knowledge about the functions of the law and mechanisms of performing those functions. For that reason, in the first part of this paper I set out an analysis of the functions of the law and their relationships to other functional subsystems of the society. I then discuss some of the salient lines of research in in sociology of the law suggested by that analysis, and the place of sociology *in* the law.

The framework I employ is that developed by Talcott Parsons and his colleagues, particularly as stated in *Economy and Society*.[1] This framework posits four major functional processes to be observed in a social system: adaptation, goal pursuance, pattern maintenance, and integration. Parsons and Smelser have identified adaptation with economic processes, and goal pursuance with political processes. Pattern-maintenance processes may very roughly, but adequately for present purposes, be identified with what we ordinarily refer to as socialization. Integrative processes are not so neatly identified with familiar patterns; but I propose to identify them in part with "the law," that is, with legal processes.

The function of the law is the orderly resolution of conflicts. As this implies, "the law" (the clearest model of which I shall take to be the court system) is brought into operation after there has been a conflict. Someone claims that his interests have been violated by someone else.[2] The court's task is to render a decision that will prevent the conflict—and all potential conflicts like it—from disrupting productive cooperation. In order to do this, the court needs three things—or, in the language of Parsons and his colleagues, the court is dependent upon three kinds of "inputs."

In the first place, the court needs an analysis of cause-and-effect relationships. It needs a way of ascertaining both the *past* relationship between the alleged act of the defendant and the alleged injury of the plaintiff, and the probable *future* relationship between the decision and the activities of defendant and plaintiff (and all persons similarly situated). I suggest that this input comes from the adaptive system, in return for an immediate output of "organic," as distinguished from "mechanical," solidarity.

In the second place, as is implied by the phrase "productive cooperation," the court needs a conception of what the division

---

1. Talcott Parsons and Neil J. Smelser, *Economy and Society* (New York: The Free Press, 1956).

2. Whether it is a district attorney claiming that the "public interest" he "represents" has been violated by an alleged "criminal," or a citizen claiming (for example) that his interest in esteem has been violated by a libel or slander, the court's procedure is essentially the same.

of labor is *for;* what the goals of the system are, what state of affairs is to be created or maintained by the exercise of power. In other words, it needs standards by which to *evaluate* the conflicting claims and the anticipated effects of a decision on the role structure. I suggest that this is the primary input from the goal-pursuance or political system, in exchange for which the court's primary output is "interpretation" of the meaning in a particular case of the abstract language of legislation, or the even more abstract language of the society's "ideals."

Finally, in order to perform its function the court needs a willingness on the part of potential litigants to *use* the court as a conflict-resolving mechanism. This motivation to accept the court and abide by its decisions is an input from the pattern-maintenance or socialization system, and the court's immediate return output is what is termed "justice."

The Law and Adaptive Processes

Adaptation refers essentially to the production of instrumental facilities for coping with obstacles to the achievement of system goals. As mentioned earlier, Parsons and Smelser associate this function on a societal level with the economic system. I prefer a somewhat different association, broader in some respects, narrower in others. I want to conceive of adaptive structures, at least for modern Western societies, as those of science and technology. (So far as I can see, this does not modify the analysis of *Economy and Society* except to give it greater scope.)

When the courts receive a signal, in the shape of a lawsuit, that there has been a clash of interests, the first requirement is "to understand it." This means two things. First, it means discovering the factual connection between the alleged harm and the event alleged to have caused it. Second, it means discovering the functional context of the action of plaintiff and defendant—that is to say, (a) the roles they are performing, (b) the functional significance for the system of those roles, and (c) the necessity (for efficient performance) of playing the roles in the manner in which the litigants had in fact been playing them. These "discoveries" are made on the basis of certain cognitive generalizations, beliefs, and theories concerning cause-and-effect relationships; and they are made with the aid of techniques for ascertaining "truth." The elaborate equipment and techniques of crime-detection laboratories; the statistics contained in a "Brandeis-type" brief; the mortality tables used in calculating potential earning power in order to assess the "damages" of a death; psychiatric examinations; public opinion polls showing the amount of confusion existing between trade-marks or brand-names—all these are examples of inputs to the legal system from the adaptive system of the society.

Not only technique and factual knowledge are involved in this input, but also cognitive theories regarding the necessity of certain kinds of behavior if certain functions are to be efficiently performed. An important example of such an input is the use by the courts of classical economic theory.

The very fact that Justice Holmes found it necessary to admonish his colleagues on the Supreme Court that the Fourteenth Amendment "does not enact Mr. Herbert Spencer's social statics"[3] is evidence that in fact the Fourteenth Amendment had, for all practical purposes, done precisely that. In interpreting concepts such as "property" and "due process" the Court for a very long time based its reasoning about economic conflicts of interest on a specific theory of what was necessary to achieve productive coordination of economic activities.[4]

---

3. *Lochner* v. *New York*, 198 U.S. 45, at 75 (1905).

4. A particularly striking example of this is provided by the famous Slaughter House cases. The first Slaughter House case consisted of a protest by butchers that the granting by New Orleans of a slaughter house monopoly to one company, with rates to be publicly fixed, deprived them of their property without due process of law. The majority of the court, holding to the common law conception of property as physical objects, denied the butchers' protests and upheld the act. A minority, led by Justice Field, dissented, but failed to meet the majority's challenge to point to a single authority for defining property so broadly as to include something so intangible as a man's "calling" or "trade."

Twelve years later, the case came up again (this time the monopolist suing because New Orleans had changed its mind); and this time Justice Field found authority for his conception of property—the authority being Adam Smith. See John R. Commons, *The Legal Foundation of Capitalism* (New York: The Macmillan Co., 1924), chap. 2.

Not only in constitutional law, but in all areas of decision-making, the courts (more or less systematically) use as a decision-making criterion, the expected impact of a decision on productive efficiency. In tort law, for example, such perennial issues as the distinction among trespassers, licensees, and invitees, or the problem of the immunity of governmental agencies or charitable institutions from liability for their negligence, are nearly always debated in the context of the question, "What will be the impact on people's ability to carry out their responsibility?"

The court utilizes these inputs of knowledge (together with the other inputs that will be discussed below) to make a decision. The decision, which will of course be binding on all persons in the same class or category as the particular litigants at bar, is an output to the adaptive system of the society. It is an output of *organization* or structure.

The decision asserts a set of rights, duties, liabilities, exposures, immunities, and privileges that either alter or reinforce the organization of roles in the division of labor. For example, the extension of the protection of the Fourteenth Amendment to corporations, regarded as "legal persons," vividly affected the adaptive machinery of the society. Other examples are the holding of minimum wage laws to be unconstitutional and the later reversal of that holding, and the holding that a state may not keep for itself certain natural resources that would benefit interstate commerce.

In Durkheim's terminology, the court's integrative contribution to the adaptive system may be regarded as an output of organic solidarity. That is, the court's contribution to adaptation is an imposition of rights and obligations *in the interests of efficient organization.* It is dependent for this, however, on knowledge of what efficient organization *is,* and what can contribute to it. For example, employers now have what is called a "qualified privilege" to defame employees, which means that they are not liable for defamatory remarks even if proved false. The ground of this privilege is that employers are thought to need freedom to express their opinions to other employers without having to worry about possible legal penalties.

How important is this freedom today for labor recruitment? What effect does it have on labor mobility? What pressures does it put on employees to see particularistic relations with employers as a safeguard against defamation? And are there different answers to these questions for different categories of employees, so that the law errs (merely on pragmatic grounds) in dealing only with the gross category "employees"?

As part of the adaptive system, sociology potentially has much to contribute to the legal system, by way of answering such questions, by way of facilitating the predictions of how people will behave when exposed to new liabilities, by way of delineating the obstacles to efficient performance of functions, and by way of understanding what kinds of actions are and are not required for meeting various responsibilities.

But even supposing that sociologists are in a position to contribute such knowledge, a further problem is raised concerning the channels of communication by which it is transmitted to the legal system, and the return channels by which a secondary output of the legal system is communicated to the adaptive system—namely, *queries,* or expression of need for certain kinds of knowledge.

The most conspicuous mechanism relied upon at present for effecting this transmission is the adversary system, which is based, at least in part, on the assumption that if each of two adversaries is motivated to get in the record all the evidence most favorable to his *own* case, the chances are maximized of getting *all* relevant considerations before the court, and of forcing on the attention of "scientists" the need for certain kinds of knowledge.

How well this system works, or the degree to which it in fact obstructs and obscures the collection of pertinent evidence, is something on which there is more folklore than scientific knowledge. Similarly, we know very little about the utility of legal education for acquainting the practicing lawyer with the possible sources of reliable knowledge, or about the nature of the obstacles he encounters in obtaining it from "experts," even if he knows the sources.

Furthermore, on the other side of the transaction, there is a difficulty in making scientists, especially social scientists, sensitive to the needs of the legal system—that is, aware of them in the first place, and responsive to them in the second. The difficulty is illustrated in the conspicuous lack of communication between lawmen and social scientists even on the same university campus. The results are that some useful raw materials for sociological analysis remain locked in the law schools and law journals; an important market for sociological knowledge remains untapped; and the quality of "organizational efficiency" put out by the legal system may fall below possibly realizable standards.

The Law and the Polity

In modern democratic societies the prototype of the sovereign may be taken to be the legislature. Legislative determination of policy—the actual uses to which power is put—is one of the primary sources of the law's conception of goals,[5] or standards for evaluating the "efficiency" of a given or anticipated role structure.

The legislature's primary input into the legal system is, in other words, a description of the ideal state of affairs for which social resources are to be mobilized through the exercise of power. The immediate corresponding output of the legal system is the *application* of general policy statements to the specific conflict at hand. This, of course, means that the courts can by no means be passive or mechanical "implementers" of the legislative policy; the statute must be interpreted, and its inter-

---

5. This statement needs to be complicated—but only slightly—by the fact that in American society the courts review legislation and pass on its legitimacy, which seems to imply that the judicial system has some source of collective goal-determination other than the legislature. The extent to which this is true is an important empirical issue to which I shall return later; but in the immediate context it is important to note that the Constitution, which is the yardstick by which the courts formally measure legislation, is itself the creature of the sovereign; it is a super-statute of a super-legislature, created independently of the courts and subject to amendment independently of them.

pretation is a creative act, giving real effect to the abstract language of the legislature. It is an indispensable adjunct to the legislative exercise of power. In return for the output of interpretation, the legal system receives from the polity a secondary input, the sanction of *enforcement*. Judicial decisions become binding on the litigants through the power of the state; and— also to be included in the concept of enforcement—it is by the legislature that the courts are *empowered* to resolve disputes and are given the facilities for doing so: courthouses, judgeships, salaries, and so on.

These interchanges, of course, do not occur in any automatic or inevitable way. The transactions between the legal system and the polity may break down. Courts may "interpret" the life out of legislative policies; or they may even ignore a statute. In turn, the polity may refuse to enforce legal decisions, and may fail to give any clear direction of public policy as a guide to judicial action. These interchanges are often precariously balanced, just as are the interchanges between the output of consumers' goods by business firms and the spending of money by households. The point is that when the exchanges are not completed smoothly, some readjustment is likely to occur, in the first place; and in the second place there will be repercussions in other subsystems of the society.

The exchange of policy directives for interpretation of such policies is especially susceptible to disruption because the legislature, subject to the influence of whimsical shifts in public opinion and to the private demands of various interest groups, often enacts contradictory policies. The court in such cases must choose between different policies of the state.

American courts, for example, are often required to choose between a policy involving the use of the police power to secure collective goals, on the one hand, and the policy of maximum individual liberty, on the other. For a long period, the courts steadily rejected the use of police power in economic affairs in favor of a policy of freedom of contract. Today, they seem willing to accept almost any legislative policy concerning economic matters, regardless of its interference with individual liberty. This is true to such an extent that Maine's famous generalization concerning a transition from status to contract may be in the process of reversal, at least as regards economic relations.[6] At the same time, the courts more frequently reject policies that attempt to place national security—or "mechanical solidarity"—above individual liberty. The decision in the *Jencks* case,[7] for example, was a rejection of the policy of protecting FBI efficiency in favor of allowing defendants maximum opportunity to defeat prosecution.

That the courts must choose between conflicting policies means they have a secondary kind of output to make to the polity in exchange for the secondary input of enforcement. In a sense, the court becomes a legitimator of legislative decisions; and this adds to the polity's dependence on a successful completion of the exchange.

This adds significance[8] to the sociological problem of locating extralegislative sources of the court's own goal conceptions. The social origins of judges and law professors probably point to one such source; another is the socialization received by lawmen in the traditions of the law, both formally in the law schools and informally in interaction with peers and clients. Further, the mechanisms by which lawmen maintain some degree of insulation from the fluctuating pressures to which legislators are exposed, and the processes of reinforcement of an independent legal self-image, are problems to which sociologists could profitably direct their attention.

The transaction between the political and the legal systems may also break down on the other side. There is no automatic guarantee that judicial decisions will be enforced. From the time when the State of Georgia sent Cherokee Indians on something close to a death march in response to the Supreme Court's declaration that Georgia could not expropriate Cherokee lands, until recently when Congress refused to empower the Attorney

---

6. Cf. W. G. Friedmann, *Legal Theory* (London: Stevens and Sons, Ltd., 1953), pp. 144–145.

7. *Jencks* v. *U.S.*, 350 U.S. 980 (1956).

8. In this context the relation between "theories of the middle range" (for example, "reference group theory") and "general theory" appears clear. It is in terms of the latter that the former take on their significance; and middle-range theories become the muscles of general theory skeletons.

General to file contempt proceedings against officials who defy
the Court's desegregation order, it has been clear that the input
of enforcement may be withheld. The withholding of enforcement under certain conditions tends to move the system in the
direction of totalitarian forms of state-court relationships, and
is hence not only a theoretically strategic but also a value-
strategic focus of sociological study.

One of the most important conditions affecting the supply
of enforcement is the need of the polity for the legitimation
by the courts. This need seems to be a function of the esteem
in which the courts are held; and that in turn seems to be a
function of the relationships prevailing between the pattern-
maintenance and the legal systems.

The Law and Pattern Maintenance

Presupposed by all that I have said so far is a third condition necessary if the legal system is to contribute to integration
through the resolution of conflicts. This is the obvious fact that
conflicts must be brought to the courts' attention. People must
be motivated to turn to the law for protection of their interests,
and this implies that they must feel that the law will in fact
give them justice. It is thus in the offer of "justice" that the legal
system makes its major output, in exchange for the input of
motivations to accept the court as a problem-solving structure.

To do the proverbial rushing in, I want to define "justice" for
present purposes simply as the subjective feeling that one has
got what's coming to him, that one has received his "due." This
amounts to saying that internalized expectations have been met.

It is perhaps in connection with these interchanges between
the legal system and the pattern-maintenance system that there
are the most familiar breakdowns. On the side of the pattern-
maintenance system, one reason for the breakdown, it is sometimes suggested, is that no one really wants what the courts offer.
As political boss Martin Lomassey put it to Lincoln Steffens, in
a remark revitalized in Merton's discussion of the political

machine, what people often want is simply *help*—"Help, you understand; none of your law and justice, but help."[9]

This dislike of justice may be put in other terms. It is a feeling that the court's conceptions of legitimate expectations are very different from one's own. And this is likely to be true, partly because of differences between the reference groups of judges and clients, and partly because of the nature of one important mechanism relied upon by the court to insure conformity to institutionalized expectations.

The mechanism I refer to is the doctrine of *stare decisis,* the doctrine that the courts are bound by their own precedents, and that lower courts are bound by the old decisions of higher courts. The justification for the doctrine is usually that it provides the best insurance that "justice" will be served by respecting the expectations that have been built up on the basis of previous decisions.

The "certainty and predictability" of the law, so important to acceptance of the law as an integrative mechanism, is sought, then, by the law's own moral commitment to precedent. This commitment, though, interferes with another condition necessary for public acceptance of the legal process: a flexibility sufficient to adapt to changed circumstances, new interests, and different dangers and liabilities attendant upon social change.

The traditional devices relied upon by the common law to balance *stare decisis* on the one hand and the need for flexibility on the other were the familiar ones of "legal fictions," "equity," and concepts of "natural law."[10] These still operate to some extent to preserve the law from rigor mortis; but a more important device in modern societies is legislation, which, as was pointed out above, constitutes an input into the legal system of policy determination from an agency more responsive than the courts to rapidly changing needs.

So important has this device become, indeed, that courts may be found rendering decisions that are labeled by the court itself as unjust and inefficient but which, the court insists, it is bound

---

9. Robert K. Merton, *Social Theory and Social Structure* (New York: The Free Press, 1949), p. 74.

10. Cf. Friedmann, *op. cit.,* pp. 320–329.

to render nonetheless, until the legislature rescues it from the consequences of a prior decision. Justice Brandeis once declared, that "It is usually more important that a rule of law be settled than that it be settled right. Even where the error in declaring the rule is a matter of serious concern, it is ordinarily better to seek correction by legislation. Often this is true although the question is a constitutional one."[11]

The rationale for this position is that the legislative procedure can give clear notice to everyone that after a certain date, rights and obligations will be changed in a certain way, whereas the courts can reverse a precedent only in the context of an actual case, which would involve injustice to the litigant who had been relying upon the validity of the court's previous judgment. The courts do, of course, still reverse decisions, on the alleged basis of new facts, as in the desegregation cases, or even on the alleged finding of simple error in previous decisions. They are, however, reluctant to do this; and such actions are not predictable enough to be relied on. Changed community sentiments regarding the meaning of "justice," therefore, tend not so readily to be reflected in judicial decisions.

Furthermore, a related aspect of *stare decisis* also contributes to the law's lack of receptivity to new claims. This is the persistence, to some extent, of the doctrine that only those *interests* will be recognized that were previously recognized. That is to say, new needs for which court protection is sought may be dismissed by the court with the deadly sentence, "Plaintiff has failed to state a cause of action," which means that he has failed to demonstrate that any court in the past has even been willing to listen to evidence on such a violation of an expectation.

The central condition responsible for such dismissal seems to be that the court's *manifest* function is to apply an already-existing law; the latent function of resolving disputes *efficiently* is seldom recognized.

Two additional mechanisms by which the court's output of justice may be kept in fairly close balance with community sentiments should, however, be noted. One is the jury system.

---

11. Felix Frankfurter, "The Social Views of Mr. Justice Brandeis," in Erwin H. Pollack, ed., *The Brandeis Reader* (New York: Oceana Publications, 1956), p. 64.

Although nominally only a "trier of facts" when facts are in dispute, the jury probably tries a good many things besides facts behind its closed doors. Without overt changes in the legal doctrines, then, justice—according to the community's views—may nonetheless be served, although, to be sure, in a mysterious and somewhat "chancy" way.

A second such mechanism is the system of communication internal to the legal system itself. I include in this both law schools and the extensive commentaries and criticisms of judicial opinions in law journals. It is commonly supposed, for example, that it was an academic article by Brandeis and Warren in the *Harvard Law Review* that was responsible for judicial recognition of a new tort, invasion of privacy.[12] To the unknown degree to which the journals are considered by the bench and bar, the legal system may be kept in fairly close touch with prevailing community sentiments—depending also, of course, on the degree to which academic jurists are themselves in touch with them.

The fact remains, however, that "the law" is for many people something to be avoided if at all possible. There is not a very good market for the law's output of justice; and—the other side of the same coin—the law is not widely regarded as the place to take one's conflicts, except as a last resort.

A deeper reason for this than any I have so far considered may be related to the fact that, almost by definition, 50 per cent of the people involved in litigation must have their expectations violated. Someone has to lose.

While the adversary system may work tolerably well as a transmission belt for inputs of facts and policy considerations, it can hardly work very well in persuading a litigant that his cause is being considered on its merits and with respect, except possibly by his own lawyer, who by definition is not in control of the situation.[13]

Furthermore, there are two related characteristics of the law

---

12. Louis D. Brandeis and Samuel D. Warren, "The Right to Privacy," 4 *Harvard Law Review* 193–220 (1890).

13. One is inevitably reminded of a *New Yorker* cartoon showing a courtroom emptying after a trial. An obviously convicted defendant sits crushed and dejected at the defense table, while his attorney shoves papers into a briefcase. Showing perfect composure, the attorney is saying cheerfully, "Well, we can't win them all, can we?"

that contribute to making its output of "justice" unpalatable. One is the fact that the legal system tends to have written into it the assumption that in any dispute one side is right and the other side is wrong. The adversary system is built on this assumption and helps to reinforce it; and the court is ordinarily empowered only to decide a winner and a loser—not to find a way to help the loser adjust to his loss, or to avoid in the future the action that led to the loss, or to alter the conditions that led to the loser's behaving as he did.

The second difficulty is related to this. An assumption implicit in the operation of the law is that once rights and obligations have been authoritatively stated, individuals have only one mode of adaptation available to them: acceptance. The assumption, in other words, is that *learning* is the only response to a deprivation.

In fact, of course, there is good reason to believe that learning—that is, a reorganization of the individual's personality system so as smoothly to adapt to the new reality—is not even a very likely response, except under special conditions such as those summarized by Leonard Cottrell[14] or those suggested by Parsons.[15]

The legal system does not include the machinery for insuring the amount of permissiveness, support, denial of reciprocity, and conditional reward required to make the court experience a learning experience.[16] To the contrary, the obscure and complicated legal procedures remain a baffling barrier to the litigant's understanding of what happened to him, except to the degree to which his attorney informally plays the role of therapist. In consequence, the major impact may be frustration,

---

14. Leonard S. Cottrell, "The Adjustment of the Individual to his Age and Sex Roles," in Theodore M. Newcomb and Eugene L. Hartly, eds., *Readings in Social Psychology* (New York: Henry Holt, 1947), pp. 370–373.

15. Talcott Parsons, *The Social System* (New York: The Free Press, 1951), chap. VII.

16. The affiliation of social workers, probation and parole officers, and mental hygiene clinicians with the courts in some areas—chiefly family problems, juvenile delinquency, and crime—is a development tending toward the filling of this gap. We remain remarkably ignorant, however, of the workings of these mechanisms, from the present point of view.

with little to prevent the frustration from leaving a permanent residue of hostility.

It is interesting in this connection, moreover, that a device that under certain conditions *could* help the losing litigant to adjust to his loss—and even, conceivably, to change his expectations and behavior—does not in fact function toward that end, and so far as I can discern, is not even intended to do so. I refer to the written opinion delivered by appellate courts, setting forth the reason for the decision. An explanation of the decision addressed to the litigants might contribute to consensus in the long run; but the legal tradition seems to be rather to address the explanation to other lawyers—who, again, may or may not attempt to translate it for their clients in a way that might gain their acceptance of it.

To the degree that there is a reluctance to accept the courts as problem-solving agencies, the question must be raised as to what in fact is substituted for them. I shall here only propose certain tentative suggestions, approaching the problem by calling attention to a fact that at first glance seems to contradict what I have just said concerning a lack of demand for the court's output.

This is the fact that, in a sense, the demand for the court's services exceeds the supply. At least this might be a reasonable way of expressing the widely publicized figures of the backlog of cases on the judicial dockets in many jurisdictions, which results in delays of up to three or four or even six years between the filing of a suit and its final settlement. Why is the supply not increased?

One reason may be found in the consideration reviewed above. Widespread skepticism about the quality of justice put out by the legal system is an obstacle to any general support for legislation to increase the number of courts. Justice costs money, and people who purchase it either have a lot of money or have a desperate need for it. Those in immediate need may not be so numerous at any given time as to be able to affect legislative behavior; and those not in immediate need may not be sufficiently impressed by the quality of the stuff to be interested in increasing its supply.

Another factor tending to prevent an expansion of facilities is the obvious fact that those with an immediate demand do not have direct access to the courts; their immediate purchase is a purchase of lawyers' services. The supply of lawyers, therefore, might be expected to be more responsive to demand for legal adjudication than the supply of courts.

Insofar as this occurs, the *de facto* system of conflict resolution tends to become, not the court system, but a system of direct bargaining and negotiation between lawyers. Conflicts may then be settled not on the basis of the considerations discussed above, but on the basis of straight bargaining power and ability to wait. Furthermore, there may be two classes of persons for whom the inadequate supply of judicial facilities is functional rather than dysfunctional. These are lawyers, who can use the very existence of delays to persuade clients to settle out of court and thus increase the turnover of cases; and defendants.

For example, a litigant who has experienced, say $20,000 worth of damages and who, let us say, has a very strong case, is put in the position of having to choose between having $20,000 six years from now or considerably less today. If he is awarded $20,000 six years later, he has lost and the defendant has gained the interest on that amount, which at 5 per cent would be a $1000 a year.

What other differential consequences for integration flow from this kind of substitution of direct bargaining and power relations for judicial review can only be a matter of conjecture, until considerably more research is done. One conjecture is that of Herbert Croly, quoted by Merton, that "The lawyer having been permitted to subordinate democracy to the Law, the Boss had to be called in to extricate the victim, which he did after a fashion and for a consideration."[17]

At any rate, a widespread attitude toward the law seems to be that conveyed by the slogan, "First thing we do, let's hang all the lawyers." The incidence of this negative view, and its sources and implications for conflict resolution, offer another fertile field for sociological research.

17. Merton, *op. cit.*, pp. 72–73.

Summary

The suggestion of this paper is that the legal system be viewed as an integrative mechanism, contributing "coordination" to the society. This contribution takes the form of certain "outputs" to other sectors of the society, in exchange for certain "inputs."

1. From the political system, goals and enforcement, in exchange for interpretation and legitimation.
2. From the adaptive system, knowledge and "acceptance of queries" as research directives in exchange for organization and "demand" for knowledge.
3. From the pattern-maintenance system, conflicts and esteem in exchange for resolution and "justice."

The legal system's effectiveness in contributing to integration is a function of the stability of these interchanges. Some factors making for instability have been tentatively suggested:

1. The possible development inside the law of goal-conceptions inconsistent with the polity's.
2. The responsiveness of legislatures to short-run fluctuations in private interests.
3. The lack of communication of accurate knowledge to courts.
4. The lack of facilities for turning litigation into a "learning experience."
5. The development in the pattern-maintenance system of values resistant to "justice."
6. The lack of channels by which demand for court facilities might lead to an increase in supply.

Finally, certain strategic areas for sociological research have been suggested:

1. Possible sources of extra-legislative conceptions of collective goals, such as the social origins of lawmen and their legal socialization experiences.

2. The mechanism of reinforcement of and support for legal "ideals" within the legal profession.

3. The channels of communication to lawmen of scientific knowledge.

4. Public perceptions of the legal system and the bases of those perceptions.

5. The reactions of individuals to the legal imposition of new liabilities.

6. The devices used as alternatives to the legal system for resolving conflicts.

It is the central suggestion of this paper that a frame of reference such as that essayed here might not only help to overcome the barriers of sociolegal stereotypes, but also point the way to areas of sociolegal cooperation that would enrich both sociology and the administration of justice.

Thomas A. Cowan

What Law Can Do
for Social Science

It is an astonishing fact of American intellectual life that
both law and social science have been able to expand so enormously in the present century without significantly affecting
each other. Executive action, legislation, and even judicial
administration invade almost every sector of human activity
without benefit of social science; and the social disciplines
range over vast areas of human behavior largely ignoring the
salient fact of legal control. There is no reason to suppose that
either law or social science will ever absorb the other. But
since each deals with human behavior and since each purports
to cover the whole domain of its subject matter, it is reasonable
to suppose that as time goes on they will come more and more
into contact. That law will long continue to go its way in
ignorance of what social science has to offer in aid of its enter-

This paper is in a sense a joint product of the Rutgers Law School Fac-
ulty Seminar on Law and Sociology. At different times and in varying ways,
Harry Bredemeier, Alfred Blumrosen, Roger Cunningham, Clyde Ferguson,
Vincent Fiordalisi, Saul Mendlovitz, Gerard Moran, Robert Rodes, and
Malcolm Talbott have had a hand in it.

prise is coming to be regarded as unthinkable by many members of the legal community. And that social science will always impose upon itself a taboo against almost all areas of human activity occupied by law is equally hard to believe.

The reasons that law and social science are virtually strangers to each other are many. Not the least among them is the fact that *law has a theory of proof that is different from the scientist's theory of proof.* Modern scientific theory of proof arose in the study of inanimate nature. Astronomy, mechanics, kinematics, physics, and chemistry are the rock-bottom disciplines on which scientific methodology rests. For centuries these subjects furnished the "matter" of scientific activities. Their apparently indispensable tool was and is mathematics—itself a creature born of land measurement, navigation, bookkeeping, and weighing and counting activities of a practical sort. Although ideally mathematics develops without avowed reference to empirical sources in external nature, these sources are never far off. Consequently, much to the astonishment of its devotees, "pure" mathematics sooner or later is discovered to have applications in the external world.

The point is that modern scientific theory did not develop in connection with the study of human behavior. The social scientist, in trying to render scientific account of this particular aspect of reality, therefore faces a dilemma. He has a choice among a bewildering array of scientific instruments of high precision and immense versatility, all of which were designed to do a job that is not his. Modern mathematics and the lore of the physical sciences are heavy baggage so far as he is concerned. But if he scraps the lot of them he is in danger of falling into the opposite peril. He may be forced into nonscientific or even antiscientific speculations of a particularized, homey, or gossipy character. If he can frankly go over to the *geisteswissenschaften* and immerse himself in the humanistic aspects of social behavior, well and good. But if he clings to science he is apt to be torn apart. How can the social scientist escape the dilemma? In other words, how can he conduct scientific investigations of human nature in spite of the heavy weight of a scientific tradition that is based almost solely on the study of nonhuman nature?

It is possible that the law's theory of proof has something to teach the social scientist. The law has gone about the job of collecting data upon which to base its decisions for a much longer time than has physical science. Its experience in seeking the "truth" from individuals ignorant of it or interested in its suppression is age-old. What of the law's methods of finding out on which of the many sides of a disputed question of fact the "truth" is more likely to be found? This type of truth will not split atoms, to be sure. But its suppression does split nations and its neglect may poison their members just as surely as radioactive fallout. In fact, law takes it as one of its primary aims to put an end to the very possibility of such racial suicide. One hears it said frequently today that without science modern life would not be possible. This of course is true since without modern science our lives would not be "modern." But that modern civilization or indeed any civilization at all is quite impossible without law is a truism that seldom needs even be stated.

Modern science is built on the prescientific labors of its ancestors. An immense amount of empirical investigation is necessary as a prelude to the emergence of generalized scientific conceptions. Until very recently it was the habit of natural scientists to ignore the history of science. And even today, when that lack is being slowly remedied, most natural scientists give the impression that all that is of major consequence to their discipline is of relatively recent origin. Aside from the work of a few monumental geniuses, the past is largely ignored and present accomplishments taken as almost entirely the contribution of contemporaries.

Fortunately for himself and for his enterprise, the social scientist has been unable to create the conditions for an equally esoteric craft. To be sure, his inability to do so is costly. The cost is nothing less than a failure to attain full professional status in his own eyes. But the gain is also incalculably great: the social scientist has escaped the fate of premature rigor. He is not yet the technician whose easily won expertise is limited by what some superior body of learning can furnish him. He still has the opportunity (and the obligation) to be a scientist. As such his concern with his own fundamental methodology must be unending.

If, then, there are these weighty reasons why social science cannot rest content to place itself solely in the right line of descent from the natural sciences of the past, if, in other words, social science cannot wholly accept the role of the continuator of a tradition based almost exclusively on a preoccupation with nonhuman nature, perhaps the need for a dual line of ancestry is indicated. And it may be that the law, with its long history of more or less successful professional or semiscientific experience with controlling human nature, is precisely the thing needed to help fill one of the basic needs of social science.

The experience of the science of biology in the medical schools is perhaps an analogue. Biology is not a creature of medicine, and presumably its development could proceed wholly in isolation from medical practice. But it is quite obvious that such a separation, which for medicine would be devastating, is not in the interests of biology either. The life sciences have gained by collaboration with medicine. It is reasonable to suppose that the behavioral sciences would have nothing to lose and perhaps much to gain by collaboration with law. As I see it, benefit might result in at least four ways, which I shall consider in the order of their growing importance. The law can help the process of social investigation (1) by sharpening up the social scientific model; (2) by supplying the social scientist's kit with another investigative tool, the art of cross-examination; (3) by providing him with a method of control, namely, legal coercion; (4) by making available to him an immense reservoir of *value judgments* on human behavior in the history of law itself and in its present body of empirical rules of decision. The rest of this paper is a brief elaboration of the first three points and an extended discussion of the last, namely, value judgments.

The Scientific Model

Suppose I call all these presuppositions or preconditions which an investigator takes with him to the job of collecting data his *a priori equipment*. I shall perhaps be pardoned this Kantian barbarism since I intend to drop it immediately. That portion of his *a priori equipment* which the investigator has

raised to the level of consciousness and formalized in a con-
ventionally acceptable scientific way I shall call his *model*. The
model then serves as his over-all major control to assure him
that his work is going to be done within the limits of scientific
precision that he has set himself.

In considering the elements of model building it is con-
venient to divide the job into two parts: formal and practical.
The formal aspects of the model are derived from the philosophy
of science, that is, from the *logic of experiment* and from the
theory of the *decision process*. Both of these disciplines are
highly abstract and the tools they use are not generally available. The influence of these activities is slow to make itself felt
in the day-to-day workings of a tradition so conservative as that
of science.

We turn then to the *practical* aspects of the model. At once
we encounter a difficulty. What *are* the practical problems of
model building, and how do they differ from the problem of
building a house, a family, or a curriculum? I am really not
sure that they do. Model building in the scientific sense is something like building a house. It calls for a number of fellows
skilled in the crafts. One could do it oneself, but the results
might be distressing.

Now, is there anything that the law-trained investigator has
to contribute to scientific model building that on the average
and over the entire profession he can do better than another?
There is, I think. It is his age-old training in the generalized art
of verbal inquiry. From the moment he enters law school until
he draws his last wicked breath a lawyer is a doubter. He begins
law training with an intensive introduction into the Socratic
method of inquiry. Each case he studies is minutely shredded.
Each aspect of it is questioned. Each rule of law is mercilessly
criticized, alternatives considered, abandoned, reconsidered, re-
abandoned. If the scientific model is the question that the scientist puts to nature, then the man whose profession is "questioning" is a very likely person to help determine whether or not
the question is put straight.

Experience bears out this theoretical supposition. Social scientists who presently are working with lawyers report that in
the work preliminary to the collecting of data, the lawyer is a

valuable ally. It is not just that the lawyer knows law in the way that the physician knows medicine and that therefore his practical assistance is necessary to guide the social investigator properly through the mazes of the law. The social scientist's model is a verbal construct, and the lawyer quickly finds that it has a grotesque resemblance to elements of his own trade. Like a legal artifact it must have internal consistency; its terms and conceptions must be precise or, if equivocal, the degree and kind of ambiguities must be in control; all dispositions must be operationally meaningful in both cases (there must exist methods for determining their likely effects); data must be gathered or the legal artifact submitted to its life experience; and finally inferences must be obtainable (the hypotheses confirmed or refuted; the artifact legally sanctioned or not).

Hence, the lawyer is apt to enter enthusiastically into the process of model building—especially as concerns its practical aspects. That he also feels free to question the bases of probability theory and to dispute all other aspects of the social scientist's competence is sad. But resolutely faced up to, he succumbs to the superior weight of the alien expertise.

Cross-Examination

The lawyer's art is adversary. The social scientist who has to bear with him in model building quickly feels the weight of this uncomfortable weapon. But it can be turned to other uses. It can be employed as an alternative or as a subsidiary method to the questionnaire in data gathering.[1]

Cross-examination, although adversary, is not necessarily aggressive. On the contrary, since the cross-examiner is after biased results, his words may be as honeyed as those the serpent used to talk Eve out of the Garden of Eden. The method of cross-examination is as old as the law itself. It purports to uncover contradictions—the peculiar mixture of truth and un-

---

1. See David Riesman's note 16 in his essay elsewhere in this volume. The work referred to was designed by and executed under the direction of Julius Cohen of the Rutgers Law Faculty.

truth that persuades courts and juries to act. I should like to see its consciously biased methods compared scientifically with the interviewer's allegedly unbiased or at any rate so-called controlled method of questioning. I suspect that its strengths and weaknesses are different from those of interviewing. If the method of cross-examination (as modified) should turn out to be a useful tool in the social investigator's kit, the enterprise would have justified itself.

Legal Control

I have long advocated an alliance between social science and law on the ground that law needs the methods of social science to strengthen its data-collecting processes and social science needs law to control or coerce experiments in human behavior.[2] Not all investigation in the behavioral sciences needs to be experimental in the sense that the investigator must have the power to manipulate his subjects. But if the social scientist can never *compel* obedience to his dictates in accordance with the necessities of his investigation, then surely he is handicapped in drawing inferences about a large and important sector of human nature: the area under legal control.

In modern times, law stands as the major means of coercing human behavior consistently with freedom. In no other way save war will modern man submit to such far-flung conscious control of his behavior. Hence, a liaison between law and social science would enable the social scientist to dictate changes in human behavior required by his model. More efficient gathering of fact for law would also result.

Elsewhere, I have argued these matters at length. One example must do here. Imagine the social scientist conducting an experiment on the relative efficiency of various legal devices designed

2. See, for example, T. A. Cowan, "The Relation of Law to Experimental Social Science," 96 *University of Pennsylvania Law Review* 484 (1948); "A Postulate Set for Experimental Jurisprudence," 18 *Philosophy of Science* 1 (1951); "The Design of Legal Experiment," 6 *Journal of Legal Education* 520 (1954).

to enforce law. Suppose he has convinced the head of an administrative agency (say the Federal Food and Drug Administration) that a scientific study of its ways of enforcing a certain regulation against contaminated food is in order. The social scientist sees in practice a whole range of administrative enforcement devices ranging from a polite letter about a new regulation to an actual criminal prosecution that, if successful, will not only put the defendant out of business but possibly also land him in jail. Then suppose the social scientist to be allowed to set up a model to study the relative efficiency of the various devices at the disposal of the agency. Enforcement can be randomized (a very delicate matter). Once data are in, new directives can go out, still in accordance with the demands of the model.

I know of no such study of the relative efficiency of alternative devices for enforcing law. There is indirect evidence that some such studies are being undertaken in secret by certain federal agencies at present. But they are being done under the blanket—a sure sign that the subject matter of the investigation may well lead to antiscientific reactions. There is no reason that carefully selected legal experiments could not be undertaken perfectly openly. They would be mutually beneficial to both law and social sciences.

Value Decisions in the Law[3]

The first three reasons for rapprochement between law and social science are easily understood. That the law-trained mind might be useful to the student of human behavior in the preparatory stages of his research, that cross-examination may turn out to be a usable tool in social investigation, and that judges,

---

3. From this point on I have ventured to allow my "affects" to spill over onto the page uncensored. I realize that I run the risk of offending sensitive people by this unscientific practice. But I have decided that with good will on his part the reader will more nearly gain an understanding of what I want to say than if I had followed in this rather unorthodox piece the customary practice of editing out emotions and feelings.

legislators, and administrators might prove useful collaborators in controlled experiments are proposals that each social scientist can consider for himself. When we come to the fourth proposal, value judgments, we are dealing with an entirely different matter.

Value judgments are presently the subject of sharpest controversy over the entire range of the sciences and the technical arts. Not only in philosophy, where the problem is absolutely critical, but also in the working sciences themselves from sociology through psychology and biology, down to chemistry, physics, and even mechanics, the question of values and their place in scientific theory is on the order of the day.

In raising the issue of value judgments in a discussion of the relation of law to social science, I am well aware that I run the serious risk of dealing in matters so obscure and intractable as practically to defy explication. This risk must be taken. In an attempt to limit the risk, however, I shall try to stick as closely as possible to familiar terms and conceptions. This means a sacrifice of the scientific clarity that conventional methods of discussion and well-recognized terms afford. But it also means that issues that are not yet ready for decision are kept open.

For example, let me first make a few common-sense observations on the nature of values. *Value is a human creation.* That the whole history of religion may well turn on this statement need not detain us. Second, *value is created by the human mind.* That this is a ridiculously simple way to dispose of the relationship of the human mind to the human body need not deter us either. Third, although the human mind is a value-creating organism, yet in contemporary scientific society, which has a most sophisticated technique for handling truth judgments, *no scientific technique exists for ranking values.* Why is this so? Why are values so intractable and yet matters of such pressing concern?

Perhaps a short discussion of the meaning of the term "value" would be helpful. There are many meanings of the simple word "value" and many compounds using the term. "Truth value" is a term of art for the logician. He speaks of two-, three-, or many-valued logics. There is little or no mystery in the way he uses the notion. The same is so for the scientist. He knows

various kinds of truth values. In addition he can assign value
to hypotheses. Some are "rich," while others are "worthless."
And he has a way of finding out which are which, namely,
scientific method. Again, he assigns values to facts, by the
orderly processing of data. To sum up, the scientist deals
familiarly with scientific laws, hypotheses, and data and each
is associated with a notion of value. Perhaps I shall be permitted to do violence to the unity of the human mind in action
by assigning each of these products (laws, hypotheses, data) to
separate functions of the mind. That is, perhaps I may be
allowed to speak of "thought values" in connection with scientific laws, of "intuition values" in connection with hypotheses,
and of "sensation values" in connection with data. This tri-
chotomy, although quite old-fashioned, may yet serve to illuminate my meaning. For example, a formulation of the scientific
process much favored in the nineteenth century and still extant
in science textbooks is to describe the scientist at work on sense-
data, which he intuitively manipulates to discover the laws of
nature. He begins with sensation values, uses intuition values
to deal with them imaginatively, and ends with truth values, or,
as I should say here, thought values. Never mind that modern
methodology has directly reversed the process. The scientist
begins with a model of his accepted truth values, that is, his
accepted conventional axioms, rules, and procedures—in a word,
his logic. Then he imaginatively utilizes intuition to furnish
hypotheses. The whole work is then tested in sensation, his
data.

What aspect of the unified human mind does this description
of the scientist at work leave out? To use another old-fashioned
expression: *it leaves out feeling.*[4] Or, as we should say, "feeling

---

4. At this point it will be evident that I have borrowed and put to new
uses the fourfold scheme that C. G. Jung used in his classification of psychological types. I run great risk in using the term "feeling," since it is
impossible to give it even a relatively precise connotation. In common
speech it means, primarily, touch; secondarily, thought, emotion, intuition,
sensation, sentiment. My general meaning is quite close to that of the word
"sympathy" as used by Charles H. Cooley. In the chapter on "Sympathy
or Understanding" in *Human Nature and the Social Order* (rev. ed.; New
York: Charles Scribner's Sons, 1922), Cooley speaks of a general concep-

values." These are the values that are "irrelevant" for the scientist at work. The methodologist (philosopher-scientist) concentrates on truth values aided by intuition values. The data-man emphasizes sensation values, aided by intuition. He who concentrates on feeling values is taken to be no scientist at all.

I take it to be a feeling judgment, an assignment of feeling value, to say of anything that it is *better* than something else. We need not inquire at the moment *why* it is better; nor how the judge knows that it is better; nor how much better it is than its alternative. I desire to concentrate simply on the judgment "this thing is better than that." What can science do with this judgment?

Many scientists say: nothing. The judgment is meaningless. That is, it is neither true nor false. To these I should say that of course it is neither true nor false—it is not a truth judgment at all. It is a feeling judgment—a judgment of value, pure and simple. Other people less intransigent than the positivist say that we must transform the statement into a truth-value judgment. Let us take it to mean one of a number of truth-value equivalents:

1. It means "this is better than that for purpose X." Then we can test the truth value of this revised statement.

2. Or it means "I think this is better than that." Then we can find out whether I truly do think so or not.

3. Or it means "under what controlled circumstances do certain people say 'this is better than that' and what are the consequences of their so saying?"

4. Or any other truth-value judgment it pleases the scientist

tion of "sympathy" that suits me very well as the general conception of "feeling." I have other irons in the fire than Cooley was there heating. In this paper I intend to emphasize the part that feeling plays in the process of *individuation*. My objective is to incorporate the individuating aspect of feeling in modern generalized scientific method. Incidentally, Cooley seems here to place exclusive emphasis upon the role of feeling rather than that of thought in the social process. As a result his work, I should think, would stand outside the main body of "scientific" sociology. He might well be discovered to be the bad conscience of the experimental social scientist. For a philosophical discussion of individuality, see William Earle, "The Concept of Existence," 62 *Journal of Philosophy* 734 (1960).

to consider an equivalent of the feeling-value judgment "this is better than that."

I think I prefer the rank positivist who tells me I am talking nonsense in saying "this is better than that" to the cheerful scientific alterer or reducer who takes the feeling value out of the judgment and, thus changed, finds it a truth judgment. I like the first better than the second, because after offering me a wearying set of alleged "truth" alternatives the second fellow too will finally tell me that the statement is nothing that science can handle. He is very apt to end by telling me that what I am talking about is an emotional afflatus. I merely emote "this is better than that." And in the presence of emotion science withdraws because science is unemotional.

It is necessary to distinguish between emotion and feeling, as I am using the latter term in this paper. When I say "this is better than that" am I being emotional? Not necessarily. It is possible to be emotional (or unemotional) about any type of value statement. I have seen scientists emotional about truth judgments (the wonderful laws of nature; nature loves logarithms). I have seen them emotional about scientific intuitions (a beautiful hypothesis, an elegant proof) and about sensations (the spectrum). No, I am not necessarily, and certainly not only, emotional about my judgment that "this is better than that." I need not care whether anyone believes me or not. Nor need I be interested in what truth-value investigations one is is induced to undertake as a result of this feeling judgment.

In the modern scientific world the function of feeling has atrophied. I believe that in classic antiquity the situation was the reverse. Men then knew what they valued. But the difference between truth and falsity was a mystery. The Sophists could baffle subtle Athenians by asking them whether a stick thrust into a tub of water was truly bent or not. Modern scientists deal freely with the question of truth, know how to go about investigating it. At the very least they know a good deal about what they don't know. But they refuse to take a stand on what is worth doing.

When judge and jury in a court of law decide for the plaintiff rather than for the defendant, they are making an over-all feeling judgment. Would anyone necessarily say that they are being swayed by their emotions? Sometimes, perhaps, but not usually. The judge and jury are acting rationally on the whole. They are making a rational judgment concerning better or worse. Truth enters into the process, to be sure, but in a peculiar way. To illustrate this point, let us consider briefly a very well-known but quite strange case. A famous movie actor was sued in a filiation proceeding in which an attempt was made to establish the actor as father of the plaintiff, an illegitimate child. The unmarried mother of the plaintiff testified that the actor had had intercourse with her at times that might well have led to the pregnancy from which the plaintiff infant issued. The actor introduced the uncontradicted testimony of eminent serologists that by the theory of blood types the actor could not have been the father. Thereupon counsel for the actor moved to have the case dismissed on the ground that the scientific evidence of his experts could not possibly be impugned by any evidence introduced for the plaintiff, and that therefore the case should not go to the jury. Nevertheless the court gave the case to the jury under instructions to consider all the testimony, lay and expert, and to decide whether the actor was the father of the plaintiff or not. The jury obliged with a verdict that the actor was indeed the father of the plaintiff infant. Thereupon the court ordered the actor to pay $75.00 a week for the child's support.

What would you say of this case? Is it a travesty on justice? Over the years the writer has gotten the most amazing reactions from scientist and lawyer. Lawyers are apt to hang their heads in shame. Scientists are apt to say "So what? The actor is rich. Somebody had to support the kid. It might well have been his."

If I say that this case represents a feeling judgment triumphant over a truth judgment, will anyone quarrel with me? Still the decision was not an emotional afflatus. If anything, the emotionality was and still is on the other side—the unfairness of saddling a man with a child not his, or the stupidity of the judges who defy the laws of nature.

I believe that law contains an immense mass of feeling judgments and I invite the social scientist to study them empirically.

I think that when feeling conflicts with fact, the former prevails in the law. The law is thus one of the great counterparts of science, since in science the conflict is supposed to be resolved the other way.

I have purposely cast the relation of science to law in terms of "thinking" and "feeling" rather than "cognition" and "affect." As already indicated, I do not want to carry the heavy burden of deciding this deep-seated philosophical and methodological dispute within the confines of a paper. I prefer to make no more than an ostensive gesture in the direction of the law. "There lies an immense complex of feeling judgments. See what you can do with it." To be sure I cannot hope that all or even many of my brethren in the law will agree that this ostensive judgment is correct. They may think of law as a mass of cognitions only. For them law's obligatoriness is a mystery. Nor am I interested in any scheme, methodological or not, to effect a compromise between those who temperamentally see cognitions in the work of science or in its subject matter and those who are temperamentally led to consider "affects" as the main subject matter of much of social investigation. I repeat: I merely want social scientists to examine the feeling life of the law to see what they can do with it or what it does to them.

I have another good reason for "pointing" to action (the law) rather than to theory (philosophy of science). All disputes I have seen about the relative place of cognitions and feelings in science are themselves highly loaded in favor of cognition. Those who favor "feelings" are told to organize and formalize their "thoughts" on the subject—in other words, to reduce feelings to cognitions. But, they could equally one-sidedly invite "cognitivists" to feel their way into a social problem and to come back with valid feeling judgments. Naturally, neither thinking nor feeling alone can adequately characterize any given item of human behavior. This can be done only in imagination. In law, which is a theory of living action, feelings are consciously and methodically generalized into living rules of conduct. Hence the invitation to the social scientist to try his luck in dealing with the feeling judgments of law.

Truth Value vs. Feeling Values

To what extent do social scientists still accept the Renaissance definition of the task of science: to measure all things measurable, and to make measurable the hitherto incommensurable? Modern measurement theory rests on probability. Is probability theory the sole indispensable adjunct to social investigation and does social science stand or fall on predictability alone? Which will yield first—contemporary measurement theory or the complexities of human nature?

It is difficult for me to see how measurement theory can fail to undergo radical change. Indeed, this process has been going on for a long while. Seventeenth-century mechanism and rationalism gave rise to a reaction in the form of probability theory. For a long time probability theory remained mechanistic and is partially so today. Indeed, rationalistically viewed, probability theory can still be stated as rigorously as any other branch of mathematics. But, as a practical matter, when probability theory is *applied* it necessitates looseness, error, go and no-go techniques. Demands for an objective teleology arise.[5]

---

5. A note in explanation of why applied science (whether probability theory or not) leads to teleology: one who applies a scientific theory does so with a purpose in mind. His job gets done more or less successfully. If the job is unsuccessful, he will on occasion blame his theoretical tools. Thus he becomes a customer for other theory, some of it (we may suppose) not yet in existence. He creates a *demand* for theory. Theory emerges to *supply* the demand. Such theorizing has an end or purpose in view. It twists and turns in an endeavor to meet the demand. It becomes evident that despite all efforts to keep theory formal, practice warps it teleologically. Theory and practice are seen to be inextricably interwoven. No matter how "pure" theory strives to be it becomes tainted with practical considerations. The unremitting attempt to keep theory pure (counsel of the ideal of perfection) must constantly fail as theory meets its fulfillment in practice. Take probability theory, for example. Only a relatively slight amount of probability theory has been able to stay in the realm of pure mathematics or pure logic. Most of it follows a progression to "pure practice." Mathematical statistics is eminently practical, as are "operations research," management science, and other forms of applied statistics in the

Probability theory must now be loosened up further. It is not enough that all sciences, including mechanics (as in cybernetics), are becoming teleological. It has become evident that somewhere or other (and where better than in the behavioral sciences?) science must come to grips with one special aspect of teleology, namely, value.

Social scientists are not happy that modern scientific theory frames all answers in the mold of one value system only: truth. True or false; false by how much; true by what percentage of likelihood? These and similar quantifications and truth-value judgments seem to exhaust scientific capabilities. We have already said that no generalized scientific methodology exists for deciding a question of better or worse. We have further said that the scientist's way of handling a better-worse problem is first to ask, "better or worse for what purpose?" and then to try to ascertain *how much* better or worse for the assigned purpose. The better-worse dichotomy in and of itself is meaningless to him as scientist. Scientists as such will not say *this* is good and *that* is bad about anything except their own scientific value system. Being human, scientists will insist that antiscientific behavior is bad and scientific behavior is good. But they can give no scientific defense for this position.

Social psychologists are entranced by the problem of human motivation, as well they might be. But do not ask them to tell you which of two examples of human motivation tends more nearly to the good. Now a natural scientist stands always ready

---

realm of human behavior. The same thing is happening to game theory.

This issue arises critically in statistical mechanics. The scientist views the behavior of particles of matter or packets of energy in the light of a twofold model. One aspect of the model is mechanical invariance; the other is statistical indeterminacy (stochasticism). Whether the scientist chooses mechanical invariance or statistical indeterminacy depends on his purpose. Sometimes he chooses both and creates a further indeterminacy, one of theory or explanation. At any rate his own purposes twist and warp theory in the interests of an end or aim he has in view. The result is to infect even mechanical invariance with teleology. *It is something useful for a purpose.* My point is that with the application of probability methods in all the sciences once more the almost universal custom, the scientist finds it increasingly necessary to find a scientific, as distinct from a mystical, place for "purpose" or "teleology" in all of his accounts of the order of nature.

to tell you which of two statements of fact lies nearer to the truth. Or he may only tell you how to go about undertaking the inquiry. Or if the inquiry is hopelessly complex he can indicate why. Or if the pursuit is vain, he may show you that you have removed yourself from the realm of scientific inquiry by failing to meet one or more of its exactions. In brief, he has a good idea of what he can and what he cannot do with natural science resources. But on the problem of value there is no received tradition in science.

The disciplines whose major concern has always been values are theology, ethics, and law. For reasons which I need not dwell upon here, theology and science have been at logger-heads for a thousand years. There is no apparent hope for a rapproachement. Ethics is more nearly neutral, but it is not supported by a hinterland since it has lost its close tie with religion. Ethical writings are thin and jejune. But law has certain advantages to offer the scientist interested in value theory. It at least is well nourished, a going concern, with more business than even its adepts wish for. It has a tradition as old as that of theology and science. It has a modern task (peaceable ordering of human relations) at least as important as that of science and probably important enough for theology to be a necessary condition for its continued existence. It is massive, consequential, and absorbed in the affairs of life. People are its stuff. Law is interested in nothing but human behavior.

Every legal disposition is a value judgment. Every statute envisages two types of relevant human behavior, the good and the bad. It enjoins the good and proscribes the bad. Every executive regulation follows the same dichotomy. So does judicial law. It is no accident that lawsuits fall naturally into biparty practice. Each side claims for itself the right. Only one side receives the accolade. The other is wrong . . . for the time being.

Every rule of judicial law can be challenged by a competitor rule. There exist devices for deciding between them. This is the judicial office par excellence. Is it not analogous to scientific method? How can value-hungry modern science possibly pass up the huge store of riches accumulated by millenia of legal practice? Can one understand an epidemiologist who shuns all plagues? My use of this analogy is, of course, not pure chance. The law is a plague for the scientist. He has reason to shun it. Perhaps in some small measure I can suggest why.

Besides that of feeling judgments there is another forbidding topic the social scientist may come upon in the law: the unconscious mind. So far as I know, social scientists still have their backs turned on this awesome beast. Social science has found a few Freudian and Adlerian conceptions such as projection, rationalization, dominance, ego, wish fulfillment, superiority, polymorphous perverse sexuality, and others readily assimilable into social science theory. But it has no place for the dominant conception of all analytical systems: the unconscious. Unconsciousness and scientific methodology are in apparent contradiction. Why?

The reason is that since the beginning of modern philosophy scientific knowledge has been equated with *conscious thinking.* This is a rationalistic ideal, which has stood despite all the other inroads made on rationalism by empirical science and by non-rationalistic cultural forces generally. The modern methodologist is purportedly engaged in conscious thinking. This is for him the highest form of scientific enterprise. True, he recognizes that without accompanying unconscious thinking (intuition) his thought would be sterile. But the role of intuition in science has itself never been consciously apprehended. Although the scientist knows that continued training affects intuition, he could not honestly say whether training aids or cripples it. In some of the most esoteric practices of natural science (say nuclear physics) it is expected that intuition will be the special endowment of youth and will be quickly exhausted.

An even more serious hazard than unconscious thinking for the scientist is unconscious feeling. If the nature of intuition is not well understood by the scientist, at least its importance to his enterprise is appreciated. A scientist without "ideas" is known to be a cripple. But what about a scientist plagued by unconscious feelings? Is he merely neurotic, or does the fact that feeling has no recognized part in the scientific enterprise have its effect on science generally? We may well suppose that it has. To begin with, feeling exerts a powerful influence on the social scientist with respect to the areas of human behavior he will be led to investigate. Human misery, injustices, inequalities, abuses, infirmities are apt to enlist his sympathy and influence his choice of subject matter of investigation. It also leads the rest of the world to suspect the social scientist's impartiality as a scientific investigator. Lawmen quickly note that only a relatively few areas of the law appear inviting to social scientists: the criminal law, family law, social security, civil rights. Conversely, among natural scientists the predominant lack of attention to feeling often leads to a callous, cold indifference to the human effects of science, to a reverence of science for science's sake. Science disclaims responsibility for the power it creates. Science can be enlisted in the service of any cause, however revolting. German science under the Nazis represents the pathological results of such "ruthless efficiency."

The methodologist is apt to be hardest hit by the disease of lack of feeling. He is taught to emphasize thought and the type of intuition that leads most readily to consistent thinking. Hence intuition as a generally creative force is sometimes throttled. More seriously, the total suppression of feeling may give his work an air of sterile, even tautological, exactitude that repels ordinary working scientists and often leaves the brilliant theorist a lonely and neglected misanthrope. Conversely, the investigator who yields too readily to intuition becomes an eccentric or a dilettante, while he who succumbs too thoroughly to the dictates of feeling becomes a special-pleader, a sentimentalist, a captious critic, or a cynic.

And now for the moral. Law is a system for organizing and systematizing feeling judgments. It attempts to offer rational alternatives to the settlement of disputes by armed might and trickery. It has a whole host of techniques for settling disputes on moral bases. It is a low-level practical morality, a minimum ethics. It puts morality into action by directing powerful currents of feeling into peaceful channels.

As the great modern exponent of the collective feeling life of mankind (religion has almost abandoned its part in this job) law stands as the dark shadow side of science—its *unconscious*. No wonder the scientist finds the law's processes dark, *irra-*

tional. Law, like morality and religion, draws it greatest guiding precepts from the unconscious feeling life of humanity, from its collective unconscious, to use Jung's phrase. Justice, injustice, right, wrong, equality, equity, security, due process, even reasonableness are all feeling-ideas, moral principles whose wellsprings are unconscious and whose appearance in events and judgments receives formal concretization in the law.

In giving objective sanction to moral principles the law brings up to consciousness and rationalizes these generalized feeling sentiments of humanity. Law is a highly rational activity notwithstanding the fact that its main guiding lines are irrational or, more properly, nonrational, that is to say unconscious, motivations.

On the other hand the dark side of the law is found in its thinking processes. Legal science is primitive, archaic, contradictory. A scientist who comes to study the law is apt to see its dark side first, that is, the primitivity of its fact-finding processes. Everything seems designed to hide the truth! In the Anglo-American legal system, the rules of evidence are relics of the childhood of Western culture. The rule excluding hearsay evidence is an example. It assumes that the only knowledge modern man can rely upon is the evidence of his own five senses. No wonder the rule against hearsay evidence is so riddled with exceptions as to be virtually inoperative. But the real question is, why is it still retained? Further, why does the law believe that truth finding should be left to adversary clash of interests? Why does the law indulge the indecent spectacle of eminent scientists contradicting one another in the area of their own expertise? Why does it permit a lawyer ignorant of the nature of science to cross-examine a distinguished expert scientific witness in the hope of catching him out in verbal contradictions? Or pretending to challenge his professional qualifications? And so on.

Well, it is quite obvious that legal science needs strengthening. Its fact-finding processes must be brought up to date. This much we in the law hope for from the scientist. On the other hand, there is also the bright side of the law corresponding to the scientist's dark or weak side. We have said that the values that law emphasizes are feeling values. Truth is a value and even possesses a certain feeling value. But the law cheerfully sacrifices truth values for feeling values. This is a partial explanation for the otherwise wholly inexplicable use of the jury as a fact-finding mechanism. The law's theory is that the jury finds facts and the judge proclaims the law. The jury is picked for its ignorance. Special competence in the area under dispute or special knowledge of the facts of the case renders a juror incompetent. How can the legal system trust the ordinary man to find out the truth concerning a complicated state of facts that skilled counsel seem intent upon befuddling? Anyone who really proposed this method as one for ascertaining truth would be certifiably mad. It is evident that the jury has another function and operates otherwise than as a scientific instrument to weigh truth. The cue is given in the test that each juror must undergo. On preliminary examination inquiry is made to test the juror's bias. The real question is: How will he *feel* about the lawsuit? Each side tries to get jurors with "right" feelings and to keep the other side from getting jurors with "wrong" feelings. No one may question a juror's motives for his verdict. The jury brings in a verdict based on collective feelings. Far from being a scientific judgment whose truth value must be verifiable by all competent to run the same test, the jury's deliberations must be kept safe from intrusion, and their verdict preserved as absolutely unique. There is no notion that another jury would necessarily arrive at the same verdict.

The result is the same if the judge acts as jury. His decision is a feeling decision. He makes a unique appraisal not in terms of truth or falsity but in terms of good or bad, or rather, better or worse. The present plaintiff's position is better than the defendant's. A unique decision.

What then of rules of law? What of the principle of equality before the law? What of the notion that in fairness similar cases must be decided similarly? This is where the social scientist enters. He is confronted with generalizations of vast numbers of feeling judgments. He is in the presence of an enormous system of value judgments extending back to the prehistory of the race. He will deal with the generalized conception of fairness, for example. What does the social scientist have to say about fairness? Does the term have any content for him? He might say that he can tell us how many people on the average in Newark think it is fair that real property be taxed on the basis of its full market value. But he would not undertake to say whether this system of valuation is fairer than another. Yet law does nothing but make such judgments and its generalizations are truly a body of knowledge and truly quite different from truth generalizations.

The generalized method of arriving at feeling judgments is persuasion. In the law persuasion is balanced. The parties try to outpersuade each other. To the scientist schooled in nonfeeling judgments this method of arriving at truth is worse than nonsense. It is downright immoral. Imagine trying to persuade a scientist-judge that one percentage rather than another represents confirmation of a hypothesis about a matter of fact when his researches tell him otherwise. He is persuaded only by his own method. To attempt to appeal to his feelings would be reprehensible. Yet he might agree that in point of fact persuasion has its inevitable place in the scientific process: what research to undertake; whether to continue in the teeth of repeated failure; how to get funds, equipment, assistance; the degree of confidence to place in his results; whether they indicate a broader or narrower field of inquiry in the sequel; how significant the results are, and so on.

Is the scientist adequately aware that his choices not only in the selection of hypotheses but also in much else of his work are influenced by feelings? Does he attempt to formalize these choices by designing a system of competing persuasions to allow him to keep the matter to be decided under control and to "keep his own feelings out of the decision"? This is how a law judge operates. A lawyer who pleads his own case has a fool for a client. How about a scientist who trusts himself to make his own feeling decisions?

Methods of Individuation

Let us assume that judicial law is a process that balances truth judgments against feeling judgments and comes up with decisions. We thus see this branch of the law as a means for reconciling the conflicting demands of truth and feeling, fact and value. Suppose further that we imagine a behavioral scientist coming to the law with the purpose of lending scientific aid to its fact-finding processes. His first discovery would be that the law's fact-finding process is so chaotic that the services of a skilled scientist would seem to be a mockery. What appears to be needed is common sense. No scientist, but a business executive, is called for to introduce some semblance of order into this madhouse.

For if we were to take seriously the law's claim that it desires to base its decisions on the facts, we would surely then do the following obvious things:

1. Abolish juries.
2. Disbar all the lawyers. Their major function is to establish bias, not truth.
3. Dismiss all the judges. They seem to believe that the way to arrive at truth is to seek a dead center in a tornado of lies.
4. Open all the jails. No one knows whether anyone in them has really committed crime, and even if the inmates are criminals no one knows whether they are better or worse in jail, or whether it would not be better for society to have them outside rather than inside jail.

In brief, why attempt to apply the methods of science to a situation that needs the junkman? Isn't any proposal for liaison between law and science a hollow sham?

Perhaps. The fact-finding methods of the law are so archaic that perhaps scientists should not be asked to bother with them. It may be that the scientist should let the fact-finding process go with the reflection that it is obvious that the law believes it has more important concerns than the ascertainment of truth. As an alternative the social scientist could look not at the law's weakness but at its strength. In the area of so-called value judgments law is strong and science is weak. I have called such judgments feeling judgments. And I should like to interest the scientist in a certain aspect of feeling judgments that I think is of importance to him. I shall approach this matter in a roundabout fashion.

The law knows general rules and it knows individual cases. It is an ideal of the branch of law called equity to reach completely individualized decisions. This ideal also operates in other areas of the law, but in them it runs more directly into competing ideals such as that of equality, which looks like an ideal of generalization. Actually, the decision at law is in its most important aspect a unique decision. The case is settled thus and so. Its value as a precedent is always dubious, always a matter for dispute. But it does settle the fate of the parties concerned, or at least purports to do so. In a word, it *individuates* them qua litigants.

Now, it is precisely the function of feeling to individuate. Feeling—as I use the term—is the name for that part of the human psyche which assigns *unique* value to things. It is the function of the human mind that assigns to things their individual worth. I do not mean by this that all objects or events are in fact regarded by human beings as unique. I mean rather that *any* object or event *may* take on a unique value by the operation of the feeling function of the human mind. The important thing about this process is that it individuates the object or event in question by assigning to it something that is ordinarily called a value but that I call a feeling value. It is the workings of this function of the human mind that I ask the social scientist to study in law.

Science is accustomed to individuate otherwise. In the history of physical science two systems of individuation have competed with each other. The first is the system of successive generalized *cernibilium,* that is, the principle that if no difference can be descriptions. Leibniz called this the *principium identitatis indis-*

discerned between what are thought of as different objects, they are in fact one. Otherwise put, the game is to come upon the singular object by successive *generalized* descriptions until only the object to be individuated possesses all of them. A trivial example is the parlor game of guessing what object a person is thinking of. Is it animal or not? Vegetable or not? And so on.

All attempts at scientific classification by the Aristotelian method of class inclusion (for example modern taxonomy) are of this order. In statistics it is always assumed that individuals are members of a class.[6] The Bertillon system of identification in law is another example of this method. Indeed, for centuries science knew no other method of classification.

With the development of modern science came a new system of individuation, by means of space-time coordinates. Analytical geometry and Newtonian mechanics popularized this method. It works by assuming that the object to be individuated can be assigned a unique point in three-dimensional space at a moment in time equally arbitrarily given.

Each of these two methods has its weaknesses. The method of individuating by successive general characteristics is obviously no good where the objects to be individuated are alike. Any atomic system such as classical mechanics, whose elements are taken to be all alike, is an example. Moreover, theoretical objections bedevil this method. For instance, one could keep on describing Socrates in general terms forever without being able to isolate his individuality. Generalized, this difficulty results because there never is a guarantee that any number of general (or class) concepts will completely isolate an individual object. This is dramatically apparent if the object keeps changing, that is, if it is in a state of *process* or is viewed dialectically.

Dialectics aside, the method of specification by general

---

6. This is explicitly so for the theory of relative frequency, which is based directly on the logic of classes. But it is implicit in the alternative systems as well. For example, subjective probability attempts to ascertain the general or class character of the probability that the specific subject assigns to an event.

attributes has a certain inherent difficulty of a logical character. Logicians have never yet satisfactorily accounted for the
relation of an individual member of a class to the class itself.
Paradoxes extant since Greek times remain to attest this failure.
Sometimes, a class has a different nature from that of its
members. The class of all Americans is not an American. Hence
the most detailed characterization of an American in general
(class) terms will not "produce" an American. But even where
the class is thought to have the same nature as its members,
difficulties arise. For example, the integers are classes (of all
units, all pairs, all triads, and so on). But the integers are also
members of a Class, namely, the Class of all numbers. Now, a
paradox appears. The number of all numbers is a Class. Is this
Class also a member of itself? If so, the Class of all numbers
increases by one. But this contradicts our original assumption
that the Class already contained all numbers. One cannot
truly individuate an object by classification. In Aristotelian
terms, the genus-species method of classification does not
succeed in isolating an individual.

The matter is also critical for law. We have said that one
of equity's chief ideals is to individuate. The same is true for
the criminal law. It seeks to individualize punishment. But the
ideal of equality before the law generalizes every effort to
individualize. Perfectly arbitrary dispositions in law are examples of complete tyrannies. *Summum jus, summa injuria.*
Therefore the magistrate tries to ascertain general grounds
for his determinations even when called on to exercise judicial
mercy as in sentencing. How to attain individuation by addition
of successive acts of generalization is one of the deepest dilem-
mas in the criminal law.

It is easy to see that these difficulties would inevitably drive
scientists to the apparently sure method of space-time coordinates. Every object in the universe can be uniquely located in
three-dimensional space at an assigned time. Don't worry about
what the object is, worry about *where* it is, and one will have
uniquely determined it. What a magnificent achievement of
the abstracting human mind! We note instantly that this
method, since it completely ignores the difference between one

object and another, is evidently good only where all objects can
be treated as alike. Paradox: individuate by destroying all
individual differences. The supreme act of generalization yields
a method of individuation. In a static universe, and with only
a static mathematics to describe it, we can only establish static
relationships among the infinite parts of our world. What if
these parts move—are we lost? Not if we have a mathematics
of motion that allows us to fix an object in space-time and
follow its motion. This gives us a method for studying the
history of particles of matter viewed as points in space. This
is surely a powerful toy. We do not know what the object is,
but we know where it has been and where it is going. We
ignore its essence, its nature, and observe its behavior. Thus
modern science, and thus the fruits of its new method of
individuation. It permits us to study the behavior of objects,
assigning them a past, present, and future history. The world
discloses itself as a vast machine whose parts in and of themselves are of no concern. What they do, how each behaves,
their action in space and time constitute our science. Apply
these conceptions to human beings and behavioristic physiology,
psychology, and sociology emerge.

The law has a counterpart, of course. A human body, evidently quite dead, is discovered with a hole in its head that
any physiologist would declare was a sufficient cause of death.
Nearby (in space and time) is a section of lead pipe that any
physicist would say could have caused the aforesaid hole in
the head if wielded by a set of biological constructs operating
by the expansion and contraction of cells called muscle cells
in a system known as the human arm, and so on. Now a different set of observers, called detectives, produce one human
being known as A who was at the spot, marked X, at time T.
A third set of observers, called prosecutors, present to a fourth
set, the grand jury, a scientific document known as an indictment, which reconstructs a given cross section of the universe,
called the scene of the crime, and locates at point X the aforesaid objects, human and nonhuman, at moment T. The murderer
is individuated. So much for space-time coordinates. Let us
hope that A is not able to produce an alternative set of space-

time coordinates (an alibi) just to make things difficult for our group of observers.

I need not belabor the reader who has come this far with me with the well-known difficulties of space-time individuation. Obviously, it works best with objects that are all alike: points or atoms. If the objects are qualitatively different, these differences must be reduced to quantitative ones (the measurement ideal of modern science). No matter that this does violence to the objects concerned. But the ideal of space-time individuation exacts further toll. It is a *world* view. "Every object (point) in the universe attracts every other object (point) directly as the product of their masses and inversely as the square of the distance between them." The universe, the whole universe, intrudes itself as the only object of observation. But it is impossible to consider a whole universe. Let us observe what we can and assume that our selection is representative of the universe. Statistics becomes an urgent necessity. We extrapolate from what few examples we have to an infinite population of the same objects.

What if we cannot get any samples at all? What if the samples (say, atoms) are too small for observation? Then apply statistical theory in reverse. From an assumed indefinitely large number of objects (say, the atoms in a drop of oil) make assumptions about the individual atoms in it, then recombine them statistically to arrive at the (assumed) behavior of that drop. No one knows or could possibly be interested in the velocity of a single atom. But put an indefinitely large number of these abstractions together and we call their behavior temperature.

Difficulties multiply. The modern view is that it is preferable to take the strain off our constructs (coordinate systems, atoms, points, statistics) and put it where it appears to do less harm: in philosophy. This leads to a relativistic, pluralistic, indeterministic philosophy of science.

Einstein attacked space-time individuation at its apparently strongest point. For millenia, science had accepted as one of its most settled convictions the irreversible character of time.

This was, we should say, the one independent variable in an otherwise precariously relativistic world. But Kant had long ago suggested that time is nothing other than a way the reasoning mind imposes order (its own order) on nature. After this, it was inevitable that someone should convince scientists that time itself is relative. Time is thus no longer a reliable means of individuation. The mathematicians had already relativized space in the non-Euclidean geometries. There is a demand, grown inexorable, for a new system of individuation. What will supply the need? *Can it possibly be that the feeling function of the human mind must now be studied to determine its role in the process of individuation?*

Individuation and Scientific Method

I have said that by the exercise of feeling the human being *individuates* an object. A value is given to it that has nothing necessarily to do with its intrinsic or extrinsic worth. Just precisely *this* clothespin or baby blanket is the one the child will not surrender under any circumstances, until suddenly the object has no value at all. It is tossed aside with complete unconcern.

The essence of such a value judgment is that it is individual. The object is said to be individuated. Now science on the other hand purports to deal solely in generalities. The scientific judgment is set forth in general terms; the judgment is public. Its truth value must be subject to check by all competent to investigate. Concerning the individual, science says nothing except that it does or does not fall into a general class of identical or similar objects or that it possesses or does not possess such and such general characteristics. This is the account that modern science gives of its work. From the most abstract inquiry in symbolic logic to the most empirical act of data gathering, concern is centered in the pursuit of the *general* and of its constituent element, the *particular*. The claims of the individual to recognition are studiously passed over. Is this inevitably the nature of science? Must its work always be restricted to the business of generalization?

If so, science can never come to grips with the most harassing dilemma the law faces, namely, the relation of the individual to the general. We have already said that one of law's most powerful ideals is the ideal of equality. This is a generality par excellence. But law also seeks individual solutions as an ideal, the ideal of equity. It seeks to ascribe a *unique* value to its determinations, as well as a *general* value. If science cannot aid the law in attaining individual solutions but insists on concentrating on general considerations, then the law must reject the aid of science, since such help is nothing but a further embarrassment to it.

A century ago, the law still had the services of Aristotelian logic at its command. An example will illustrate the point. (1) He who takes and carries away the goods of another with intent to convert them to his own use commits larceny. (2) At a certain time and place, X did take and did carry away, etc. (3) Therefore, X is guilty of larceny. With a little juggling, this statement can be placed in the form of a valid syllogism. The law used the form to give order to its processes. The first statement was for the law a *general* proposition or, as we should say, a rule of law; the second is a *particular* proposition of fact; the third is a unique decision. No embarrassment was experienced in passing from a general, through a particular, to an individuated proposition because logic itself sanctioned the process.

This species of logic has all but disappeared from modern life. During the last hundred years all the processes of logic have been generalized. There are no differences of a basic character between the individual and the general that can be represented in modern logic. The modern logician would say that the above example of a legal syllogism and the logical form upon which it was based is really psychological. He would be apt to say that our example is really an instance of the transitivity of implication, that if a implies b, and b implies c, then a implies c. There is no difference for him between major premise, minor premise, and conclusion save the form of the over-all proposition. And each is a *general* proposition or some *generalized* function. For him there is nothing at all unique or individual about the conclusion *so far as logic is concerned.*

Since modern logic cannot handle the individual as object or proposition, then modern science cannot do so either. For the philosopher the matter is as simple as that. The following conclusion is equally simple: either science must continue to ignore what its logic is incapable of handling, *or else logic must change.* Is it quixotic to suggest that nothing in the history of science would lead us to suppose that the second alternative is forever beyond the bounds of science?

I think not. Logic has completely changed its character in the last hundred years in response to the demands of generalization. It has all but become absorbed in mathematics, itself an empirical generalizing activity of the purest sort. If logic could be rescued from the mathematicians, there is no reason to suppose that its processes, now infinitely more complex, might not be turned to the aid of those scientific activities which demand not only generalization but also individuation. And I am prepared to suggest further that among such activities is scientific methodology itself.

I suggest that scientific method will be forced to turn to a consideration of the individual *to the extent that scientific method replaces measurement theory with decision theory.* A decision is a unique or individual event. After the decision comes into existence, it may be generalized. But not before. Measurement theory generalizes before decision and insists that decision is nothing but the outcome of generalization. For such a theory, a decision is always a leap in the dark, or, if you will, a miracle. It is analogous to classical empiricism's theory of induction, the process by which particulars (or individuals) become generalized. Only here, the process is reversed.

However, if one starts with the concept of the decision as individual, then, in order to escape regress to classical empiricism on the one hand, and to hold off the onslaughts of generalizing rationalists (the present-day decision theorists) on the other, it may become necessary that logic intervene and come to our aid with a theory of the relation of the general to the individual.

The Sociology of the Individual

While this war is being fought out in the clouds, what should the ordinary everyday working social scientist do? Surely he should not await the outcome of struggles at such rarefied heights. He should, I think, come directly to grips with the individual within the compass of his present scientific instruments. Fortunately his methodology is flexible (never mind that generalizers regard it as sloppy). Being flexible it is suited as well to the logic of the future as to the logic of the past, even if the logic of the present appears to be too much for it. The social scientist can address himself to the sociology of the individual!

At this point, I have surely fallen down the well, haven't I? The sociology of the individual is a contradiction in terms, is it not? I think it is not. Let us look at the matter obliquely. A sociologist who is asked to deal with the individual may think he is completely justified in saying that the individual is a matter for psychology, not for sociology. I say this is not so. The psychologist has the same scientific bias as the sociologist. *The psychologist as scientist does not deal with the individual either.* He deals with generalized aspects of the behavior of human beings and as scientist feels that he has no more to say about the *individual* than has anyone else. Of course, the psychologist admits that he is concerned with mind and that in some sense mind is in the single human being. But all his investigations lead him to general propositions, not individual ones. He is no more concerned with the individual human mind than the biologist is concerned with the individual living being. Even in the study of subjective states of mind, the psychologist feels constrained to deal only in general propositions.

I must admit that this proves no more than that the sociologist cannot saddle the psychologist with the problem of the individual. It does not prove that the sociologist can or should handle it himself. I believe the sociologist should handle the individual because unless he does he cannot do his important job with law. Moreover, unless and until the sociologist learns to handle the individual object or event methodologically he will not be able to use decision theory. For it is precisely the failure of the decision theorists to make room for the individual (the decision is an individual event, is it not?) that keeps their speculations beyond the reach of empirical investigation. They will remain rationalists until they can show empirically-minded investigators how to go to work. And I say (on my own authority, to be sure, yet with passionate conviction) that a willingness to handle the individual is absolutely necessary in order to bring decision theory down out of the clouds.

To sum up, it will not do to attempt to solve the problem of individual choice by increasing general specifications. On the other hand, the imposing structure of modern generalized science could not be scrapped without untold loss. The way out of the difficulty is for scientific theory to expand so as to accommodate both generality and individuality.

What have social scientists to say about the individual? I would attempt to outline an empirical research program for them if I had any competence in that kind of work. I have none. But I do have confidence that social scientists can come up with something, especially in law, when and if they turn their attention to the job.

Will the social scientist be utterly lost in what may seem to him the vast jungle of feelings that is the law? Nowhere else does anything like an orderly system of value judgments of a feeling kind exist. I invite the social scientist to try his luck with it. He may lose his head, but perhaps his heart will carry him safely through.

Hans Zeisel

Social Research on the Law

The Ideal and the Practical

Viewed from the distance, legal decisions may appear to involve no more than a syllogism: this is the rule, these are the facts; hence, this is the verdict. To be sure, every so often, when a case is clear and simple, the syllogistic form of the argument will correspond to its substance. But where the law grows and changes, through cases that are under dispute, whatever remains of the syllogism becomes a mere pretense.[1] What matters, then, is how the new rule will fit into the community's sense of justice; how it will affect the parties involved and such future behavior as it sets out to control, Such an appraisal falls into the realm of the social sciences, especially when one includes in its orbit the study of the legal process itself, of legislation, judicial decision, and administration.

1. "The pretense is that the law is a system of known rules applied by a judge." Edward H. Levi, *An Introduction to Legal Reasoning* (Chicago: University of Chicago Press, 1949), p. 1.

For many decades, whenever the social scientist would come to the lawyer and tell him that he could help him with his job, the lawyer could rightly ask what he could bring into the bargain that the lawyers did not possess: special knowledge of society, special techniques, simply more brains? On all these points, the social scientist in modesty had to withdraw. It is only during the last three decades or so that he has been able to stand up under such scrutiny. He now has in his possession a set of tools that has proved useful in exploring all kinds of social institutions and that should therefore prove useful with respect to the law as a social institution.

Tool Chest of the Social Scientist

These tools are helpful in a variety of ways. First, some tools have greatly widened the area of analyzable data. Systematic interviewing on facts, decisions, and motivations, aided by techniques that probe levels below the consciousness barrier, are providing us with raw material heretofore simply not available. New conceptual frameworks have made it possible to deal more rigorously with such data, which heretofore, because of their sheer variety and complexity, seemed to defy precise analysis. Mathematical statistics, through the development of sampling techniques and canons of inference, has enabled us to deal in more precise terms both with the new data and with the newly developed concepts. Lastly, and perhaps most importantly, a set of analytical tools has opened the realm of the social sciences to the controlled experiment, and, even more significantly, to a series of analytical techniques that are logically derived from the experiment without actually requiring one.

To be sure, some social scientists[2] will argue, not without

2. The term social scientist is used here in the narrow and somewhat improper sense: the economist has long ago become a partner in the law; but the economics department, in the medieval separation of our universities, had so much a life of its own that one easily forgets how clearly it is one of the social sciences. We seem to be headed, though, for a reintegration that will include even history, the social science now exiled into the humanities.

merit, that the application of this tool chest to problems of the law by no means exhausts the potentialities of a sociology of law. Sociological inquiry, in their view, is not confined to these techniques. Although the nineteenth-century tradition of theorizing on the basic relationship between law and other aspects of society has somewhat abated, Parsons and others continue this distinguished tradition. But if I read the signs correctly, the main thrust of sociological inquiry into the law, in this country at least, will follow the narrower if safer road of empirical research, rather than the broad speculative tradition, although ultimately the two should link up.

The following discussion will try to illuminate the potential usefulness of this tool chest of the social sciences for the study of the law. This discussion will also reveal some of the difficulties under which such research efforts labor, and point up some of the means of overcoming them. The examples will suggest that the tools can almost never be used in their pure form, because natural and social obstacles usually prevent the ideal research approach. Forced to operate against such odds, and limited to data that are never perfect, social science research requires at every turn ingenuity and prudence: ingenuity in overcoming the obstacles and prudence in judging how far the research design can be carried without breaking down—that is, in judging when half a loaf is better than none. The natural sciences are, of course, not free from these difficulties, but the social sciences have more of them. This is so partly because the controlled experiment must always remain the exception rather than the rule, and partly because the theoretical structure of the social sciences is still in its infancy. It provides, therefore, less aid in judging how far a set of imperfect data will go.

All the examples to be discussed below are taken from the Jury Project of the University of Chicago Law School.[3] They

3. The Jury Project, which operates under a grant from the Ford Foundation, is under the direction of Professor Harry Kalven, Jr. Its findings are being reported in a series of volumes, published by Little, Brown and Co., in Boston. The first volume, *Delay in the Court*, by Hans Zeisel, Harry Kalven, Jr., and Bernard Buchholz, appeared in 1959; two more (see footnote 5) are in preparation; more are to follow.

are presented here not so much for their end results but for the help they provide in illustrating methodological points.[4]

Examples of Social Science Methods

Since most analytical devices are derived from the basic design of the controlled experiment, we will begin our series of examples with such an experiment. It will help us to see the strength and limitations of this paradigm of all research instruments. One effort of the Jury Project was directed toward a celebrated point of controversy between the law and psychiatry: the possibility of reformulating the prevailing law on insanity as a defense to a criminal charge. A series of experiments was designed to learn how such a change in the law would affect jury verdicts.[5] In most courts, if a defendant is seeking acquittal on the grounds of insanity, the jury is instructed to apply the M'Naghten rule. This rule requires that in order to find the defendant insane it must be shown that he did not know what he was doing or did not know that what he was doing was wrong. Since 1954 the courts in the District of Columbia have been applying a different test, known as the Durham rule. The Durham rule states that in order to find the defendant

4. For a bird's-eye view of the tool chest of the social sciences, the following reading list will prove useful: Marie Jahoda, Morton Deutsch, Stuart W. Cook, *Research Methods in Social Relations* (2d ed.; New York: Henry Holt, 1959); Leon Festinger and Daniel Katz, *Research Methods in the Behavioral Sciences* (New York: The Dryden Press, 1953); Paul F. Lazarsfeld and Morris Rosenberg, *The Language of Social Research* (New York: The Free Press, 1955); Harold H. Anderson and Gladys Anderson, *An Introduction to Projective Techniques* (Englewood Cliffs, N.J.: Prentice-Hall, Inc., 1951); Hans Zeisel, *Say It with Figures* (4th ed.; New York: Harper & Brothers, 1951).

5. One of the volumes in the Jury series will report on this study. Under the supervision of Fred L. Strodtbeck, the Jury Project has developed a technique of controlled experiments by use of mock cases. The example cited in the text is one of several lines of inquiry and will be reported in an early forthcoming volume by Rita James. The other experiments together with an evaluation of the method will be reported in a subsequent volume by Fred L. Strodtbeck and Harry Kalven.

insane it must be shown that "the act was the product of a
mental disease or a mental defect."

The ideal way of answering our question would be through
a controlled legal experiment. One would want to have all court
cases in which insanity is raised as a defense assigned ran-
domly—that is, by some lottery—either to the M'Naghten or to
the Durham test. This would be the classic form of the experiment: keeping the cases through random selection as equal as
possible, and changing only the experimental variable. Whatever difference there would be in the two groups of verdicts
could then be attributed to the difference in the court's instructions.[6] Since such an experiment would meet insurmountable
obstacles, a substitute design had to be developed that would
come as close as possible to the original one.

A mock trial based on the real Durham case was tape-
recorded; the recording contained all parts of the trial from
opening statement to the judge's instruction to the jury. The evidence left no possible doubt that the defendant had committed
the act—it was burglary, as in the original Durham trial. Three
recorded versions were produced that were identical except for
the judge's instruction to the jury. In the first version, the judge
instructed the jury according to the M'Naghten test; in the second version, according to the Durham test; and in the third
version, the jury received no instructions from the judge on
the issue of responsibility.

Jurors were selected by lot from the jury pools of three
metropolitan areas. They were told that instead of serving on
a real trial, they would deliberate on an experimental case.
After listening to the recorded trial, the jury deliberated until
they reached a verdict.

Each of the three experimental versions was run a number
of times, resulting in verdicts summarized in a table of the
structure shown in Table 1. The actual numbers are omitted
from this table in deference to the forthcoming publication,

6. Cf. "The Case for the Official Experiment," in Zeisel, Kalven, and
Buchholz, *Delay in the Court*, chap. 21; also, Hans Zeisel, "The New York
Expert Testimony Project: Some Reflections on Legal Experiments," *Stan-
ford Law Review*, vol. 8, no. 4 (1956), p. 730.

Table 1
Effect of Different Instructions on Insanity
on the Jury's Verdict

Verdict of the Jury	M'Naghten (Per cent)	Durham (Per cent)	No Instruction (Per cent)
Guilty	...	...	...
Insane	...	...	...
Hung jury	...	...	...
Total	100	100	100

the core of which it forms. The question is whether the percentage of guilty verdicts, and conceivably that of hung juries, changes if the instructions on insanity are changed. The numbers that will be eventually inserted will reveal the answer, and will thereby aid in the decision on the merits of the respective rules. Advisedly, we say that these numbers will aid in the decision rather than decide the issue, because the outcome of the trial is but one of the factors on which the over-all judgment must be based.[7]

It is generally instructive to consider the problems raised by the interpretation of this experiment. The first difficulty arises from the degree of unreality introduced by replacing an actual trial with a mock trial. To be sure, the jurors are real jurors; and the deliberations often last for many hours, occasionally ending in bitter recriminations or in a hung jury. These are factors that give confidence in the earnestness of the experiment. But it is difficult to say exactly what differences may be expected when an hour-long taped condensation, in which all visual and many auditory details are lost, is replaced by a real trial.

In one respect, of course, the mock experiment is more nearly perfect than the "natural legal experiment." In the mock experiment everything except the judge's instructions *is* equal for the whole series of replications. In the "natural legal ex-

---

7. The issues in the debate are well joined in the University of Chicago Law School Symposium on Insanity. The participants were Edward De Grazia, Harry Kalven, Jr., Wilber G. Katz, Herbert Wechsler, Henry Weihofen, Dr. Frederic Wertham, and Dr. Gregory Zilboorg. [*University of Chicago Law Review*, vol. 22, no. 2 (1955), pp. 317–404.]

periment" the cases would be different. They would be comparable only as a group, thereby increasing the uncertainty of the findings.

But this is only the beginning. Suppose we were satisfied that real trials of this case confirmed the results of the mock trial. What could we say about other trials, that is, trials in which any of a thousand details were changed? Would the result repeat itself if the defendant were a murderer instead of a burglar, a woman instead of a man, a Negro instead of a white man, and so on? How are we to know which circumstances affected the outcome of the experiment and which did not? Short of repeating the experiment under all these circumstances, we must guess.

It is important to realize that in this respect the contrast with the natural sciences is only one of degree. Often a laboratory experiment must be repeated to learn whether a difference in temperature, in humidity, or in any of a thousand conditions would change its outcome. But in the natural sciences more is known about factors that conceivably could or could not affect the experiment.

Thus, the experiment in the social sciences, and especially in the law, labors under these handicaps: its performance under optimal, natural conditions is seldom possible; mock experiments or approximations must suffice, and it is difficult to estimate how close to reality the approximation in fact is. The second difficulty arises from the need for generalizing. Little is yet known as to the permitted degree and direction of such generalizations. As our experience with such experiments and our substantive knowledge of the field increases, these difficulties lessen. Every new experiment is in itself a step in this development.

Our second example is an "experiment" even further removed from the natural one. The question is one of theoretical and practical concern to lawyers. Do juries in some regions or cities give higher damage awards in comparable tort cases than in other regions or cities? Since there are some 60,000 civil jury trials held each year in the United States, it seemed tempting simply to compare the average awards made in different states or cities. The first obstacle that arose was that only few courts have ever recorded this type of information. On closer inspection, it turned out that this was not a key deficiency. Even if the data were available they would mean little, because the cases that came to trial varied so immensely that "average awards" had little meaning. We thought, then, that certain of the more frequent standard injuries, such as a lost leg, might supply a sufficient number of comparable cases. But it soon became clear that these legs were lost by young people, old people, rich ones, poor ones, men, and women. Hence, the value of a leg varied almost as widely as the value of all injuries. Since it is not feasible to try the same case fifty times in fifty different courts, what was one to do?

In place of the unobtainable comparable verdicts, the research device eventually resorted to was a plan to use *estimates* of these verdicts by informed experts. Experts can be useful provided that the particular request is within the expert's routine experience, and that individual idiosyncrasies do not endanger the result. All of these safeguards were incorporated in the design. Five personal injury cases were described in such detail as is customarily requested by the insurance adjustor who evaluates claims. Through the cooperation of three nationwide insurance companies these five cases were then submitted to their local adjustors with this question: "How much, judging from your experience, would you expect a jury in your court to award for this case?" The question was asked for a selected number of courts that together constituted a representative sample of various regions and community sizes.

The logical chain that supports this research approach runs as follows. The adjustors make their living by being right on the types of guesses that were asked. These guesses are informed by continuous comparison with the subsequent court verdicts, if the claim should reach that stage. If one conceives of the ongoing jury trials as a series of "experiments," our experts extract the essence of the experience and apply it to five standard cases. We attempted to eliminate personal idiosyncrasies by submitting several cases, with the intention of using an average, and by having in each case *three* experts, representing the three cooperating insurance companies. We could, therefore, expect that if these verdict-guesses showed systematic variations, they would truly reflect geographic variations in jury behavior. In fact, as Table 2 shows, such variations did emerge.

Table 2
Regional Variation of Estimated Jury Awards
for Identical Claims
(In per cent deviation from the national average = 100)

City Size	West	Midwest	South	East
Large	+20	+2	0	+19
Medium	+8	—11	—9	+10
Small	0	—21	—15	—6

Awards for identical claims vary roughly between 80 per cent of the national average in the rural South and Midwest, and 120 per cent in the metropolitan cities on the East and West coasts. If one were to translate this table into a formula, one would say: add 10 per cent to the average if the trial takes place on the East or West coast; add another 10 per cent if it is conducted in a large metropolitan city; subtract 10 per cent if it is conducted in the South or Midwest, and another 10 per cent if it takes place in a rural area.

Our third example is of a different sort. A problem was answered by resorting to already existing, if somewhat hidden, data. This is a promising method for the law since it accumulates a great quantity of statistical data in the ordinary course of its business. But the mode of analysis is again patterned after the design of a controlled experiment. The question was: are certain cities of the United States more "claim-conscious" than others? The term refers to the propensity of some people to try to make a law claim out of an accident that other people might merely shrug off.

The first step was to obtain information on the number of claims resulting from the primary injury cause: the motor vehicle accident. Court data, if available, would not suffice since an unknown number of claims never reach the court. An insurance company would be a better source, but one company might have selective coverage in certain areas. It was essential to obtain insurance data for a cross section of the entire industry. These data showed that the number of claims per insured car varies widely from city to city and state to state; but then so may the number of accidents per car. Even after the number of claims was related to the number of accidents, the number of claims per accident still showed wide variations. Since the gravity of accidents could also vary, an independent corroboration had to be found. It was postulated that if one city was more claim-conscious than another, this should show up in matters other than motor vehicle accidents. The corresponding claim frequency was, therefore, established for accidents occurring in department and chain stores. When the two sets of data were confronted, it transpired that the order that ranked areas by the frequency of claims per automobile accident looked surprisingly similar to that for claims from store accidents.

The final piece of evidence came from still another comparison. It was learned that a considerable number of claims are raised as second thoughts, sometime after the insurance company is first notified. The proportion of these "second-thought" claims was also found to vary from city to city. But it turned out that the variation in the over-all number of claims compared well with the variation in "second-thought" claims, strongly suggesting that one was a cause of the other.[8] From these comparisons a fairly consistent rank order of the cities emerged, with Philadelphia leading the field among the larger cities and Detroit emerging as the least claim-conscious. Thus, for the first time evidence was produced on the hitherto elusive phenomenon of claim-consciousness.

The statistics used in this analysis were simple—only percentages, ratios, and measures of rank correlation. Yet the design of proof, simple as it may look in retrospect, is shaped after a series of hypothetical experiments. First, given a set of comparable automobile accidents, will the number of claims vary? Since accidents cannot very well be induced for experimental purposes, actual accidents had to serve. But without

---

8. For the statistician: all these rank-order correlations showed coefficients of approximately 0.7.

prior control, one could not be sure that the accidents *were* indeed comparable. Hence, an indirect assurance had to be sought from the claim ratios arising out of different types of accidents. Finally, the analysis of insurance records revealed a category of claims that, hopefully, could explain and thereby confirm the variations in claim-consciousness. And although each of the three types of data used had flaws that could make any conclusion hazardous, together the three sustain well the structure of proof.[9]

The examples, so far, have dealt with two controlled experiments and one investigation based on data that had to be found in records originally compiled for different purposes. The two experiments illustrated the degree of simulation forced upon the investigator by a variety of legal and factual barriers. The aim of the third investigation was like that of the second: the discovery of regional variations. But here, although no experiment was conducted, the data were analyzed *as if* they had been collected in the course of an experiment.

Our final example is provided by a survey—the technique that more than any other has been identified with social science research. The survey analysis is also patterned after that of the controlled experiment, but its method of data collection is basically different.

The survey described below was designed to solve a central problem of the jury study: What, if any, difference is there between the way a jury and the way a judge decide the same case?[10] Again, if we were unencumbered by practical difficulties, we would have each case tried twice: once by a jury, and once by a judge, but this is obviously an impossible procedure.[11]

Retreating somewhat, one might simply compare the verdicts of the cases tried before juries with the judgments in cases

---

9. For details see "Claim Consciousness," in Zeisel, Kalven, and Buchholz, *Delay in the Court*, chap. 20.

10. The study will be published under the title, *The Jury, the Judge, and the Criminal Law*, by Little, Brown and Co.

11. Once in a long while a case may indeed be tried twice—once with and once without a jury—after the appellate court had ordered a new trial and the defendant then waives his right to trial by jury. But these instances are rare; besides, on retrial, no case is ever quite the same.

tried without a jury. The comparison could be made easily enough from court records, but it would have little meaning. The cases tried with juries are significantly different from the cases in which the defendant decides to waive the jury. Far from being a random assignment, it is the defendant himself, or his counsel, who decides whether he wants a jury or not. Hence, any observed difference in verdicts would reflect not only the different mode of trial but also a difference in the type of case. We would have no way of separating the two, especially since the defendant's choice between jury and judge trial is determined partly by the expectation of the very difference which we want to study.

As a third possibility, one might think of assigning cases at random, that is, by lottery, to a jury or to a judge, so as to insure comparability of both groups of cases. But this again would not be feasible, since it would deprive the defendant of the constitutional right to make his own choice.

Retreating even further, one might consider asking for the expert opinions of lawyers and judges whose business it is to try cases with and without juries. This expertise is in fact abundantly available in much writing on the jury. On the whole, however, this writing reflects a lack of reliable information. It remains on the level of bland generalities, evoking from other authors opposing views that are equally plausible.

In the design that was finally adopted, we asked the presiding judge in a large number of jury trials to tell us how he would have decided the case had he tried it without a jury. This operation proved feasible and resolved one of our major problems, namely, that judge and jury verdicts had to be compared for the same type, if possible the same group, of trials. In a way, this research plan placed each defendant before two types of adjudicators, the jury and the judge. In addition, we asked the judge for two types of data designed to assist in finding out *why* in some trials judge and jury arrived at a different verdict. For each case, the judge was asked for a detailed description of the trial and for the judge's own assessment as to why he and the jury differed.

To be sure, the judge's decision is a hypothetical one ("If

you . . .″), which raises the general point of when such "if-questions" may be relied upon. They vary between two extremes. Situations in which the problem is not raised in the respondent's mind, other than by our inquiry, will clearly yield artificial responses. But where the problem is raised and answered in the respondent's mind quite independently of our inquiry, we may rely on the answer. Our particular survey clearly represents the extreme case that is most favorable to the "if-question." As a rule, the judge is so deeply involved in the trial over which he presides that he forms his opinion anyway; our asking for it merely puts it on paper.

There is an interesting, if minor, wrinkle in the request we make to the judge. Although we ask him to put his judgment down before the jury returns, we cannot be sure he follows these directions. Some judges might be affected by the jury's verdict, in the sense that they report agreement with the jury even though they might have disagreed had they given their answer before the jury returned. But this, by definition, would involve only verdicts on which the judge was not too firm. Thus, our data probably under-report the marginal, minor disagreements. Whatever disagreement we do find is free from such volatile dissent. On consideration this should be an advantage. The general principle underlying the solution of this minor problem of methodology is of some importance. Faced with the absolute impossibility of insuring the *ideal* behavior (answering before the jury's return) one tries to gauge the bias that may result from the mode of response that was in fact followed.

But within this general solution of the research design, other difficulties still remained. One concerned the impossibility of obtaining a perfect sample. Since these difficulties too are typical of many social science research operations, their discussion should be helpful. In an operation such as this we are bound to end up with what one might call a "Kinsey-sample."[12] We cannot possibly expect a perfect sample of all jury trials, because we must rely on the voluntary cooperation of the presiding

---

12. Cf. the review by Zeisel of Kinsey's "Sexual Behavior in the Human Female," *University of Chicago Law Review*, vol. 21 (1954), pp. 517–525.

judges; and since for a variety of reasons some will not cooperate, we must be satisfied, if we can, with the reports from those who do.

How, then, should we have proceeded? We might have assessed the limitations and decided which generalizations could and which could not be made within these limitations. But one must not expect this decision ever to yield a sharp dichotomy; rather it will be one of degree of confidence. Often the degree of such confidence, although argued and discussed in procedural terms, is not measurable; it will simply remain a qualitative caveat.

How were we to assess the accuracy of our sample? We compared, first, the distribution of various crimes in our sample with published trial statistics. This did not lead us far, because only few states had such statistics. Then we tried to learn whether the judges who refused to cooperate (because it is these judges who raise the issue of a nonrepresentative sample) might be expected to judge cases differently from the judges who did cooperate. This comparison could not be made directly, of course, but it could be done indirectly in the following manner. Among the judges who did not cooperate we have some who did so only reluctantly, after a considerable amount of correspondence and persuasion. By comparing these reluctant cooperators with those who cooperated from the beginning, we try to gauge the difference between cooperators and noncooperators. We assumed that the reluctant cooperators stood somewhere between the willing cooperators and those who refused; and we projected the difference accordingly.

Finally, there remain difficulties with respect to the collected data that do not derive from the sampling problem. They derive from the length of the questionnaire and the manner in which it is answered. Looked at in one way, ours was a brief questionnaire—a mere forty questions designed to summarize what may have been a week-long trial. But we were satisfied that it was the longest questionnaire that had a reasonable chance of being filled out by a busy judge. Then, there is the loss of direct communication in a mail survey, which does not allow for personal contact with the judge. Yet, if our judges were to

answer these questions for every jury trial before them, we had
to permit them to answer, at their convenience, in the modest
intervals between trials. The general principle here is to exert
prudence in deciding on the proper compromise between accuracy and feasibility. Its exact position was dictated by the
limits of cooperation that could be expected from the judges.

Table 3 is the over-all basic table that emerged from this
survey as to criminal cases. Judge and jury agree on their
verdict in 80 per cent (13 + 67) of the cases, and disagree in
20 per cent (18 + 2). The disagreement is almost entirely
one-sided. In 18 per cent (of a total of 20 per cent), the jury
acquits where the judge would have convicted; only in 2 per
cent is it the other way around. As a result, if all jury cases
were tried without a jury, the rate of acquittals would be cut
approximately in half, from its present level of 31 per cent to
15 per cent. This table, although interesting in itself, is but the
starting point of the analysis proper. Our quest is for the reasons why judge and jury at some times agreed and at others
disagreed.

Table 3
Agreement and Disagreement between Judge and Jury
on the Question of Guilt of Criminal Defendants
(Percentages of the Total Number of Cases Tried)

JUDGE Would Have:	JURY Acquitted	JURY Found Guilty	Total Judge:
Acquitted	13%	2%	15%
Found guilty	18%	67%	85%
Total jury:	31%	69%	(Total 100%)

As mentioned above, we had two avenues for answering this
problem. One was to compare—on the analogy to an experiment
—trials that *had* a certain characteristic (for example, a superior defense counsel) with trials that *did not,* and see whether
the proportion of judge-jury disagreement was higher in the

one group than in the other. Since any or all such factors in any combination could affect the difference between judge and jury verdicts, the logic of survey analysis demands that all these factors be separated from one another and looked at in isolation. This requires a great many cases. Even 1200 jury trials dissipate fast if one has some forty factors to deal with, and all but two of them have to be held constant if the two groups are to be compared with each other. Even with this sacrifice in numbers, we could not be sure that these two groups of cases would not be adulterated by some unknown spurious factor that might be present relatively more often in one group than in the other.

Such are the torments of survey analysis. They are inherent in all surveys, but they are worse in the field of law, because of the richness of its context. As always, imperfect data require outside support, either from other knowledge that is available about the subject matter, or possibly even from other data in the same survey. In our case, we had asked the judges for their assessment as to what moved the jury to a different verdict. We thus had another source in addition to the cross-tabulation of the assorted factors from which to approach our solution. We could look at the judge's assessment of the reasons for the jury verdict in the individual case.

Both types are logically related to each other, and both are derived from the basic analytical pattern of the controlled experiment. An example will make this clear. Suppose we wanted to test the hypothesis that the odds for the defendant's acquittal increase if counsel for the defense is superior to the prosecutor. In an ideal experiment we would assign to a random half of the cases a defense counsel superior to the prosecutor; and to the other half, counsel whose abilities were well matched. If superiority of counsel would indeed affect the outcome, we would expect that 40 per cent of the acquittals would have superior defense counsel and that 30 per cent would not.[13]

Not all cases with superior defense counsel end in acquittal and not all cases without such counsel end in conviction—a

13. The percentages in Figure 1 reproduce, somewhat simplified, the subsequent findings of our investigation.

clear indication that other factors also play a part. But the
percentage of acquittals with superior counsel is higher than
in the cases without such counsel, indicating that superiority
of counsel has some effect. In only ten out of every 100 cases
will this superiority become effective: the difference between
40 and 30 percentage points. In the 60 out of 100 superior-
counsel cases in which the defendant was convicted, quality
of counsel obviously did not help; and in 30 out of the 40 cases

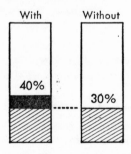

Figure 1

where he was acquitted, he would have been acquitted without
superior counsel, as a comparison with the "without" group
shows. Thus, only ten cases remain for which a competent
observer might be able to pick out and declare: "In *these* cases,
it was the superiority of defense counsel that was responsible
for the acquittal." This is, in effect, the "reason assessment" that
we asked the judge to perform.

     The analysis of survey data proceeds in analogy to the ex-
perimental design, with one important handicap. In the true
controlled experiment, the two groups (with and without superior counsel) would have been established by a lottery process so as to keep them as much alike as possible, except for the
deliberately introduced difference in the quality of counsel. In
the survey analysis, we must be content with proceeding *as if*
the two groups were alike.[14] But in our case the survey pro-

---

14. For an elaboration of this rationale, see Part II, "Tools of Causal
Analysis," in Zeisel, *Say It with Figures, op. cit.*

vided a rare opportunity for bolstering our confidence in this as-if procedure. When cross-tabulations and "reason assessment" were confronted on particular cases, they matched rather closely. In terms of our discussion, the judge in most instances *was* able to identify the ten out of 100 cases (40 per cent minus 30 per cent) in which the superiority of counsel was the *cause* of the acquittal. Actually, only in 10 per cent of all trials will it happen that defense counsel is superior; hence the 10-percentage-point difference from Figure 1 affected only 10 per cent of all cases. Since 10 per cent of 10 per cent is 1 per cent, superiority of defense counsel affects the verdict in approximately only 1 out of 100 trials. But however far, by outside support and internal cross reference, we may be able to reduce the danger of spurious causal inferences, this danger remains an irremovable flaw in any survey analysis.

Potentialities of Social Science Methods

What does our examination of some social science research on the law add up to? The social science tool chest is bound to provide better answers to the old questions that the law has raised, and to answer new ones that heretofore seemed beyond the reach of empirical analysis. These new data are provided either by sampling surveys or experiments, or are rediscovered by analyzing available data originally collected for quite different purposes. Sampling statistics now permits us to make inexpensively precise measurements of large universes without imposing the necessity of counting, in census fashion, every unit of that universe. To be sure, all these techniques have their limitations, in the range of data yielded, in the accuracy affected by social and legal obstacles, and in the important factor of costs, which we have not mentioned thus far.

When efforts are directed toward the discovery of causal connections, reasons, and motivations, social science research is put to its hardest test. Great inventiveness and good judgment are needed in deciding on the proper research approach, which inevitably must fall short of the ideal one. But the very necessity of such deliberate compromise will lead at least to a more precise formulation of the problem, of the data required for its analysis, and, finally, of the mode of analysis itself. It will also lead to a more balanced assessment of how distant the eventually available evidence is from the ideal one.

These examples of empirical study on the effects of laws and of the legal process itself should strike a familiar chord among lawyers. Both briefs of counsel and opinions of the courts refer often to the expected effects of the favored or opposed ruling, and not infrequently adduce "social science" evidence in support. A considerable amount of social science research has thus come into the law in the course of litigation. The Brandeis brief, filed in 1908, defending the constitutionality of limited working hours for women, is considered an early landmark for the use of social science in legal argument. The footnote on social science studies in the 1954 decision of the United States Supreme Court on school desegregation is one of the more recent instances, although in both cases the citation of empirical data was more conspicuous than essential. Of greater relevance, though less visible, has been the use of social science research in the area of economic litigation. Market and price surveys in antitrust cases, consumer surveys in trademark suits and in proceedings before administrative agencies, have become standard procedures of the law.

Another link with the law has been established by ad hoc committees of legislative bodies, which have at times produced important social science monographs. Studies of such institutions as insurance, investment banking, and public utilities provide some of the better examples. A parallel development took place in the academic field. Sociological jurisprudence, emphasizing the engineering aspects of the law, if it did not gain much ground, received at least acceptance of some of its principles. Later on, the legal realists, in more concrete if less systematic fashion, carried on this point of view by contrasting the alleged purpose of legal institutions with their actual effects, thus contributing their stimulus toward empirical inquiries into the law. In the law schools, empirical social research, after a start at Columbia, Chicago, Yale, and Johns Hopkins, has now reached a second phase. The case histories of this paper were selected to represent this second phase. It is characterized by the inclusion of topics that are not necessarily in the passing limelight of litigation or in the political debates of the day; by an aspiration to use the very latest developments in social science technique; and by a sober realization of the limitations of such inquiry into the law.

The yield from these efforts is still modest. But as the tools are sharpened, and as new roads of research on the law are opened, the overall effectiveness of the endeavor is bound to increase. In many ways this will make the task of the law easier: some questions will now become answerable with more precision. In other ways it may make the law's task more difficult: questions that had been raised and answered by rough guesses and approximations may now reveal more of their true complexity and hence defy simple answers. In the long run the new research methods should prove their value. If these efforts are carried on with integrity and skepticism, some training in the methods of social science research might soon become part of the legal scholar's required education.

Fred L. Strodtbeck

Social Process, the Law, and Jury Functioning

During the past thirty years no attempt to graft one of the core behavioral sciences of anthropology, or sociology to law has enjoyed continued success at any major law school,[1] al-

I should like to acknowledge my collaborator, Harry Kalven, for his discussion of various sections of this paper and for his assistance in the legal sections. The paper is based upon materials from the volume, *Social Process in the Law: A Study of the American Jury*, by Fred L. Strodtbeck and Harry Kalven, to be published by Little, Brown and Company.

1. This question has been treated in a broader historical perspective by Brainerd Currie in Parts I and II of his articles, "The Materials of Law Study," and in Part III of this series he discusses in detail the Columbia Law School excursion into the social sciences in the mid-twenties and thirties; see *Journal of Legal Education*, vol. 3 (1951), pp. 331–383, and vol. 8 (1955–56), pp. 1–78. Professor Robert Angell assisted this group in collecting supplementary readings treating of the family; see Albert C. Jacobs, *Cases and Other Materials on Domestic Relations* (Chicago: The Foundation Press, 1933). In retrospect, the sociological materials that were included expose the sociological framework as being thin and uneven. In addition, the coordination of these materials with legal cases left much

though there have been notable successes in medicine. A brief study of the history of the failures in law suggests that it may be fatal for the behavioral scientists to adopt the role of expert witnesses. The all-consuming questions of the law go well beyond extrapolations that may be validly made from behavioral science theories; and the price of failing to recognize the fundamental absence of relevant research may continue to be an early request to "step down, please." The alternative to service as an expert witness is active collaboration between the behavioral scientist and lawyer in legal research. This alternative is not without difficulties of its own; it may well not succeed either, but it does have the attraction of not having previously been tested and found wanting.

To make clear the potentialities of such collaboration, it may be helpful to behavioral scientists to characterize traditional legal study as a unique sort of factor analysis. Prior appellate rulings are studied somewhat like the pronouncements of a presumably rational oracle. The rule must be teased from the context of the specific instances. In traditional legal analysis all judges are regarded as fungible replicates, rational, well motivated, and, like the analyst himself, deeply concerned to determine whether the rule as it is currently understood applies to the case in question.[2] Sifting cases and statutes is a normative, retrospective exercise, and generalization beyond a limited aspect of law is ordinarily not sought. There are differences in

---

to be desired. The *Journal of Legal Education* has recently published a number of notes treating of this problem. See, in particular, David F. Cavers' review of Beutel's *Some Potentialities of Experimental Jurisprudence as a New Branch of Social Science,* in the *Journal of Legal Education,* vol. 10 (1957), pp. 162 *et seq.*

2. The assumptions of day-to-day legal analysis may at more reflective moments be criticized with urbane candor. Dean Levi exposes the multifaceted nature of any particular case in his *Introduction to Legal Reasoning* (Chicago: University of Chicago Press, 1949). The late Judge Frank's *Law and the Modern Mind* (New York: Brentano's, 1930) is a famous statement of the extreme realist position. Despite its disarming simplicity of structure, Karl Llewellyn's *Bramble Bush* (New York: Oceana Publications, 1951) is a provocative and mature statement of the problem. Lon Fuller creates imaginary appellate rulings and opinions in his *The Problems of Jurisprudence* (Brooklyn: The Foundation Press, 1949) to characterize and illuminate the most frequently recognized judicial styles.

method, but despite these differences law shares with social science a deep commitment to the understanding of the consequences of a law.

Let us take as an example the *McCollum* case[3] which concerned the use of "released time" from school for religious education. In his opinion Justice Frankfurter first asserts his belief that released time "sharpens consciousness of religious differences" among children, and then finds that the Constitution proscribed relations between church and state in order, among other objectives, to prevent such consequences.[4] Social scientists are generally familiar with comparable reasoning in the segregation cases, effects of loyalty programs, and so forth. These examples from the field of education[5] can be matched in many other areas. Study of the language of the decisions suggests that assertions about a rule imply a model of behavior, and if one may read the temper of the field from the status accorded certain judges such as Holmes, Brandeis, Cardozo, or Learned Hand, the more explicit and accurate the comment upon the behavioral consequences, the better the opinion and the more revered the judge.

It is not, however, to be concluded that the interest of the law in behavioral consequences is the same as that of behavioral science. For example, in the released-time decision cited above, one is not warranted in believing that Justice Frankfurter and the Court would have been interested in knowing the exact percentage of children in which a sharpened consciousness of religious differences arose after institution of a released-time program. Would not one child have been sufficient? Or, to take the stated basis for the decision one step further: a social scientist's demonstration that released time

---

3. *Illinois* ex rel *McCollum* v. *Board of Education of School District Number 71, Champaign County, Illinois,* 333 U.S. 203 (1948).

4. Social scientists might wish, as an exercise in jurisprudence, to reread the First Amendment. Then, reflect a moment on the distance between the Constitution and the ruling in this case, and, in turn, upon the implications this has for the judge's job.

5. See Harry Kalven, Jr., "Law and Education," *The School Review,* vol. 5 (Autumn, 1957), pp. 287–303.

results in a reduction of sharpened religious consciousness would not cause a reversal of the decision. Thus, there is no inherent error in the court's taking judicial notice of behavioral science findings without, in any way, relinquishing the case law line of argumentation.

It is staggering to recognize that each of the one million or so recorded cases could probably be fruitfully illuminated by an empirical footnote. One might further assume that behavioral studies for such purposes would be comparable in cost and complexity with the study that would have been required to appraise the effects of released time. Thus, to those about to conclude that collaboration of law and behavioral science is overwhelmed before it begins, we are here suggesting that it is fallacious to assume that the normative operations of the law require such precise behavioral information. One does not have to stress that it is beyond our present resources to bring useful investigation to bear on every problem encountered by the courts, if one at the same time believes such rigor would so often prove gratuitous.

One can guess that each day the courts encounter a score of problems that might conceivably be illuminated by social science research; and in business, government, and medicine comparable requirements arise. Some would argue that if the limited energies available were channeled to solve these substantive problems, the autonomous development of the behavioral sciences would be impeded. Concerning such arguments, it is one thing to argue the need for theory-directed inquiries pointed toward the rounding out of our accounting schemes, but it frankly takes quite a bit of faith to believe that the more abstruse and general the behavioral science theory, the greater the relevance to law. On the other hand, if one attempts to husband scarce resources by working on some "crucial" issues, this tactic also implies faith in our present ability to identify such issues. In short, what we require is a strategy whereby an effective relationship between law and behavioral science might be obtained.

A Strategy for Law-Sociology Research

As one searches for relevant criteria for the selection of an area of joint inquiry between law and sociology, the study of law as a profession comes easily to mind. We were not inclined to pursue this lead, in part because others are presently so engaged, and more importantly because only a minimal toleration of sociology by law is required to carry out such studies. We believed a fuller commitment by law *and* sociology was desirable. We felt that more would follow from our findings if they excited the lawyer's lawyers in the field, even if the substantive issues were too technical for a general audience. This contrasts with studies of professions that are generally less informative to the profession than to outsiders.[6]

We are now disposed to believe that we were attracted to the study of the jury by the fact that legal and behavioral elements intersect in the jury in a manner that is more complex and more immediate than that implied above in the discussion of the behavioral assumption in law. The jury renders verdicts like a judge, but it is still controlled by the judge. The jury is given the rule of law to apply, and it brings to its evaluation of a case the varying perspectives and social experiences of laymen. The lay character of the jury is a device by which the law expressly seeks to attain a definite, even though difficult to define, jurisprudential objective. Although the law cannot very easily contemplate abolishing the jury, it has wide prerogatives in the way in which it shall select and control the jury.[7]

---

6. At no time at Chicago was it believed advisable to use the sociologists to teach in the Law School; hence, there was no need for a heroic search for an assignment that might have led to an early course on law as a profession. As a point of interest, the existence of the project in the Law School has not affected law teaching in any way, save that during some of our early difficulties the regular faculty had less time to devote to it. In the Social Science Division, Allen Barton offered the course, "Sociology of the Legal Profession" (Spring, 1957), while he was associated with the project.

7. We are here encouraging the reader to ponder questions between

Concerning Experimental Replication

Since trials are ordinarily never repeated without change, a regular jury deliberation is always a response to a unique stimulus. This provides no guide for separating idiosyncratic from recurrent elements, and no determination can be made of the relation between any segment of the trial and the eventual verdict. Although the crystallization of jury procedure stretches back some six centuries, it is almost certain that the grounds on which procedural changes were from time to time instituted were insufficient to support valid conclusions in the particular instance. Nor, throughout this period, could the important decisions of attorneys during trials ever have been reliably assessed. A stratagem that under controlled conditions could have been demonstrated to give positive results in 80 of 100 cases might have failed in an unreplicated instance and been discarded. Faulty stratagems that were once used successfully might eventually be discarded by a practitioner who had opportunities to try them in many trials; but other practitioners might retain them for want of having accumulated enough information. It is in this way that the sensitive accumulation of usages by both the bench and bar inextricably mixes half truths and false beliefs about juror behavior with the winnowed insights of a several-hundred-year-old institution.

The radical contribution of the experimental perspective arises when any trial is considered to be a potentially reproducible event. Any trial could be given to a very large number of juries, or judges, in order to obtain a distribution of verdicts. For example, in a negligence case with clear liability, the distribution of verdicts would be a frequency diagram of amounts awarded the plaintiff. In criminal cases, the distribution would

the extremes of "Should the jury be permitted to take notes?" and "Should the question of negligence and damages be separated?" instead of "Should the jury system be abolished?" This latter question ordinarily has about the same clarifying effect on the discussion of the jury that "Would you want your sister to marry a Negro?" has on the discussion of race relations.

be the percentage of guilty and not guilty verdicts. For the civil case with equivocal negligence, and this is the preponderant pattern both in practice and in our experimentation, there is first the percentage of defendant verdicts, and then the distribution of awards to the plaintiff for the remaining verdicts. These latter distributions present certain statistical difficulties, but this in no way reduces the analytic value of thinking of the distribution of verdicts that would result if, within the same jurisdiction, a given case were repeatedly tried before different juries, or different judges.

Whatever prior strength was inherent in the search by the case method for comparable elements in the different cases still exists under this new perspective. The change is to be found only in the increased precision with which elements identified as important for appellate review of jury decision may be assessed. In this sense the case method is not supplanted; it is revised in a crucially important detail. A complex of factors of potential importance now takes on the additional dimension relating to whether it would shift one or five hundred verdicts in a thousand replicated trials. The difference between a concern with all possible factors and the narrower concern with factors that make a shift in a specified percentage of the verdicts is a difference that admits to consciousness an ordering of factors by their pragmatic effects. When this is done, one opens a window on the prospects of greatly increased control. It legitimates adding the paraphernalia of experimental inquiry to the tools of the scholar who formerly worked only at his desk.

In this connection it is appropriate to report that in our attempts in Chicago to simulate real trials with mock jury trials, we encountered no problems concerning the propriety of the research. The courts in Chicago, St. Louis, and Minneapolis provided space and jurors for the experiments and the judges cooperated by instructing the jurors. In contrast with some other forms of opinion assessment, this approach is exceptionally successful in avoiding the respondent who has never heard of the topic under study and furthermore is not interested. This success is in no small part due to the compulsion that is a part of the institutional atmosphere of the court. There is no newspaper reading, no whispering, and no conspicuous dozing as the jurors listen to the recorded trial under the watchful supervision of the bailiff. The disposition to evaluate what comes to one's attention is mobilized by the structure of the trial itself, and jurors easily form individual verdicts. Later in the deliberation some defend their interpretation more than others, but in all cases the culture of the jury room and the requirement of unanimity adds weight to the belief that every opinion counts.

It is possible to use the recordings of the deliberations and postdeliberation reports to demonstrate the deep involvement of the jurors in the procedure and in defense of their interpretation of the case. This is important because the lack of face-to-face contact with the principals in the courtroom might have been expected to more seriously "reduce involvement" in the deliberation. The deliberations collected prove to be quite similar to those recreated from juror interviews and to those obtained in the ill-fated recordings of actual trials.[8] The verdict results conform well to experiences of judges and attorneys, and the movement in verdicts when equity considerations are changed are in the direction that would be predicted from common-sense expectations. The questions of the validity of our experimental results are probably no better solved than they were after our first year of operation, but with greater experience we find our concern about validity is now much lower. We have

---

8. In 1954, during the early part of our research, we recorded, by means of concealed microphones, five jury deliberations in a Federal Court jury room in Kansas. The recordings were made with the permission of the judges and attorneys involved in the cases; the tapes were sealed for two years, and when they were eventually presented, the identity of the court and participants was masked. However, when the jury tapping became known to the public, there was an indignant outcry in editorial columns, and by the radio commentator, Fulton Lewis, Jr. Members of the research team were called to Washington to testify before a subcommittee of the Senate Judiciary Committee. As a result of these hearings Public Law 99 was passed making it illegal for anyone not a member of the jury to record, observe, or listen to the proceedings of a United States Jury while it is deliberating. For a more detailed account of reactions to these recordings see Waldo W. Burchard, "A Study of Attitudes toward the Use of Concealed Devices in Social Science Research," *Social Forces,* vol. 36 (December, 1957), pp. 111–116, and "Lawyers, Political Scientists, Sociologists—and Concealed Microphones," *American Sociological Review,* vol. 23 (December, 1958), pp. 686–691.

experienced a growing fascination with the interplay between legal constructs, behavioral theory, and the empirical results of the inquiry, which may be illustrated with three examples. The first treats of participation in the deliberation; the second, of the response to attorney fees, and the third of the willingness to discount a plaintiff recovery in a negligence case.

Relative Participation in Jury Deliberation[9]

Small-group theory holds that for groups to define and achieve their goals they must control the use of their primary group resource, their common time together. Only one or, at most, a few persons can talk at any given instant and be understood. Who talks and how much he talks is, within limits, determined by the reactions of the remainder of the group to the speaker. Acts that are perceived as relevant to the solution of the group's problems are generally favorably received and the responsible speaker is encouraged to continue. Over the long run, participation tends to become differentiated, with a small fraction of the group's members accounting for most of the participation.

In the jury situation there is not only the widespread norm that group members should act toward one another as equals but also the reinforcement of the presumption of equality by the requirement that the verdicts be unanimous. Equal and responsible participation in the deliberation is an institutionalized expectation. Therefore, if there is evidence that the status differences of the larger community become manifest in the deliberation, then it may be expected that a similar generalization of status will also be found in other situations where status differences are manifestly recognized.

9. See Fred L. Strodtbeck, Rita M. James, and Charles Hawkins, "Social Status in Jury Deliberations," *American Sociological Review*, vol. 22 (December, 1957), pp. 713–719, for a report on other concomitants of differentiation by participation.

With regard to the details of the technique, the deliberations were recorded with two microphones to facilitate binaural identification of individual participants. The protocols were fully transcribed, and from the protocol each speaker's contributions were unitized into discrete acts, which are roughly the equivalent of simple declarative sentences but also include nonverbal gestures noted by the observer.

Since there are twelve persons in the jury, one-twelfth, or 8.3 per cent, of the total acts is the pro rata expected percentage for each juror, which provides the baseline against which the effects of external status may be appraised. The higher the average participation of an occupational group, the greater their relative share of the common resource of time. It may be seen in Table 1 that in all occupations males talked more than females, and the amount of participation was sharply differentiated between higher-than-expected values for proprietors and clerical workers and lower-than-expected values for skilled and unskilled laborers.

Table 1
Percentage Rates of Participation in Jury Deliberations by Occupation and Sex of Juror

Sex	Proprietor	Clerical	OCCUPATION Skilled	Labor	Combined
Male	12.9	10.8	7.9	7.5	9.6
	(81)	(81)	(80)	(107)	(349)
Female	9.1	7.8	4.8	4.6	6.6
	(31)	(92)	(28)	(62)	(213)
Combined	11.8	9.2	7.1	6.4	8.5
	(112)	(173)	(108)	(169)	(562)*

* Numbers of jurors are shown in parentheses. Twenty-six of 588 jurors from the 49 juries used were not satisfactorily classified by occupation and are omitted.

While the moderately differing values in Table 1 are averages based upon the scores of more than 500 persons, within any particular deliberation there was a very steep differentiation between the most- and least-speaking jurors. For example, in 82 per cent of the juries the top three participators account for one-half or more of the total acts, the remainder being distributed among the other nine members. It is to be emphasized that the averages of Table 1 are descriptive of the relative participation of the occupation and sex groups, but do not reflect the wide variation within a jury.

The meaning of levels of participation may be viewed from still another perspective. After the deliberation, the jurors were asked to answer a battery of questions reporting their personal satisfaction with the quality of the deliberation and the tone of interpersonal relations. The level of an individual's satisfaction was positively correlated with the level of his own participation ($r = 0.52$, $P < 0.05$). The involvement that high participation represents in the jury is not unlike the investment in the affairs of the larger community by higher-status persons; both are instruments for group-derived satisfactions.

As a further commentary upon the interpretation of participation levels, responses to the postdeliberation question, "Who do you believe contributed most to helping your group reach its decision?" were tabulated by occupation of the person chosen. The average number of helpfulness votes received by occupation groups closely parallels the participation by occupation groups. The correlation between votes received and participation is about 0.69 when sets of individual values are correlated. Male clerical workers get slightly fewer votes than their participation would appear to warrant and male skilled workers get slightly more, but the overwhelming impression is that votes received as a helpful juror, like participation, influence, and satisfaction, parallels status differentiation in the larger society. Thus, contrary to the conception that one man dominates the jury or that many jurors are coerced, the picture emerges that in the retrial in the jury room the jurors work like responsible citizens, with democratic recognition of competence where it is found.

The Question of Attorney Fees

The differentiation discussed above is a somewhat static structural result of the social process in the deliberation. It is well to consider how a substantive topic fares in this same process. Attorneys frequently ask, "Does anticipation of attorney fees cause jurors to raise their awards?" An answer to this question that is in accordance with our understanding must necessarily go beyond a "yes" or "no" and include consideration of social process.

Before illustrating this, it should be indicated that in the experimental transcripts there are no references to attorney fees and, in addition, instructions concerning attorney fees are not given by the court. In this regard the transcripts accord with the practice of the courts, for in both state and federal jurisdictions attorney fees are not ordinarily recoverable as either compensation or costs and the practice is not to tell this to the jury. The courts tend to reason that nonrecovery enables parties to submit doubtful and disputed cases to the courts without being threatened with the entire legal costs in the event of a loss.

Insofar as it is possible for the jury in some instances to include an amount for attorney fees and in other instances not, the effect of the nonrecovery doctrine may be an increase in the variability of awards. On the other hand, if it can be shown that substantially all juries either "include" or "exclude" attorney fees when itemizing damages, then the attorney fees would affect not the variability, but rather, the level of awards. If attorney fees are included when the plaintiff is given an award, the legal argument that holds that the present "no instruction" practice is equal in its effects on both parties would be disproven.

One might guess that the essential question would be easily resolved by looking at a few deliberations. To show the complexities that attend such inspection, two pages from the deliberation of Doyle Case jury #12 will be quoted. One juror favors holding the plaintiff's recovery to between 20 and 25 thousand. The jurors speaking are identified here by the numbers assigned them:

12: Yeah, usually all of them [lawyers] take, most of them take a third.

6: However, the reduction in the amount awarded will be proportionate to what the lawyer is going to take. I mean he will take less . . .

8: He is going to take something out of that . . .

6: He will take less, of course, as the amount is reduced.

4: Yeah, but that will lessen her amount, too.

5: I don't think so . . .

12: They take a third regardless of how big or small.

4: That is right.

11: They take their percentage regardless, don't they? I mean, it is either 10 or 20 percent.

4: Regardless, they take it from the full amount—the award.

12: It is one-third. If they take $100, if they get $100,000, or if they get $25,000, it's still one-third. All lawyers take one-third.

4: One-third?

6: Yeah, it's proportionate to the amount awarded.

9: Yeah, but don't some of them . . .

8: What she is pointing out is that if *you* award $50,000, they will take $17,000 out.

12: Oh, I see. . . . That is right.

4: That's right.

8: Whereas if you award $30,000, they'd only be taking $10,000 out.

12: Oh, I see . . .

8: See, she'd be ending up with $20,000 out of $30,000 award, or she'd be ending up with $33,000 out of a $50,000 award. Well, that would be proportionate, one-third from the. . . . It's like when you're going to buy something, and you get a discount. You buy it a little bit more expensive because you're going to get more money's worth.

6: That is right.

12: I didn't understand that [before].

8: Now, there were a few who said $25,000, and one who said $20,000, uh, this discussion around the table. . . . Have you folks changed your minds in any way? That you feel that because of the expenses that you might not have thought of—the lawyer's expenses and things like that—would you agree that she get closer to $50,000, or do you still. . . .

3: Well, the reason I said $20,000, I, er, wasn't thinking about, expenses.

8: Yeah.

3: That's what I meant.

8: Course, that brings you back into the case where if she did get $50,000, and she was given *supposedly*, had to give a certain amount, well, say, $17,000, to her lawyers, it would leave her $33,000. Of that amount there's approximately $10,000 which she has spent between hospital bills, doctor bills, and her loss of pay. So that brings it down around $23,000, which she would have cash.

· · · · ·

8: Then are we all agreed that a $50,000, verdict would be a fair amount? Anybody in disagreement?

In this way, by comments from eight of the twelve jurors, it was made clear to those who favored 20 to 25 thousand that the plaintiff would, because of attorney fees and specific costs, only receive $33,000 if a verdict of $50,000 were given. This weakened the 20-to-25,000 position insofar as it implicitly said, "The figure you favor is about right; you'll have to award $50,000 for her to receive it." The person who favored the $50,000 may have done so because of his wish to compensate the plaintiff for pain and suffering, or loss of future income— not necessarily attorney fees. Although there is strong reason for believing that the attorney-fee consideration enabled this jury to resist a lower award, it is not at all clear that exactly one-third was added for attorney fees. At the same time the reality of attorney fees is no mystery to the jury.

In another set of experimental trials, which involved a facial injury to an infant child, the damage request was varied. At the $10,000 low level of the damage request, only one of the seven juries that found for the plaintiff mentioned attorney fees. At the $75,000 equitable level, mentions were made in seven of nine juries; and at $150,000, the high-level request, the percentage of mentions declined again, there being only four of seven. Thus, while nearly all jurors indicate a willingness to award attorney fees on an individual postdeliberation questionnaire, they find it most salient to mention them when deliberating under an equitable damage request. If the request is too low, *or* too high, there are less frequent mentions of attorney fees. This suggests an interesting double bind; as one comes closer to a supervised, equitable action, the jurors have a heightened consciousness of the reality of legal costs, which, in turn, the law holds they should not consider.

It must be remembered that these data are from cases in which there is a "silent" instruction on fees. How much the jury's behavior could be changed if one were to extend the experimental treatments by adding an instruction expressly telling the jury *to award* fees and by alternately adding an instruction expressly telling them *not to award* fees is not clear. There is a suggestion from some of our data on comparative, as contrasted with contributory, negligence that if the law legitimates an equitable tendency of the jury, it makes the tendency more pronounced. By analogy, legitimating the awarding of fees would argue for predicting an increase in damages. Again there is a suggestion from an experiment with instructions to disregard insurance that if the law makes expressly illegitimate an equitable tendency of the jury its efforts to control jury behavior may boomerang. By analogy, expressly forbidding the awarding of fees would also argue for predicting an increase in damages. And, as against either prediction, there is the healthy skepticism, generated by the deliberations we have studied, that the jury cannot be easily moved as a group to itemize damages as it sets a fair award. In any event, the continued use of the silent instruction provides a prime example of the society's leaving to the jury a policy dilemma it is unwilling or unable to resolve. And the jury in this instance, as is so often the case, treats the dilemma with an eye on both equity and reality.

Willingness to Discount Plaintiff's Recovery

A final example, which also demonstrates that questions about jury behavior are simultaneously questions about the law, arises in the postdeliberation response of jurors, as in the second example above, who have heard the action by David Conway, a child of three, to recover damages for facial injuries suffered when his bed caught fire as a result of the alleged malfunctioning of a vaporizer. David's mother could be thought of as having contributed to the accident if any of the following were construed as failure to use "reasonable care."

1. Placing the vaporizer on a fabric pot holder;
2. Putting a croup tent over the spout of the vaporizer;
3. Putting the vaporizer too near the crib;
4. Leaving the vaporizer unattended while she did the washing; and
5. Using a one-year-old cord.

The general legal doctrine involved is that of imputed negligence. The issue is whether this is an instance under which David and his mother are so closely associated, so much on "the same team," that if the negligence of the mother combines with the negligence of the manufacturer in causing an injury to David, the mother's negligence can be imputed to or charged against David when he seeks redress against the manufacturer. Assuming for the moment that we are operating under the rule that the contributory negligence of the plaintiff is a complete bar to his claim, the question is whether the negligence of the mother so "stains" David as to bar his suit against the manufacturer.

The doctrine of imputed negligence has had a long and checkered career at common law. Until about seventy-five years ago the doctrine flourished in several recurring situations: the negligence of the bailee was imputed to the bailor, the negligence of the parent was imputed to the child. The early cases were characterized by rather mechanical reasoning in terms of the "identity" of A to B and were not concerned with the possible harshness of the full contributory negligence defense. In any event, the doctrine has almost completely yielded to criticism, and today there has been a full reversal of the policy, in almost all jurisdictions, in the bailment, passenger, and child-parent situations. The reform would appear to have liberalized the law and made it more sensible. But, unfortunately, now that the issue is clearly resolved in favor of the plaintiff there

are some lingering doubts as to whether this result is really so
sensible after all. If the parent has been significantly negligent,
is it so obvious this should have no bearing on the recovery by
the family against a third party? This policy question is thus an
inviting one on which to poll the jury since, in this case, the
formal rule of law may be more favorable to the plaintiff than
the jury's common-sense view would dictate.

Unfortunately, the legal picture is complicated by the possible relevance of two other legal doctrines: comparative negligence; and proximate cause. The common law makes any
contributory negligence that was causal a 100 per cent defense.
It remains possible, however, that the sensible jury will make
a *double* departure from the legal rules in the imputed negligence case. It will impute negligence where the law today would
not but it will then moderate the consequences by using some
sort of *comparative* negligence where again the law would
not. Under the comparative doctrine, the plaintiff's recovery
is reduced in proportion to his contribution to the accident in
question.

The second strand in the legal tapestry—that of proximate
cause—makes it curiously difficult to state what result the
formal legal rules dictate in our case. The formula is that the
manufacturer is liable only for so much of his negligence as
is "the proximate cause" of the harm. It almost defies analysis
—and has for a century—to state simply what this new policy
consideration encompasses. But it does offer the jury legitimately the option of deciding that although both the mother
and the manufacturer were negligent in causing harm to David,
the manufacturer is not liable because the mother's contribution was so impressive as to render the manufacturer's too
trivial to make it fair to hold him. The upshot is that in this
case a jury could decide that the mother's negligence inter-
vened and dominated so much as to insulate the defendant
from liability. Hence, the child could not recover because of
the mother's negligence even though the mother's negligence
was not being imputed to him. If so, one final point needs to
be underscored. If the jury is going down the proximate cause
road, although it can then legitimately bar the plaintiff it

cannot legitimately reduce his recovery because of the mother's negligence. In law her negligence either was or was not the supervening cause. If it was not, he should recover in full; and if it was, he should recover nothing.

Turning to the data to determine the line of juror reasoning, it is to be noted that a slight majority (52 per cent) of the 144 jurors who believed the mother to have failed to use "reasonable" care in three or more of the five acts previously enumerated would discount, whereas only 28 per cent of the 114 jurors who faulted the mother on two or fewer instances would discount. Stated as a rule that would best account for the majority of their decisions, it appears that the jurors reason thus: impute negligence and discount the award where the parent's negligence is perceived as relatively great; follow the law and disregard the parent's negligence where the parent's negligence is perceived as relatively low. Since over the past one hundred years the law has done a complete reversal on imputation of negligence of parent to child, and neither its original position nor its present has seemed to critics and commentators to be altogether satisfactory, it is indeed arresting to note that jurors operate so as to effect their own complicated compromise of the law's policy dilemma.

Jury Study and the Sociology of Law

Each of these three examples illustrates a different facet of the problem of collaboration between law and behavioral science. To start with a critical example, one commentator has expressed the opinion that research operations of the type that result in the differential participation findings discussed previously constitute a pushing of small-groups approaches to the forefront of legal sociology "less for the sound knowledge it can offer than for the opportunity it presents to apply sophisticated research technique."[10] It may be granted that at the

10. See Philip Selznick, "The Sociology of Law," in Robert K. Merton, Leonard Broom, and Leonard S. Cottrell, Jr., eds., *Sociology Today* (New York: Basic Books, Inc., 1959), p. 120.

time this study began law had no highly articulated expectation about power and influence in the jury beyond some interest in knowing the percentage of juries that were dominated
by one man. But even though law had not raised the question,
our legal collaborators have shown a very great interest in
the results. On the other hand, given the availability of an
almost representative, highly motivated adult population seriously engaged in a discussion requiring unanimity—why should
this not hold a particular interest for the behavioral scientist?
There are very few instances in which face-to-face behavior
has been carefully studied in the exact institutional context
to which findings are to be generalized.

Concerning attorney fees, one of the recurring legal jokes
has it that juries arrive at damages by setting the attorney fee
and multiplying by three. Our techniques of inquiry touch a
narrow point of vocational interest by indicating this is not
the case, but much more fundamentally our techniques indicate
that it is necessary for jurors to elaborate a rationale for final
consensus. Jurors who have advocated verdicts distant from
the group mean must move closer if unanimity is to be reached.
It is a rule of the jury that members must not abjectly concede;
they must show they have been seriously convinced. While
the device of admitting that attorney fees had been overlooked
serves to bring the jurors inclined to a low award to a higher
figure, it reveals its true role in social facilitation by not mov-
ing to a higher award other jurors who might also have "for-
gotten." It is indeed probable that if a way were found to
remove the salience of attorney fees from the closing negotia-
tions, some other damage consideration would be given a
similar function.

The final example treating of the comparative discounting
of the award reveals the jury operating extralegally in the
service of the defendant rather than the plaintiff. It shows
clearly that one may be lulled by the sonorities of the dictum,
"the jury considers questions of fact and accepts the law as
given," into neglect of a social process that deserves to be
better understood. A view of the delicate interplay between
the role of law and the lay sense of equity in this one narrow

area of negligence actions changes one's strategy of research. The notion that broad generalizations about decision-making could be transferred to this context seems increasingly doubtful. As the general theories of disease of the eighteenth century have given way to the nearly autonomous and differentiated theories of today, so may it be with the cause of justice. It may not be wise for all who investigate to pursue the interrelation between the legal rule and the social sentiment in increasingly specific situations, but we are personally curious to know a great deal more about the civil negligence field.

Our personal view on this point is in one sense a general view, for although the field of jury study is highly appropriate for law and behavioral science collaboration it is not uniquely so. Other areas pursued with industry will certainly produce comparable results. Our personal view goes to the mode of operation. Sober, behavioral fact gathering, expensive and difficult as it is, provides the inherently persuasive basis for the acceptance of the sociological theory that may have guided the inquiry and interpretation. There are some who are impatient with sociological craftsmanship and who wish to proceed quickly beyond fact finding to what they perceive as the "scholarly objectives" of a sociology of law.[11] It may be observed that policy responsibility and scientific detachment are ill-suited to one another. Should not the social scientist, who has taken the pains both to learn the law and to observe legal behavior from the perspective of his discipline, at the same time consider seriously the wisdom of making the information available as a scientific report—free of the "oughts" of policy

---

11. See Selznick, *loc. cit.*, p. 124. And on p. 122: "This means that we should avoid the temptation to present social-science knowledge as based on the specific results of a limited survey or experiment, for any one of the latter may be vulnerable while the basic generalization remains firm. The general agreement among social scientists regarding the damaging effects of segregation is actually based, not on specific studies of Negroes and whites, but on a theory of personality and on quite diverse, though logically related, empirical work. The very need to defend our own conclusions should recall us to basic theory." The present position is just the opposite; it is here argued that the appropriate defense, sociologically, lies in the data and, until more relevant data are available, frank skepticism is to be encouraged.

recommendation? The jurisprudential responsibility for normative policy does not have to be gobbled by the sociologist making legal studies. One can agree that the stubborn difficulties inherent in questions of policy can never be resolved by consideration of the facts—either standing alone or in the context of sociological theory. The frontiers of collaboration can accommodate legal doctrine and sociological theory without resulting in an interpenetration that will erase the unique prerogatives and responsibilities of the respective disciplines.

William M. Evan

Public and Private
Legal Systems

Virtually all legal scholars and many political scientists
view law as being inextricably interwoven with the state, and
the state, having a monopoly of coercion, is identified as the
sanctioning agent of law. Accordingly, phenomena analytically
similar to law that do not fall within the framework of the
state have been either largely neglected or else conceptualized
in unrelated terms.[1] And the sanctioning power pervasively

This paper is a product of a general study in the sociology of law,
which was supported by a grant from the Russell Sage Foundation. The
author wishes to express his gratitude to this Foundation for making this
study possible. He is also indebted to Harry C. Bredemeier for many invaluable suggestions.
    1. "Private government is not only a legitimate but a much neglected
subject of inquiry by political science." Earl Latham, "The Group Basis
of Politics: Notes for a Theory," in Heinz Eulau, Samuel J. Eldersveld,
and Morris Janowitz, eds., *Political Behavior: A Reader in Theory and
Research* (New York: The Free Press, 1956), p. 235. "Before the rise of
the modern state, the existence of a plurality of legal orders was probably
too obvious to be remarked on. But even after the claim of the state for
the monopoly of lawmaking made itself felt, the existence of nonofficial
systems of law was recognized. . . . But an investigation into the real

exercised by associations less inclusive than the state has been inadequately explored. With its stress on the sovereign state as the source of positive law, analytical jurisprudence has played a dominant role in the articulation of this conception of law.

Certain scholars, however, have departed from the prevailing view of law; two are especially noteworthy. Ehrlich, one of the earliest students of the sociology of law, conceived of law as consisting primarily of rules by which persons in society order their conduct and only secondarily of "norms for decisions" developed by the courts and of legislation enacted by the state. These rules or "facts of the law," as he called them, are developed by various "social associations"—families, clans, religious organizations, corporations, labor unions, employer associations, political parties, social clubs, and so on. It is the "inner order of the [social] associations" that is the "basic form of law."[2] Similarly, Weber's view of law includes a "legal order" that falls outside the province of the state.

> We categorically deny that "law" exists only where legal coercion is guaranteed by the political authority. . . . A "legal order" shall rather be said to exist wherever coercive means, of a physical or psychological kind, are available; i.e., wherever they are at the disposal of one or more persons who hold themselves ready to use them for this purpose in the case of certain events; in other words, wherever we find a consociation specifically dedicated to the purpose of "legal coercion."[3]

Ehrlich[4] and Weber,[5] as well as other scholars,[6] acknowl-

---

structure of these legal systems, representing, so to speak, as many states within the state, is completely neglected." Alexander Pekelis, *Law and Social Action: Selected Essays,* ed. by Milton R. Konvitz (Ithaca, N.Y.: Cornell University Press, 1950), p. 68.

2. Eugen Ehrlich, *Fundamental Principles of the Sociology of Law,* trans. by Walter L. Moll (Cambridge, Mass.: Harvard University Press, 1936), p. 37.

3. Max Weber, *Law in Economy and Society,* trans. by Edward Shils and Max Rheinstein (Cambridge, Mass.: Harvard University Press, 1954), p. 17. See also Introduction by Max Rheinstein, p. lxvii.

4. Ehrlich, *op. cit.,* pp. 61–82.

5. Weber, *op. cit.*

6. See, for example, Charles E. Merriam, *Public and Private Govern-*

edge the efficacy of the sanctions at the disposal of nonstate associations such as the church, the corporation, the trade union, and the professional association. A case in point is the reluctance of labor arbitrators confronted with a grievance involving discharge from employment to sustain the penalty because they regard it as the functional equivalent in industry of "capital punishment."[7]

In this paper we shall consider some implications of a conception of law and legal systems that is not exclusively identified with the state in an effort (a) to reconceptualize law and legal systems in general normative and social-structural terms and (b) to identify some problems and formulate some hypotheses in the sociology of law.

A Sociological Conception of Legal Systems

Sociologically, a legal system consists of at least (a) a body of norms governing the expectations and actions of the members of a given social system and (b) a set of specialized statuses to which are allocated different normative functions.

The set of norms of a legal system may vary with respect to the extent of knowledge on the part of objects (those to whom the norms apply); extent of acceptance by objects; extent of application to objects (whether they apply to all members or to special categories of members of a social system); severity of sanction provided; amount of conformity by objects, and so on.[8] Likewise the relations among norms comprising the legal

---

ment (New Haven, Conn.: Yale University Press, 1944), p. 9. "The state can throw a man into prison. But an employer can take away his job. As the state can deprive a man of his life, the church can threaten his happiness for the future and make him extremely uneasy and unhappy while he lives. The state may tax, but the monopoly may raise prices and lower standards." Quoted in Robin M. Williams, Jr., *American Society: A Sociological Interpretation* (New York: Alfred A. Knopf, 1951), p. 206, n. 7.

7. Robert H. Skilton, *Industrial Discipline and the Arbitration Process* (Philadelphia: University of Pennsylvania Press, 1952), p. 29.

8. Cf. R. T. Morris, "A Typology of Norms," *American Sociological Review*, vol. 21 (1956), pp. 610–613.

system may differ. For instance, they may be logically and substantively independent of one another, contradictory, or reciprocal. A reciprocal relation is one in which the norms, directed to different individuals in interaction, reinforce one another—for example, norms relating to the rights of a member of an association that correlatively set forth the duties of its officers.[9]

The set of specialized statuses of a legal system may also differ in various respects, as in number, distribution of functions, and pattern of organization. Regardless of differences, three normative functions—universal in the type of social system to be discussed—are performed by the occupants of specialized legal statuses: legislative, judicial, and executive. By legislative function is meant the authority to innovate norms; by judicial function, the authority to interpret existing norms; and by executive function, the authority to enforce norms with the aid of institutionalized sanctions. Complementing the set of specialized legal statuses in which is vested authority over the normative processes is the nonspecialized status, the occupants of which constitute the "laity" or the rank-and-file members of a social system.

In combination, the norms and the specialized legal statuses constitute the structure of a legal system. It is evident that such a legal system has some of the attributes of a formal organization.[10] Hence, unlike Ehrlich, we would not characterize the family, at least of the type common in industrial societies, as a legal system, if only because the statuses are not functionally specific relative to the three analytically distinguishable normative processes. Formal organizations differ in many respects, one being the character of their legal systems, a question which we shall presently consider.

---

9. Wesley N. Hohfeld, *Fundamental Legal Conceptions* (New Haven, Conn.: Yale University Press, 1923), pp. 23–114.

10. Cf. Philip Selznick, "The Sociology of Law," in Robert K. Merton, Leonard Broom, and Leonard S. Cottrell, Jr., eds., *Sociology Today* (New York: Basic Books, Inc., 1959), pp. 115–127. "Some of us who have worked in that field [sociology of administration] have discovered that in studying formal organizations we were also studying legal systems," p. 118.

A Typology of Legal Systems

Given the structural elements of a legal system set forth above, various typologies might be constructed. For present purposes we shall classify legal systems along two dimensions. Implicit in our discussion is a distinction between legal systems on the basis of jurisdiction, namely, whether they are public or private. A public legal system has its locus in the formal structures of the state such as the judiciary, the legislature, the executive, and the administrative agency; its jurisdiction extends to all inhabitants of the territory of a society. A private legal system, on the other hand, has its locus in a formal organization relatively independent of the state; its jurisdiction officially extends only to the organization's members.

The second basis of classification involves a vague, multidimensional but important distinction between democratic and undemocratic types of legal systems. A democratic legal system includes at least three attributes: (a) the separation of powers, (b) "procedural due process of law," and (c) the consent of the governed. The first two attributes have the function of delimiting the authority exercised over the members or the "laity" of the social system. Through the separation of powers, the three normative functions are so distributed as to prevent a concentration of authority in one and the same status.

Procedural due process of law, as distinct from substantive due process, relates to a complex of norms protecting the rights of parties in the prosecution and adjudication of a dispute.[11] Incorporated in the Bill of Rights in 1791, the Due Process Clause protects the citizen against the exercise of arbitrary power by the federal government. These rights were extended after the Civil War, via the Fourteenth Amendment, to citizens vis-à-vis their state governments. Parties to a dispute are assured

---

11. Morris D. Forkosch, "American Democracy and Procedural Due Process," *Brooklyn Law Review*, vol. 24 (1958), pp. 176–195; Robert L. Hale, *Freedom through Law* (New York: Columbia University Press, 1952), pp. 228–239.

a "fair" and "impartial" trial through such guarantees as the right to notice of hearing, the right to confront witnesses and to cross-examine them, and the right to introduce evidence on one's behalf.[12] The significance of this constitutional doctrine for democracy has recently been underscored by a legal scholar who states that "due process may almost be said to be a sufficient cause for our democracy."[13] Justice Frankfurter has expressed a similar view in asserting that due process is one of the "indispensable conditions for the maintenance and progress of a free society."[14]

Consent of the governed, the third attribute of a democratic legal system, not only affords the laity a veto power through the electoral process, but also implies the right to dissent. Institutionalization of dissent protects the minority among the laity as well as among the officials performing specialized normative functions.[15]

A democratic legal system as defined here—one characterized by the separation of powers, procedural due process, and consent of the governed—maximizes the probability that the institutionalized rights, immunities, and privileges of all members of a social system are protected. On the other hand, an undemocratic legal system, or one lacking these three properties, provides for none of the safeguards against unlimited and arbitrary authority. The occupant of one and the same status in a social system may perform legislative, executive, and judicial functions; there is no institutionalized procedure for impartially adjudicating disputes; and the occupants of statuses that do not have specialized legal functions, the laity, have little or no formal veto power over the officials performing executive, legislative, and judicial functions. Weber's monocratic type of bureaucratic organization is obviously closer to the undemocratic than to the democratic type of legal system.[16]

12. Forkosch, *op. cit.*, p. 212.
13. *Ibid.*, p. 173.
14. Quoted in Forkosch, *ibid.*, p. 189, n. 43.
15. For a discussion of institutionalization of dissent, see S. M. Lipset, M. Trow, and J. Coleman, *Union Democracy* (New York: The Free Press, 1956), pp. 238–269, 416.
16. Max Weber, *Theory of Social and Economic Organization,* trans. by A. M. Henderson and Talcott Parsons (New York: Oxford University Press, 1947), pp. 337–341.

These two dimensions for classifying legal systems yield four ideal types: (1) public democratic, (2) public undemocratic, (3) private democratic, and (4) private undemocratic. Examples of public legal systems that are formally democratic are the municipal, state, and federal courts, legislatures, and executive branches of government in the United States and other countries with polylithic states. By contrast, the public legal systems of societies with monolithic states are formally undemocratic. Private legal systems that are formally democratic are exemplified by such organizations as trade unions, professional associations, and trade associations. With respect to its employees, the industrial or business organization is an example of a private undemocratic legal system.

This typology of legal systems suggests several general classes of problems for the sociology of law. First, what are some significant structural and functional similarities and dissimilarities among legal systems, public and private? Second, what are the interrelationships between public and private legal systems? Third, what are the interrelationships between public legal systems? Fourth, what are the interrelationships between private legal systems? Fifth, under what conditions do legal systems, whether public or private, undergo transformation from an undemocratic into a democratic type, and vice versa? Sixth, under what conditions do legal systems, democratic or undemocratic, undergo transformation from a public to a private type and vice versa? Although the typology may point to other problems, those enumerated have the merit of dealing with basic problems of normative and structural change about which we have relatively little systematic knowledge.

Some Problem Areas in the Sociology of Law

We shall briefly consider four of the classes of problems suggested by our typology because they readily lend themselves to the identification of problems of sociological significance. This discussion is intended merely to illustrate the kinds of problems that a developing sociology of law might embrace.

COMPARATIVE STUDY OF LEGAL SYSTEMS

Comparative studies have been made by legal scholars of public legal systems, either of total systems (judicial, legislative, and executive components) or of subsystems. Thus, for example, Wigmore examines a great variety of public legal systems; Orfield compares the public legal systems of Scandinavian countries; and Hoebel compares the public legal systems of several preliterate societies.[17] An illustration of a comparative study of a subsystem of public legal systems is McRuer's work on judicial process.[18] Since these studies tend to be descriptive in nature, they provide data only for comparative sociological analysis.

Characteristically, Weber developed a classification of analytical categories for his comparative and historical analysis of different public legal systems.[19] His fourfold classification—concerned with law making and law finding, two of the three normative processes—is based on the interrelationship between two dimensions: formal-substantive and rational-irrational.[20] We may infer from Weber's analysis that democratic legal systems may have the attributes of either a formally rational or a substantively rational system, though perhaps not of a formally irrational or a substantively irrational type.

The three attributes of a democratic legal system discussed above—separation of powers, procedural due process of law, and consent of the governed—provide the bases for a comparative

17. John Henry Wigmore, *A Panorama of the World's Legal Systems*, 3 vols. (St. Paul, Minn.: West Publishing Co., 1928); Lester B. Orfield, *The Growth of Scandinavian Law* (Philadelphia: University of Pennsylvania Press, 1953); E. Adamson Hoebel, *The Law of Primitive Man: A Study in Comparative Legal Dynamics* (Cambridge, Mass.: Harvard University Press, 1954).

18. James C. McRuer, *The Evolution of the Judicial Process* (Toronto: Clarke, Irwin, 1957).

19. Weber, *Law in Economy and Society, op. cit.*, pp. 61–64.

20. See Rheinstein's penetrating analysis of Weber's typology, *ibid.*, pp. xlvii–lxiii.

study of public and private legal systems. In the case of public legal systems we may examine the structural differences and similarities between the democratic and the undemocratic. For example, do democratic legal systems have a higher rate of turnover in key specialized statuses? Is this true of legislative and executive statuses but not of judicial statuses, which may require greater stability of tenure to guarantee the incumbents the necessary autonomy in their role performance? Correlatively, is the status sequence[21] of occupants of specialized statuses in democratic legal systems characterized by a higher rate of transition to nonlegal or lay statuses than is the case in undemocratic legal systems?

Other differences between these two types of legal systems may be observed in the structure of the legal profession, the judiciary, and the civil service. A legal profession that does not enjoy a high degree of autonomy vis-à-vis the state cannot effectively train recruits to uphold the normative system in a disinterested manner. Similarly, if the court system is organized on the principle of a chain of command, the lower courts are not likely to venture independent interpretations of law for fear that they may be overruled by the higher courts. This hierarchical mode of organization facilitates extralegal control of the judiciary. And if the civil service is not sufficiently professionalized and hence does not administer the law efficiently and in accordance with universalistic standards, it, too, is susceptible to extralegal control. Are such propositions true?

Related questions may be raised about private legal systems. The high degree of variation among formal organizations of a private character points to a general problem: in what types of private organizations do we find an approximation to a democratic legal system, and in what types an approximation to an undemocratic legal system?

A distinction between administrative organizations and voluntary associations, as advanced by Moore,[22] provides a fruitful

21. Robert K. Merton, *Social Theory and Social Structure* (rev. ed.; New York: The Free Press, 1957), pp. 370, 380–385.
22. Wilbert E. Moore, "Management and Union Organizations: An Analytical Comparison," in Conrad M. Arensberg, *et al.*, *Research in Industrial Human Relations* (New York: Harper & Brothers, 1957), pp. 119–

preliminary approach to this problem. In administrative or work organizations, in which membership is a direct source of livelihood, the legal system tends to be undemocratic. Authority with respect to normative processes is not limited by any of the three attributes of a democratic legal system. Ruml, for example, in analyzing the structure of corporate management, observes that "the Someone who represents the Company [to potential stockholders] gets his authority from a superior source in the Company's management, a source which *combines legislative, administrative, and judicial powers.*"[23] In voluntary associations, on the other hand, in which membership is generally based on shared norms and values, a democratic legal system tends to predominate. To take but one subclass of voluntary associations, occupational associations are likely to be closer approximations to the democratic type of legal system than are industrial organizations.

A more refined typology of formal organizations than the distinction between administrative organizations and voluntary associations is obviously necessary. A comparison between an industrial organization and a university, both of which are administrative organizations, would show marked differences in their legal systems, with the former resembling an undemocratic legal system and the latter a democratic legal system. This contrast is due to differences in organizational goals—the production of goods versus the creation and dissemination of knowledge—and to a corollary difference in occupational structure. A university generally has a higher proportion of professional personnel than an industrial organization; this is conducive to the growth of an "occupational community"[24] with norms and a social structure consistent with that of a democratic legal system.

Voluntary associations, as in the case of administrative or-

130. See also William M. Evan, "Dimensions of Participation in Voluntary Associations," *Social Forces*, vol. 36 (1957), pp. 150–152.

23. Beardsley Ruml, "Corporate Management as a Locus of Power," *Social Meaning of Legal Concepts*, no. 3, ed. by Edmond N. Cahn (New York: New York University School of Law, 1950), p. 227. [Italics added—W. M. E.]

24. Cf. Lipset, Trow, and Coleman, *op. cit.*, pp. 83–140.

ganizations, also differ greatly. Thus a comparison of a professional association with a trade union would probably yield evidence that the former more closely approximates a democratic legal system than the latter, if only because the norms of a professional occupation engender the development of a more cohesive and self-governing occupational community.

A comparative approach to private legal systems might fruitfully inquire into the extent of members' knowledge of norms, the extent of their acceptance of the norms, and the extent of nonconformity. How different are private legal systems in their profiles on these three variables? With respect to knowledge of norms, it may be hypothesized that the laity of an undemocratic legal system is likely to be more informed about the duties pertaining to its status and less informed about its rights, privileges, and immunities, whereas in a democratic legal system no such difference obtains, or the reverse may be true. It may also be hypothesized that in a democratic legal system a higher proportion of the laity approves of and conforms to the norms.

Such comparative inquiry would probably show that the number of persons who perform the functions of legislators, executives, judges, and lawyers in private legal systems is larger than we generally assume; it would probably identify a larger number of litigants, a higher incidence of litigation, and many more sanctions being invoked than we tend to associate with the organs of public legal systems.

INTERRELATIONSHIPS BETWEEN PUBLIC
AND PRIVATE LEGAL SYSTEMS

The relationship between public and private legal systems has usually been conceived of and examined in terms of the role of pressure groups in the legislative process, or in terms of the government's regulation of private organizations, especially business organizations. It also has long been observed that public legal systems confer on private legal systems rights, duties, privileges, and immunities through the process of granting a charter of incorporation, license, permit, franchise, and so on.[25] Several modes of interrelationship, however, have been neglected.

First is the increasing tendency for the norms of private legal systems to be judicially recognized, as for example, in a medical malpractice suit in which the code of ethics of the American Medical Association is invoked; in a suit involving the internal relations of a trade union in which the union's constitutional provisions are accorded legal status by the court; or in a suit by a student against a college or university in which the institution's disciplinary rules are judicially recognized. Such judicial recognition, particularly under a system of common law, results in precedents, that is, in the growth of new legal norms guiding judicial decision-making. The adoption, as it were, of the norms of private legal systems by public legal systems is functionally equivalent to the conferral of rights on private legal systems.

A second interrelationship is the diffusion of norms in letter or spirit from private to public legal systems. Although such diffusion is probably less common than judicial recognition of the norms of private legal systems, this is an important source of growth of the norms of public legal systems. An example of such diffusion is the incorporation of the "law merchant" into common law and statutory law.[26] Diffusion of norms should be distinguished from the process associated with the concept of pressure groups. Whereas the concept of pressure groups connotes an "enactive" and intended process of change, diffusion connotes a "crescive" and unintended process. The tempo of effect of pressure groups on public legal systems may be gradual or rapid. The suffragette movement is an example of a pressure group whose effect was gradual as compared with the "right-to-work law" pressure groups whose effect, at least in eighteen states, was relatively rapid. By contrast, the diffusion of the

25. With respect to the history of the corporation, it should be noted that "it is a matter of dispute . . . whether the British Crown created corporations or found and assumed the control of preexisting collectivities." Adolph A. Berle, Jr., "Historical Inheritance of American Corporations," in Ralph J. Baker and William L. Cary, *Cases and Materials on Corporations* (3d ed.; Brooklyn: The Foundation Press, 1958), p. 1.

26. Louis L. Jaffee, "Law Making by Private Groups," *Harvard Law Review*, vol. 51 (1937), p. 213.

"law merchant" to the public legal system was a very gradual and unintended process. Another distinction is that pressure groups are associated primarily with one or two structural components of public legal systems, namely, legislatures and administrative agencies, whereas the diffusion mechanism applies to all structural components of public and private legal systems.

A third form of interrelationship involves the flow of personnel between public and private legal systems. Public legal systems of necessity recruit officials of private legal systems who have the required expertise to administer laws transferred from or modeled after those of private legal systems, as in the case of professionals serving on occupational licensing boards, or business executives serving in such administrative agencies as the Securities Exchange Commission, Federal Trade Commission, or Interstate Commerce Commission.[27]

Private legal systems in turn seek to recruit professionals with experience in public legal systems, possibly because of their knowledge of "secrets of the office." Thus, for example, corporations and trade unions may wish to recruit officials of the National Labor Relations Board in the hope that it will help them in their relationships with the agency. Such transfers of personnel may lead to a transfer of norms between public and private legal systems. In other words, the status sequence of officials of public and private legal systems probably serves as a mechanism for the transmission of norms from one type of system to another.

A fourth interrelationship between public and private legal systems is the emergence of administrative agencies in response to the emergence of private legal systems. In the United States, where this development occurred later than in some European countries, there has been a steadily increasing multiplication of administrative agencies or independent regulatory agencies since the establishment of the Interstate Commerce Commission in 1887. Regulation by administrative agencies entails a conferral of both rights and duties on private legal systems.

Private legal systems are obviously not all of equal impor-

---

27. *Ibid.*, p. 231; Walton Hamilton, *The Politics of Industry* (New York: Alfred A. Knopf, 1957), pp. 51–62, 141.

tance as sources of new legal norms and organs in public legal systems. Those which are rooted in certain institutional spheres have greater effect on public legal systems than others with different institutional bases. For example, the legal systems of trade associations, professional associations, and trade unions, because of their links with economic institutions, presumably have more effect on public legal systems than the legal systems of, say, educational, familial, or recreational organizations.

The converse of this mode of interrelationship, namely, the impact of the public legal systems on private legal systems, is well known. However, two interrelationships are noteworthy. First is the diffusion of "procedural due process of law" from public to private legal systems. This process is more readily observable in trade unions than in corporations—for example, in the growth of internal and external appellate review procedures in trade unions such as the Upholsterers International Union and United Automobile Workers.[28] Berle, however, claims that

[T]here is being generated a quiet translation of constitutional law from the field of political to the field of economic rights. . . . The emerging principle appears to be that the corporation, itself a creation of the state, is as subject to constitutional limitations which limit action as is the state itself.[29]

If in fact this process of institutionalization is under way, we may expect that public legal systems will eventually impose a duty on corporations to conform to procedural due process of law in their internal relations.

The second interrelationship, even less obvious, is the emergence of private legal systems as unanticipated consequences of decisions by public legal systems.[30] Two contrasting

28. See, for example, *First Annual Report of the Public Review Board to the Membership of the UAW*, 1957–1958, no publisher given.

29. Adolph A. Berle, Jr., "Constitutional Limitations on Corporate Activity," *University of Pennsylvania Law Review*, vol. 100 (1952), pp. 942–943; also *The 20th Century Capitalist Revolution* (New York: Harcourt, Brace & World, 1954), pp. 77 ff.

30. For an analysis of the impact of public legal systems on private legal systems, see William M. Evan and Mildred A. Schwartz, "Law and the Emergence of Formal Organizations," forthcoming.

examples of this process will suffice: the rise of the League of Women Voters, following the passage of the Nineteenth Amendment, with its functional consequences for the public legal system; and the formation of the White Citizens' Councils, following the desegregation decision of the United States Supreme Court, with their dysfunctional consequences for the public legal system.

INTERRELATIONSHIPS AMONG PRIVATE LEGAL SYSTEMS

The proliferation of private organizations and hence private legal systems, particularly in the United States,[31] has resulted in an increase in the frequency and types of interorganizational relations. Of the various types of interrelations two will be mentioned because of their effect on public legal systems. One entails a marked inequality of power in the relationships between two or more private legal systems; the other, an approximation to a balance of power. In the former type of relationship, the weaker party may choose one of several alternatives: submit to the domination of the superordinate power; seek alliances—as in the case of international relations—to effect a shift in the balance of power; or have recourse to a unit of a public legal system to redress wrongs of the more powerful private legal systems or to augment its relative power. The latter course of action is illustrated by the National Automobile Dealers Association's efforts, through the courts and legislatures, to curb the power of the three large automobile manufacturers to dictate the terms of contracts and to cancel contracts.[32] In other words, inequality in power relationships among private legal systems is a major source of pressure on public legal systems to introduce normative and organizational changes.

Where there is an approximation to a balance of power between two or more private legal systems, that is, where organizational relationships are of a coordinate rather than a

---

31. Kenneth E. Boulding, *The Organizational Revolution* (New York: Harper & Brothers, 1953).

32. See, for example, Joseph Cornwall Palamountain, Jr., *The Politics of Distribution* (Cambridge, Mass.: Harvard University Press, 1955), pp. 107–158.

superordinate-subordinate character, one possible consequence is the growth of a degree of consensus regarding goals that eventuates in a merger or a federation. In the absence of a high degree of consensus regarding goals, an approximation to a balance of power may lead to the growth of a partial legal system for the purpose of resolving intersystem conflicts. Private tribunals for labor and commercial arbitration are notable examples of this process. The more the parties approach an equality of legal and power status, the more effective these tribunals are as conflict-resolving mechanisms. It may be hypothesized that if the formal legal equality of the parties in these tribunals is not accompanied by equality in economic and political power, the effectiveness of the arbitral process is diminished.[33]

Such mechanisms develop among private legal systems because of the incompetence of units of public legal systems to cope with the technical problems of private legal systems, the cost and delay of litigation, the lack of legislation or precedents applicable to the novel problems confronting private legal systems, or because of the importance of maintaining flexible relationships, which action by components of public legal systems would make difficult.[34] Bypassing the courts, private arbitration tribunals handle 70 per cent—according to one estimate—of all civil litigation in the United States.[35] And in the case of labor arbitration, the grievance machinery of which it is a part is administered by a large number of management and union personnel, for example, approximately half a million shop stewards perform the function of "counsel" for aggrieved workers.[36] It is small wonder

33. For a related discussion, see William M. Evan, "Power, Bargaining and Law: A Preliminary Analysis of Labor Arbitration Cases," *Social Problems,* vol. 6 (Summer, 1959), pp. 4–15.

34. See, for example, Harry Shulman, "Reason, Contract and Law in Labor Relations," *Harvard Law Review,* vol. 68 (1955), pp. 999–1024; also "The Arbitration Process," in Joseph Shister, *Readings in Labor Economics and Industrial Relations* (2d ed.; Philadelphia: J. B. Lippincott Co., 1956), p. 249.

35. Soia Mentschikoff, "The Significance of Arbitration—A Preliminary Inquiry," *Law and Contemporary Problems,* vol. 17 (1952), p. 698.

36. Neil W. Chamberlain, *Labor* (New York: McGraw-Hill Book Company, 1958), p. 609.

that this private judiciary with its evolving body of private law is recognized by public legal systems. For instance, the New York Civil Practice Act takes cognizance of private arbitration tribunals, specifies procedures, and makes their awards enforceable by the courts.

TRANSFORMATION OF LEGAL SYSTEMS

Reconceptualizing law and legal phenomena in these general normative and social-structural terms generates the insight that the frontier of growth of the law in a modern industrial society such as the United States is not—as is often assumed —only in public legal systems but also in private legal systems. In addition, it suggests several general hypotheses regarding the transformation of legal systems.

First, as private legal systems extend their sphere of jurisdiction beyond their institutional base, the potential for competition and conflict with other private legal systems in the affected institutional sphere increases. Thus, for example, as corporations, trade unions, and churches increase their political activities, their relations with one another and with political parties may become marked with conflict. And conflict, in turn, may continue unresolved; it may elicit efforts at cooptation of the leadership of the threatening organization; or it may call forth the mediating action of other private legal systems or of public legal systems. In the event the public legal system intervenes, new norms arise, whether through legislative enactment, judicial decision, or executive or administrative action. We may also hypothesize that the more each private legal system seeks to extend its sphere of jurisdiction, the more safeguards are thereby erected against the monopolization of power by public legal systems. However, a democratic public legal system can, among other things, protect the rights of the laity of private legal systems against the exercise of arbitrary and autocratic authority.

Second, the progressive differentiation of specialized statuses with respect to the normative processes results in an acceleration of the rate of growth of norms of public and private legal systems. But the multiplication of rules and officials that we associate with the trend toward bureaucratization need not necessarily endanger the rights of the laity if limitations on authority are preserved through the three democratic mechanisms—separation of powers, consent of the governed, and procedural due process.

Third, private legal systems of a democratic type are transformed into undemocratic types under such *exogenous* conditions as the following: (a) if there is a monopolization of power in a given institutional or subinstitutional sphere; or if there is an oligopolization of power in the absence of countervailing private legal systems; (b) if relationships with other private legal systems are principally with those of an undemocratic type of superior economic or political power. Conversely, private legal systems of an undemocratic type are transformed into democratic types under such *exogenous* conditions as the following: (a) if countervailing power in the form of a private legal system develops within a given institutional or subinstitutional sphere to counteract monopolization or oligopolization of power among private legal systems; (b) if relationships with other private legal systems are primarily with those of a democratic type or with those of an undemocratic type of equal or inferior economic or political power.

Fourth, public legal systems of a democratic type are transformed into undemocratic types under such *exogenous* conditions as the following: (a) if the autonomy of private legal systems declines to the point where they cannot challenge the authority of the public legal systems; (b) if there is a monopolization of power among private legal systems in the various institutional or subinstitutional spheres, or if there is an oligopolization of power without the development of countervailing private legal systems; and (c) if most private legal systems are transformed from democratic into undemocratic types.

In the last two hypotheses, with their implicit *ceteris paribus*, we have drastically limited the exogenous conditions of a legal system to relationships with other legal systems in the environment and to the structure of these systems. Obviously other exogenous as well as endogenous factors are operative in the transformation of a legal system from a democratic to an undemocratic type and vice versa.[37]

Conclusion

The traditional view of law as an integral part of the state has tended to obscure the fact that law exists in nonstate contexts as well. Taking as the point of departure the legal concepts of Ehrlich and Weber, we have presented a sociological conception and typology of legal systems that bridges the developing field of the sociology of law with that of formal organization. To illustrate the research potentialities of this approach, we have examined four problem areas suggested by our typology: comparative study of legal systems, interrelationships between public and private legal systems, interrelationships among private legal systems, and the transformation of legal systems.

Inquiry into the processes whereby public and private legal systems are transformed will throw light on the general sociological problem of the conditions under which new norms and organizational structures arise and old norms and organizational structures decline. Of particular significance and promise is a comparative study of the structure and functioning of private legal systems and their interrelationships with private and public legal systems. Although these problem areas in the sociology of law may appear new, Ehrlich, one of the earliest students in this field, indirectly suggested them over four decades ago when he asserted that "the center of gravity of legal development . . . from time immemorial has not lain in the activity of the state but in society itself, and must be sought

37. See, for example, the illuminating analysis by Seymour Martin Lipset, "Some Social Requisites of Democracy: Economic Development and Political Legitimacy," *American Political Science Review*, vol. LIII (1959), pp. 69–106.

there at the present time."[38] In a sense, Ehrlich's perspective combined with the approach outlined in this paper suggests the need for research on the conditions under which political pluralism—as a type of social system, not as a political philosophy—survives or perishes.

---

38. Ehrlich, *op. cit.*, p. 390.

Alfred W. Blumrosen

Legal Process
and Labor Law

Some Observations on the
Relation between Law and Sociology

For many years lawyers and sociologists have discussed the relation between law and sociology. But the development of a routine working relationship between the disciplines has not proceeded apace with the discussion. Projects that stem from this relationship can still be individually identified. Only a few in law or sociology are professionally identified with the relationship. There is no doubt that the theoretical work on the relationship that has taken place in the last few years is a necessary precondition to the development of self-consciously integrated activity. But one suspects that the concept of a routine working relation between law and sociology (and this may mean between law professors and sociology professors) is still limited to the self-chosen initiates, and has not become part of the routine kit of working tools of either profession.

There are undoubtedly many reasons for this situation. We know that the relation between lawyers and sociologists is highly complex.[1] The purpose of this paper is to explore one such reason: a lack of adequate understanding on the part of sociologists of certain aspects of the legal system that are conducive to the development of a viable relation with sociology.

The legal system presents many facets. Some of them are such as to incline most observers to throw up their hands in hopeless withdrawal. But there are elements within the legal system that are conducive to a viable working relation between law and sociology—elements that may lead sociologists to take a more sustained interest in the legal dimensions of the material they are exploring.

My purpose here is to explore these elements of the legal system. To what extent is the legal system prepared to receive and use the results of ongoing sociological research? To what extent may the legal system provide material useful to the sociologist in his continuing study of human behavior? Some sociologists hold an image of the legal system that would yield negative answers to the above questions. I suggest that there is one image of the legal system that has much to offer the sociologist who will work with it. This is the image of a legal system conscious that doctrines represent and reflect policy decisions, that policy decisions require choice among competing values, and that, in making such choices, the social and institutional context is important. Such a legal system recognizes that the doctrines it has evolved are not self-sufficient, but rather are abstractions useful in guiding the decision-maker as he sifts the implications of the case before him to reach the most appropriate decision. This legal system is prepared to put the various agencies of law—legislation, administrative, executive, as well as less formal mechanisms such as mediation and arbitration—to work in resolving problems not capable of adjustment through the conventional judicial process.

---

1. See, particularly, the 1958–1959 *Annual Report of the Russell Sage Foundation* (New York: Russell Sage Foundation, 1959), pp. 9–16.

This image does not represent the whole story of the legal system, nor does it describe fully the behavior of lawmen and their institutions. But there is an element of reality in this image, and it is this element which is important. For it is this facet of the legal system that makes possible a genuine reciprocal relationship between law and sociology. In this relationship the policy choices made by the legal system may be integrated into ongoing sociological research, while the law may take advantage of the detailed knowledge of social institutions developed by sociology.

But it is necessary first to demonstrate the reality of the image of the legal system suggested here. The demonstration will consist of two parts: first, an overview of the general course of American legal history, and then specific examples of the concern of law for value, consequence, and institutional context, to be drawn from the field of labor law.

A Perspective of Legal History

James Willard Hurst, historian of the University of Wisconsin Law School, has described the changing pattern of the legal system in a way that demonstrates how factors other than abstract legal doctrine have come to predominate during this century in the process of judicial decision:[2]

. . . In the first half of the nineteenth century, within the confines of a "judicial" power limited to disposition of particular disputes, the courts did the vast job of fashioning a body of common law for the main affairs of everyday life. They defined the bases of rights in real property; they laid the foundations for the law of business contracts and commercial instruments; they shaped rudimentary doctrine for such fields of new importance as the law of negligence or of the conflict of laws. From the logic and decisions of John Marshall, in the third quarter of the century the judges made good their title to pass on the constitutionality of legislation; and they used

2. J. Willard Hurst, *The Growth of American Law: The Law Makers* (Boston: Little, Brown and Co., 1950), pp. 185–189.

the power to such effect as to make it a material factor in the social balance of power. To 1937 judicial review continued to be a tangible influence on what the legislature did and how it did it, especially in regard to economic regulation. This was nonetheless true, though the effects of judicial review were often misconstrued; its long-range influence was overrated, and what was in practice only delay was sometimes treated as an effectively definitive veto. But, through the drama of judicial review, the courts made the idea of constitutional limitations one of the most powerful elements in our political thinking.

· · · · ·

The interpretation of statutes offered a truly creative job for the judges. But the chances of events long obscured the creative opportunity. The legislature and its works fell far in popular standing in the second quarter of the nineteenth century. But at the same time the newly forming states felt the urgent pressure of practical needs for law to meet their everyday needs and the everyday problems of the people. The response to this pressure afforded the first great manifestation of judicial lawmaking in the United States. Out of this period of policy leadership, the courts learned confidence in their own capacity to decide what was best for the community. For example, in the late nineteenth century, judges were not inclined to look favorably on legislation which, like the married women's property acts, changed doctrine which judges had made the law of the land. There was more involved than a conflict of policy ambitions. Social conservatism brought the full flowering of due process doctrine at the end of the century; the same impetus also inclined the courts, where they were not ready boldly to declare social legislation unconstitutional, to interpret it so restrictively as to narrow its effect.

· · · · ·

. . . This depreciation of the statute book was promoted by the pre-eminence of case-made, judge-made law in the formative first half of the nineteenth century; and this was reinforced, first, by the office-apprentice system of legal education, and then by the spread of the case method in the law schools. Legislation was an intrusion on a symmetrical system of learning properly found only in the Reports. One could to general satisfaction summarily distinguish a cited case if he could brush it aside as merely "turning on the particular statute involved."

. . . . .

But it was in the trend of events that statutory interpretation should form one of the positive contributions of the courts to the making of law. Only the legislature—with its control of the purse, its powers of investigation, and its varied array of benefits and sanctions —could begin to cope with the demands made on government after the 1870's. But experience taught that the best-drawn statute was only the starting point of effective regulation; this was inevitable, out of the limits set by language and men's foresight, as well as by the infinite variety of events and causes. The measure of understanding, sympathy, and vigor with which the executive or the judges implemented a statute decided how far it became a living fact of the community life.

Between about 1880 and 1920 legislation again became, as it once had been, the main growing point of the law in the United States. By 1920 administrative legislation shared this distinction. In either case, after 1880 the leadership in making general policy had passed from the courts; their creative opportunity had become the subordinate, but essential, task of imaginative, firm implementation of legislative policy.

The decisions after 1900 began to reflect a more affirmative and practical, a less negative and literal, approach, in response to the pressure of this shift in the political situation. Tangible witness of the change was in the shifting techniques of interpretation. The canons of construction whose elaboration filled the pages of nineteenth-century treatises began to disappear from judges' opinions. After 1920 it became hard to assemble from the Digest any substantial citations to so familiar a late-nineteenth-century shibboleth as the rule that statutes in derogation of common law must be strictly construed. Before it had explicitly validated the change, in practice the Supreme Court of the United States began to drop the barriers to full use of the history of a statute as light upon its meaning. Where there had been absolutely phrased rules of competency that barred use of hearings, debates, committee reports, there appeared by the 1930's more or less explicit recognition that almost any official source contemporary with the passage of a statute might be used in its interpretation. The effect of such background evidence was to be gauged by its credibility, and not by its compliance with formal rules of competence.

. . . . .

In the law at least, mere technique guarantees no one result; there remains inescapably "the sovereign prerogative of choice." In 1940 as well as in 1890 the interpretation of statutes inevitably demanded that the courts share in making policy. One could still find examples —one was the restrictive interpretation of state statutes which curbed the use of the injunction in labor disputes—where judges hostile or distrustful toward the legislative judgment clearly shaped construction to minimize the effect of a statute. Only the naive could not see that in adroit hands the "history" behind an act might be read in different ways: the new technique of using legislative history in interpretation might widen, rather than narrow, the judge's discretion.

Nonetheless, the new approach lent itself less than the old to manipulation in the interests of the judge's personal values. It was most insistent on a demonstrated basis in fact, for the interpretation given the legislation. And in any case its basic importance was that it showed a shift in the prevailing attitude toward statute law. Late-nineteenth-century judges rationalized their interpretations under abstract canons of construction which had no necessary relation, and required no showing of any specific relation, to the legislation in question. Clearly, there was a drastic change in approach, when courts sought to view an act in terms of its own particular genealogy, and in effect to fashion their principle of construction from the materials of the statute's own environment and origins.

The change perhaps reflected the pragmatism which characterized thought in the United States after the turn into the new century. Certainly it evidenced a shift in the climate of opinion affecting the balance of power. Perhaps the judges merely shared the self-doubt of their generation. Perhaps they yielded more or less consciously to the weight of events which had thrust the initiative in policy on the legislative and executive branches. In any case, in the second quarter of the twentieth century judges plainly lacked the serene self-confidence and assurance of wisdom and rightness with which their predecessors had made a native common law and, firmly and sometimes arrogantly, had explicitly or under guise of interpretation wielded a veto over legislative judgment.

Thus, Hurst's perspective on legal history reflects a gradual widening of the range of materials relevant to the legal decisional process, a widening that, by now, has reached the stage of openly embracing information concerning consequences of alternative decisions and institutional context. Implicit in the first paragraph of Hurst's description of the making of the early common law is the necessity of a system of values that would enable the courts in creating the common law to choose between competing contentions presented to them. The free use of policy considerations in the formative years of our legal system has perhaps been obscured by the judicial techniques of the late nineteenth and early twentieth centuries. But today, overt discussions of policy considerations have regained significance in opinions of the courts, and are accepted as determinants of the scope of legal doctrine. And where policy choice is made the touchstone of the decision, the sociological contribution to the formulation of wise policy may play its overt and important role.

Changing Legal Conceptions Concerning the Organization of Employees

The formative years of the common law in the field of labor relations saw economic policy bulking large in the decisions. In these first labor cases the policies dictated that unions be condemned as criminal conspiracies. Today, different policies have dictated a different status for the American union.[3] But the process by which this status is determined continues to have its roots in the policy choices of the lawmakers.

---

3. More detailed reference to most of the material discussed herein can be found in Alfred W. Blumrosen, "Group Interests in Labor Law," 13 *Rutgers Law Review* 432-484 (1959); "Legal Protection for Critical Job Interests; Union-Management Authority versus Employee Autonomy," 13 *Rutgers Law Review* 631 (1959); "Public Policy Considerations in Labor Arbitration Cases," 14 *Rutgers Law Review* 217 (1960); and "Legal Protection against Exclusion from Union Activities," 22 *Ohio State Law Journal* 21 (1960).

An excellent analysis of many problems in labor law, which would appeal to one not trained in the law, is Charles O. Gregory, *Labor and the Law* (2d rev. ed.; New York: W. W. Norton & Co., 1961).

LABOR UNIONS AS CRIMINAL CONSPIRACIES

At the headwaters of American labor law stands the cord-wainers case[4] tried in the Mayor's Court in Philadelphia. In 1806 the judge charged the jury that it was criminal for workers to band together to raise their wages.

A combination of workmen to raise their wages may be considered in a twofold point of view: one is to benefit themselves. . . . The other is to injure those who do not join their society. The rule of law condemns both.

Recorder Levy described the "law of supply and demand" and said of it,

[These are] the usual means by which . . . prices . . . are regulated. . . . To make an artificial regulation, is not to regard the excellence of the work or the quality of the material, but to fix a positive and arbitrary price, governed by no standard, controlled by no impartial person, but dependent upon the will of the few who are interested; this is the unnatural way of raising the price of goods or work. . . . It is an unnatural, artificial means of raising the price of work beyond its standard, and taking an undue advantage of the public.

There can be no misunderstanding the judge. While the criminal conspiracy doctrine is applied because it is law, it is law because collective action of workers would interfere with the operation of the market, and this is the evil that the criminal law must prevent. Economic policy bulks large in the decision.

But it was not abstract economic policy that led the courts in those formative years to apply the criminal conspiracy doctrine to collective employee action. Rather it was their estimate of the consequences of such concerted action for the behavior of the market that concerned the judges. This was

---

4. *Commonwealth v. Pullis*, Phila. Mayor's Court, John R. Commons and Eugene A. Gilmore, *A Documentary History of American Industrial Society* (Cleveland: A. H. Clark, 1910), vol. 3, pp. 59–248.

made clear by Judge Roberts in his charge to the jury in a criminal case against the Pittsburgh cordwainers.

Confederacies of this kind have a most pernicious effect, as respects the community at large. They restrain trade: they tend to banish many artisans, and to oppress others. It is the interest of the public, and it is the right of every individual, that those who are skilled in any profession, art, or mystery, should be unrestrained in the exercise of it.[5]

One can disagree with the economic policies followed by these judges. But one cannot deny that they were consciously following economic policies.

There is another dimension, one involving political theory, in one of these early cases. In 1836 Judge Edwards sentenced some tailors in New York for criminal conspiracy.[6] To him, collective employee action was un-American.

Associations of this description are of recent origin in this country. Here, where the government is purely paternal, where the people are governed by laws of their own creating; where the legislature proceeds with a watchful regard to the welfare not only of the whole, but of every class of society; where the representatives ever lend a listening ear to the complaints of their constituents, it has not been found necessary or proper to subject any portion of the people to the control of self-created societies. . . . Every American knows or ought to know that he has no better friend than the laws and that he needs no artificial combination for his protection. . . . They are of foreign origin, and I am led to believe are mainly upheld by foreigners. . . .

Self-created societies are unknown to the constitution and laws, and will not be permitted to rear their crest and extend their baneful influence over any portion of the community.

Criticism of this statement was sharp, both as to its facts and as to the political implications of the court's philosophy.

A New York newspaper took issue with the court's discussion of the sources of union support.

---

5. *Commonwealth v. Morrow*, John R. Commons and Eugene A. Gilmore, *A Documentary History of American Industrial Society* (New York: Russell and Russell, 1958), vol. 4, p. 81.

6. *Ibid.* at 315.

Men must shut their eyes to events passing around them if they think it is a few foreigners or only foreigners that compose our Trades' Union. . . . At any rate even if the Union is popular among our workmen from other climes, we have reason to believe it is countenanced and supported by the great majority of our native born.[7]

Here then, is an early criticism that a court misconceived the facts of industrial life.

De Tocqueville, touring America at about the same time, had a different perspective on private associations in this country— one that was to dominate the future of our thinking about associations far more than Judge Edwards' paternalism.

. . . the most democratic country on the face of the earth is that in which men have in our time carried to the highest perfection the art of pursuing in common the object of their common desires, and have applied this new science to the greatest number of purposes. Is this the result of accident? or is there in reality any necessary connection between the principle of association and that of equality? Aristocratic communities always contain, among a multitude of persons who by themselves are powerless, a small number of powerful and wealthy citizens, each of whom can achieve great undertakings singlehanded. . . . If men living in democratic countries had no right and no inclination to associate for political purposes, their independence would be in great jeopardy; but they might long preserve their wealth and their cultivation; whereas if they never acquired the habit of forming associations in ordinary life, civilization itself would be endangered.[8]

Thus, in the formative period the legal system in America had condemned collective employee action on policy grounds in order to protect the free market, which was regulated by "supply and demand" to allow free access to all trades, and (perhaps) to discourage the development of private associations as such. The doctrine that carried this condemnation was that of criminal conspiracy, but the policy elements behind it were clear.

---

7. *Ibid.* at 330.
8. Alexis de Tocqueville, *Democracy in America* (New York: Oxford University Press, 1947), pp. 319–321.

THE DEMISE OF THE CRIMINAL CONSPIRACY DOCTRINE

The decision that wiped away this "law" is the highly technical opinion in *Commonwealth* v. *Hunt*,[9] decided in 1842 by the Supreme Court of Massachusetts. One who sought proof that the lawyer's craft was narrow, that the courts were blind to the broader implications of judicial decision, might think he found it in *Commonwealth* v. *Hunt*.

Chief Justice Shaw of Massachusetts analyzed an indictment against the bootmakers and found that it charged only that a group of men were associating together. This, he stated, was not criminal unless they had done this either for an unlawful end or to achieve a lawful object by unlawful means. The men might be associating to refuse to work where alcoholic beverages were used. Then he examined the objectives charged in the indictment, and found that it alleged an intent to impoverish one Horne, who refused to join the union, by causing his discharge. But this might be merely legitimate competition and did not demonstrate an unlawful objective. The case against the workers was dismissed.

The opinion does not recognize the struggle of workers to achieve self-organization through collective bargaining. Nothing indicates, even remotely, that economic policies lay behind the development of the law of criminal conspiracy as applied to labor organizations.

Aside from the fact that the Massachusetts Supreme Court took a year to deliberate the case, one would not know from reading the opinion that the case involved anything other than a run-of-the-mill problem of the adequacy of a criminal indictment.

But Chief Justice Shaw was not blind to the implications of his decision. In the same month in which he decided the *Hunt* case, Shaw said this in another opinion:

In considering the rights and obligations arising out of particular relations, it is competent for courts of justice to regard considera-

---

9. 45 Mass. (4 Met.) 111 (1842).

tions of policy and general convenience and to draw from them such rules as will, in their practical application, best promote the safety and security of all parties concerned.[10]

On policy matters Shaw was not, by any stretch, pro-worker or anti-capital. The words quoted above are the peroration to the adoption in America of the infamous "fellow servant" rule, which prevents an employee who is injured because of the negligence of another employee from recovering against his employer for the injuries. To overcome the effects of that decision, the nation, state by state, would adopt statutes that did away with it. But this was not to happen for sixty years, and in that time Shaw's policy of protecting industry from its human overhead left losses from industrial accidents on the shoulders of workers and their families.

Walter Nelles, nearly thirty years ago, described Justice Shaw this way:

He was liberal in the sense that another great Tory judge, Lord Mansfield, was liberal; his eyes were wide open to what was going on in the world; he was impatient of narrow legalism, well though he could use it; he wanted law to promote fair dealing in business transactions; he wanted enterprise to prosper; he was sagaciously alert to promote these and other interests which seemed to him to be those of the supposed entity called "society." Holmes wrote of him: "The strength of that great judge lay in accurate appreciation of the requirements of the community whose officer he was. Some, indeed many, English judges could be named who have surpassed him in accurate technical knowledge; but few have lived who were his equals in their understanding of the grounds of public policy to which all laws must ultimately be referred."[11]

What then led Shaw by his technical decision in *Hunt* to overthrow the criminal conspiracy doctrine and make it possible for worker organizations to exist within the law?

Nelles suggests that in the local economic climate, the risk

---

10. *Farwell* v. *Boston & Worcester R.R.*, 45 Mass. (4 Met.) 49, 59 (1842).

11. Walter Nelles' discussion is found in an essay entitled, "Commonwealth v. Hunt," 32 *Columbia Law Review* 1128 (1932).

of effective union organization was small, but enterprise needed worker support to secure passage of protective tariff legislation. This support might have been denied had the case been decided otherwise. The decision, then, served the interests of the expanding business community much as had the decision in the fellow servant case.

THE ERA OF THE LABOR INJUNCTION

Freed from the shackles of the criminal law, labor unions were allowed to exist. But during the next seventy-five years, their activities were hamstrung by judges restraining the civil rather than the criminal aspect of their behavior. Utilizing the injunction, during the last quarter of the nineteenth century, judges imposed serious limits on what unions could do in furthering their organizational objectives. Professor Gregory, of the Law School of the University of Virginia, describes the era this way:

But perhaps the most alarming feature of the labor injunction . . . was the ease with which its use increasingly tempted judges to dispense with any well-founded independent theory of illegality. . . . They came to look at much of organized labor's economic coercive activity as enjoinable in itself, without bothering to find or to state in their opinions that it was also unlawful. This was an unfortunate tendency which fed on itself. It seemed to lead many courts to grant sweeping injunctions on the basis of personal or class dislike of organized labor's economic program instead of in accordance with settled standards of law. A process of this sort lent itself admirably to the use of the illegal purpose doctrine.

. . . many courts asked to issue injunctions unfortunately slipped into the custom of using as standards their own notions of what they believed to be good or bad as a matter of policy. In this way too many judges began to think of labor union activity as something enjoinable in itself. . . . This unwholesome state of affairs, where labor unionists never knew just where they stood under the shadow of a brooding and undefined judicial power, involved an almost certain threat of suppression to most of organized labor's bargaining and organizational program, without benefit of any legislative declaration of policy or, indeed, of any rules of the game that might be called law.[12]

---

12. Gregory, *op. cit.*, 102–103.

The result was that unions looked to the legislatures for protection in their efforts to organize the workers. Some legislatures responded by recognizing the rights of workers to organize, to be free of the hated "yellow-dog contract," and to be protected in their jobs if they organized. But this legislation was then scrutinized for its constitutionality by those same courts whose substantive law was being rejected.

LABOR LEGISLATION INVALIDATED BY THE SUPREME COURT

The Supreme Court twice struck down such legislation. The first decision, in 1908, *Adair* v. *United States*,[13] was written in narrow technical fashion. It made three points that are relevant here:

1. The Court held that a statute prohibiting discharge for engaging in union activities violated the employer's liberty of contract. It disturbed the "equality of right" between worker and employer.

It was the legal right of defendant, Adair—however unwise such a course might have been—to discharge Coppage because of his being a member of a labor organization, as it was the legal right of Coppage, if he saw fit to do so—however unwise such a course on his part might have been—to quit the service in which he was engaged, because the defendant employed some persons who were not members of a labor organization. In all such particulars the employer and the employee have equality of right, and any legislation that disturbs that equality is an arbitrary interference with the liberty of contract which no government can legally justify in a free land.

2. Furthermore, Congress had no power to legislate concerning union activities. Its power to regulate interstate commerce did not include the power to protect employees' rights to organize because there was not a sufficient relation between interstate commerce and the organization of workers.

But what possible legal or logical connection is there between an employee's membership in a labor organization and the carrying

13. 208 U. S. 161 (1908).

on of interstate commerce? Such relation to a labor organization cannot have, in itself and in the eye of the law, any bearing upon commerce with which the employee is connected by his labor and services. Labor associations, we assume, are organized for the general purpose of improving or bettering the conditions and conserving the interests of its members as wage-earners—an object entirely legitimate and to be commended rather than condemned. . . . One who engages in the service of an interstate carrier will, it must be assumed, faithfully perform his duty, whether he be a member or not a member of a labor organization. . . . It is the employee as a man and not as a member of a labor organization who labors in the service of an interstate carrier.

3. The Court refused to assume that Congress was concerned with the pressure for reform or the demand for relief from the harsh common law.

Will it be said that the provision in question had its origin in the apprehension, on the part of Congress, that . . . if it did not insert in the statute some such provision as the one here in question, members of labor organizations would, by illegal or violent measures, interrupt or impair the freedom of commerce among the States? We will not indulge in any such conjectures.

On their face, these three prongs of the *Adair* case seem to verify the worst that can be said of the "legalism" of American law. The equality of freedom of contract protected by the opinion was abstract only, and was deprived of reality by the superior bargaining power of employers. The application of this reasoning served to perpetuate the power of those who had it by preventing the growth of unions strong enough to demand to share that power.

The second point in the opinion was unrealistic. By what warrant could the Supreme Court determine that labor organizations were not relevantly related to interstate commerce, when history had already demonstrated that, particularly in the railroad industry, labor disputes had led to the disruption of commerce? Furthermore, in the same year as this decision, 1908, the same Court, in another case under another statute, declared

that labor union activities were combinations that restrained
interstate commerce.[14]

The third point is equally unrealistic. Why should Congress
not consider the effects of its legislation on the desires and
probable behavior of those being regulated? Why should it not
be concerned lest violence break out along the railroads, in
pursuit of what it conceived to be a proper demand? The Court
was, in effect, telling politicians in Congress that it would
ignore the operation of the political process altogether, in a
manner that reflected the 1836 thinking of Judge Edwards.

The opinion has an air of unreality about it, a refusal to
recognize and accept political and economic facts, an adherence
to doctrine without regard to the realities that underlie the
issues before it. The opinion fails to expound the policy considerations that underlie it, but this does not prove that there
were no such considerations involved.

Adair was not to be the last word on the subject. Some state
courts and legislatures went right ahead in their effort to
protect workers against the superior bargaining power of employers. These lawmakers forced the Supreme Court to disclose
its policy perspective.

LAISSEZ-FAIRE DOCTRINE OF THE COURT

In 1912, four years after the *Adair* decision, the Kansas
Supreme Court passed upon a state statute that prohibited employers from entering into "yellow-dog" contracts whereby employees agreed to refrain from union activities while working for
the employer.[15] It was argued that under the *Adair* decision the
government could no more prohibit contracts not to engage in
union activities than it could prohibit the firing of an employee
for such activity.

But the majority of the Kansas Supreme Court placed their
technical legal training at the service of what they conceived
to be important policy considerations. They believed that the
legislation before them was justified because of the inequality

---

14. *Loewe* v. *Lawlor,* 208 U.S. 274 (1908).
15. *State* v. *George,* 87 Kan. 752 (1912).

of bargaining power between unions and employees. They took note of this inequality in their opinion. They were bound to follow the *Adair* decision, but they were not bound to construe it broadly. Instead, they drew a narrow line around the *Adair* decision, holding that it dealt only with the discharge of workers. Therefore, it did not apply to a statute that prohibited the making of yellow-dog contracts.

Faced with this pressure from Kansas, the Supreme Court finally explained its policy considerations behind the *Adair* case. In *Coppage* v. *Kansas*[16] came the flowering expression of the judicial policy of *laissez faire*. The Court denied, as follows, the legitimacy of the attempt to support labor organizations:

But no attempt is made, or could reasonably be made, to sustain the purpose to strengthen these voluntary organizations, any more than other voluntary associations of persons, as a legitimate object for the exercise of the police power. They are not public institutions, charged by law with public or governmental duties, such as would render the maintenance of their membership a matter of direct concern to the general welfare. If they were, a different question would be presented.

As to the interest of the employed, it is said by the Kansas Supreme Court (87 Kansas, p. 759) to be a matter of common knowledge that "employees, as a rule, are not financially able to be as independent in making contracts for the sale of their labor as are employers in making contracts of purchase thereof." No doubt, wherever the right of private property exists, there must and will be inequalities of fortune; and thus it naturally happens that parties negotiating about a contract are not equally unhampered by circumstances. This applies to all contracts, and not merely to that between employer and employee. Indeed a little reflection will show that wherever the right of private property and the right of free contract coexist, each party when contracting is inevitaby more or less influenced by the question whether he has much property, or little, or none; for the contract is made to the very end that each may gain something that he needs or desires more urgently than that which he proposes to give in exchange. And, since it is self-evident that, unless all things are held in common, some persons must have more property than others, it is from the nature of things impossible to

16. 236 U.S. 1 (1915).

uphold freedom of contract and the right of private property without at the same time recognizing as legitimate those inequalities of fortune that are the necessary result of the exercise of those rights. . . .

Now we can understand the three positions in the *Adair* case. Equality of freedom of contract was an essential bulwark of the constitutionally protected system of private property. The argument of the majority in *Coppage* is succinctly analyzed by Robert Rodes as follows:

In holding that the state cannot forbid the yellow-dog contract, Pitney, speaking for the majority in *Coppage,* restates the whole individualistic philosophy, and the interests it does and does not recognize. It will not be held, he says, that the state has an interest in fostering labor unions, since there is no reasonable relationship between unions and the health, safety, morals, or welfare that have been traditional police concerns of the state. . . . To be sure, the worker may need the job more than the employer needs to hire him, but this situation inheres in the difference between their respective estates, which in turn inheres in our constitutionally protected economic system. If we are to protect a person against the weakness of his bargaining position as such, our object is to level the differences of estate that the Constitution protects when it protects property.[17]

The difficulty with *Adair* was that the Court was unwilling to articulate its policy perspective. When forced to do so in *Coppage,* it responded vigorously, denying that the group interest of the workers provided a justification for legislation that interfered with freedom of contract, because a contrary holding would weaken the economic system to which the Court was committed.

The extreme in denial of legal protection for the collective interest of employees came in the Supreme Court's decision in *Hitchman Coal & Coke Co.* v *Mitchell*[18] in 1917. The Court upheld an injunction against a union attempt to organize employees who had agreed to work under "yellow-dog" contracts.

---

17. Robert Rodes, "Due Process and Social Legislation in the Supreme Court—a Post-Mortem," 33 *Notre Dame Lawyer* 5 (1957).
18. 245 U.S. 229 (1917).

Injunctive relief to protect the yellow-dog contract, if carried to its logical extreme, would have prevented the emergence of the strength of organized labor because it would have allowed employers to use the courts to prevent union organizational campaigns altogether.

THE BEGINNING OF LEGAL RECOGNITION
OF EMPLOYEE RIGHTS

In 1921 the court was asked to extend the *Hitchman* case to prohibit all union organizational campaigns. In the *American Foundries*[19] case the employer sought to enjoin peaceful picketing and persuasion of his employees to strike even though they had not promised to refrain from union activity during their employment. If this argument had been accepted, it would have dealt a deathblow to legal protection for interests of the group, for it would have denied any opportunity to organize employees for collective action. But the argument went too far, and Chief Justice Taft, in what has become a classic labor law opinion, recognized that the union did have sufficient interest in labor-management relations to justify peaceful persuasion of employees.

Is interference of a labor organization by persuasion and appeal to induce a strike against low wages under such circumstances without lawful excuse and malicious? We think not. Labor unions . . . were organized out of the necessities of the situation. A single employee was helpless in dealing with an employer. He was dependent ordinarily on his daily wage for the maintenance of himself and family. If the employer refused to pay him the wages that he thought fair he was nevertheless unable to leave the employ and to resist arbitrary and unfair treatment. *Union was essential to give laborers opportunity to deal on equality with their employer.* They united to exert influence upon him and to leave him in a body in order by this inconvenience to induce him to make better terms with them. They were withholding their labor of economic value to make him pay what they thought it was worth. The right to combine for such a lawful purpose has in many years not been denied by any court. The strike became a lawful instrument in a lawful

19. *American Foundries* v. *Tri-City Council*, 257 U.S. 184 (1921).

economic struggle or competition between employer and employees
as to the share or division between them of the joint product of
labor and capital. To render this combination at all effective, employees must make their combination extend beyond one shop. *It
is helpful to have as many as may be in the same trade in the same
community united, because in the competition between employers
they are bound to be affected by the standard of wages of their
trade in the neighborhood.* Therefore, they may use all lawful propa-
ganda to enlarge their membership and especially among those
whose labor at lower wages will injure their whole guild. [Emphasis
added.]

Here is the beginning of acceptance by the Supreme Court
of the underlying economic realities as justifying collective employee action. In 1921 the Supreme Court accepted what the
Kansas court had said in 1912 about the inequality of bargaining power. But the picketing permitted by the court was narrowly confined. The Court remained concerned with the effect
of its decisions. In another case, decided the same year, the
Court applied the Sherman Anti-Trust Act to prohibit union
action that prevented interstate commerce.[20] It construed narrowly legislation that restricted the power of the court to issue
injunctions against unions for the following reason:

. . . An ordinary controversy in a manufacturing establishment,
said to concern the terms or conditions of employment there, has
been held a sufficient occasion for imposing a general embargo upon
the products of the establishment and a nation-wide blockade of the
channels of interstate commerce against them, carried out by inciting
sympathetic strikes and a secondary boycott against complainant's
customers, to the great and incalculable damage of many innocent
people far remote from any connection with or control over the
original and actual dispute—people constituting, indeed, the general
public upon whom the cost must ultimately fall, and whose vital
interest in unobstructed commerce constituted the prime and para-
mount concern of Congress in enacting the antitrust laws. . . .

The opinions in these cases are a far cry from the dry technicalities of the *Adair* case. The new adjustment of relations

20. *Duplex Co.* v. *Deering,* 254 U.S. 433 (1921).

between unions and employers presaged in the *American Foundries* case was finally crystallized by the highly influential New York Court of Appeals in 1927.[21] The court refused to enjoin union efforts to induce workers to breach a yellow-dog contract and to organize. Thus the *Hitchman* principle was rejected. The court reasoned:

The purpose of a labor union to improve the conditions under which its members do their work; to increase their wages; to assist them in other ways, may justify what would otherwise be a wrong. So would an effort to increase its numbers and to unionize an entire trade or business. It may be as interested in the wages of those not members, or in the conditions under which they work, as in its own members because of the influence of one upon the other. All engaged in a trade are affected by the prevailing rate of wages. All, by the principle of collective bargaining. Economic organization today is not based on the single shop. Unions believe that wages may be increased, collective bargaining maintained only if union conditions prevail, not in some single factory, but generally. That they may prevail, it may call a strike and picket the premises of an employer with the intent of inducing him to employ only union labor.

LABOR LEGISLATION ADOPTED AND ACCEPTED

Ultimately, a genuine problem of political theory emerged from the struggle of labor organization against the policies of the courts. What institution held the power to make ultimate policy concerning the organization of the economic system? The Court had assumed, in *Adair* and *Coppage*, that the power lay with it, and had proceeded to destroy or cripple legislative efforts to alter the policies that they had set. Thus the drive of organized labor for freedom to expand organization became entwined with the political principle of legislative supremacy in economic matters.

The last Republican Congress before Roosevelt asserted its dominance in the area. By stripping the federal courts of most of their power to issue injunctions in labor disputes in the Norris-

---

21. *Exchange Bakery & Restaurant* v. *Rifkin*, 245 N.Y. 260, 157 N.E. 130 (1927).

LaGuardia Act[22] Congress defined the public policy of the United States in no uncertain terms.

> Whereas under prevailing economic conditions, developed with the aid of governmental authority for owners of property to organize in the corporate and other forms of ownership association, the individual unorganized worker is commonly helpless to exercise actual liberty of contract and to protect his freedom of labor, and there to obtain acceptable terms and conditions of employment, wherefore, though he should be free to decline to associate with his fellows, it is necessary that he have full freedom of association, self-organization, and designation of representatives of his own choosing, to negotiate the terms and conditions of his employment, and that he shall be free from the interference, restraint, or coercion of employers of labor, or their agents, in the designation of such representatives or in self-organization or in other concerted activities for the purpose of collective bargaining or other mutual aid or protection; therefore the following definitions of, and limitations upon, the jurisdiction and authority of the courts of the United States are hereby enacted.

The retreat of the judiciary from the foreground of policy-making in labor law, which began in 1932, was turned into a route in 1935. The Wagner Act[23] not only gave explicit legal protection to the rights of employees defined in the Norris-LaGuardia Act, but it entrusted the implementation of these rights to a newly created administrative agency. The effect of this congressional decision was to strip state and federal courts of most of their jurisdiction over labor relations matters, except as they sat in review of administrative decision. The Wagner Act recognized the legality of employee organization and created the conditions that would allow unions to prosper by prohibiting employer conduct inconsistent with the growth of the organization. Congress recognized and protected the privileges and the powers of the group to inflict economic harm and to bargain for employees. The Supreme Court upheld the legislation against a claim that such a law exceeded the constitutional power of Congress.

---

22. 47 Stat. 70 (1932), 29 U.S.C. § 101 *et seq.* (1952).
23. 49 Stat. 449, 29 U.S.C. § 151.

In meeting the constitutional issues in the *Jones and Laughlin* case[24] in 1937, Chief Justice Hughes dealt with the argument presented some thirty years earlier by Justice Harlan that the activities of a labor organization did not sufficiently bear on interstate commerce to justify congressional regulation. To counter this point, Justice Hughes said,

> Experience has abundantly demonstrated that the recognition of the right of employees to self-organization and to have representatives of their own choosing for the purpose of collective bargaining is often an essential condition of industrial peace. Refusal to confer and negotiate has been one of the most prolific causes of strife. This is such an outstanding fact in the history of labor disturbances that it is a proper subject of judicial notice and requires no citation of instances.

This risk of paralysis of the processes of production justified congressional regulation of labor-management relations. What Chief Justice Hughes relied upon in determining the constitutional question of the scope of congressional power was the fact that employees demanded recognition for their organizations and would take strenuous action if recognition was not forthcoming, a factor which the *Adair* case had refused to recognize.

Congress and the Court had drawn diametrically opposite conclusions concerning the relationship between the public interest in continued production and the interest of employees in collective action. The Court had considered them inconsistent and limited employees accordingly, under the Constitution and under the Sherman Act. Congress considered them as complementing each other and therefore protected employee rights in the Norris-LaGuardia and Wagner Acts. The Sherman Act thesis of the Court and the Norris-LaGuardia-Wagner Act thesis of Congress could not long coexist in the same legal system. Under standard doctrines of construction of laws passed in sequence, the later expression of legislative policy had to govern.

And this is the result, although it is not too satisfactorily rationalized by the Supreme Court. Where union activity is pro-

---

24. *Labor Board* v. *Jones and Laughlin,* 301 U.S. 1 (1937).

tected from injunction by the Norris-LaGuardia Act, it is not a violation of the Sherman Act.[25] Thus the Court deferred to the congressional policy of protecting the interest of employees by promoting their organizational rights.

LEGAL AWARENESS OF STRUCTURE
AND FUNCTIONS OF UNIONS

As unions grew and flourished under legislation of the 1930's their structure and function changed from that of the previous era. The Court has recognized this development. The characteristics of the union as spokesman for the collective interest of employees were eloquently described by Justice Murphy in *United States* v. *White*[26] in 1944. At issue was the question whether a union official could refuse to produce the union's books on the grounds of self-incrimination. This depended upon whether the union was so far identified with the members as to justify extension of the personal privilege, or whether it was more of a separate unit, along the lines of the corporate entity, which was not entitled to the privilege. Justice Murphy concluded that the privilege was not available.

Structurally and functionally, a labor union is an institution which involves more than the private or personal interests of its members. It represents organized, institutional activity as contrasted with wholly individual activity. This difference is as well defined as that existing between individual members of the union. The union's existence in fact, and for some purposes in law, is as perpetual as that of any corporation, not being dependent upon the life of any member. It normally operates under its own constitution, rules and by-laws which, in controversies between member and union, are often enforced by the courts. The union engages in a multitude of business and other official concerted activities, none of which can be said to be the private undertakings of the members. Duly elected union officers have no authority to do or sanction anything other than that which the union may lawfully do; nor have they authority to act for the members in matters affecting only the individual rights of such members. The union owns separate real and personal property,

---

25. *United States* v. *Hutchinson*, 312 U.S. 219 (1941).
26. 322 U.S. 694 (1944).

even though the title may nominally be in the names of its members or trustees. The official union books and records are distinct from the personal books and records of the individuals, in the same manner as the union treasury exists apart from the private and personal funds of the members.

Furthermore, the Supreme Court has shown awareness of labor relations problems. In *Ford Motor Co.* v. *Huffman*,[27] in 1953, the Court noted the functional needs of the union in negotiating collective bargaining agreements with employers.

Any authority to negotiate derives its principal strength from a delegation to the negotiators of a discretion to make such concessions and accept such advantages as, in the light of all relevant considerations, they believe will best serve the interests of the parties represented. A major responsibility of negotiators is to weigh the relative advantages and disadvantages of differing proposals. . . . The bargaining representative, whoever it may be, is responsible to, and owes complete loyalty to, the interests of all whom it represents. . . . Inevitably differences arise in the manner and degree to which the terms of any negotiated agreement affect individual employees and classes of employees. . . . The complete satisfaction of all who are represented is hardly to be expected. . . .
Compromises on a temporary basis, with a view to long-range advantages, are natural incidents of negotiation. Differences in wages, hours and conditions of employment reflect countless variables. Seniority rules governing promotions, transfers, layoffs and similar matters may, in the first instance, revolve around length of competent service. Variations acceptable in the discretion of bargaining representatives, however, may well include differences based upon such matters as the unit within which seniority is to be computed, the privileges to which it shall relate, the nature of the work, the time at which it is done, the fitness, ability or age of the employees, their family responsibilities, injuries received in course of service, and time or labor devoted to related public service, whether civil or military, voluntary or involuntary. . . .
The National Labor Relations Act, as amended, gives a bargaining representative not only wide responsibility but authority to meet that responsibility.

27. 345 U.S. 330 (1953).

Congress legislated extensively concerning permissible scope
of union activities in the Taft-Hartley Act of 1947. The function
of the courts since then has largely been one of interpretation
of this legislation, which is administered primarily by an administrative agency. The attitude of the Supreme Court toward this
administrative tribunal, the National Labor Relations Board,
will be discussed shortly. It is important to note here that the
Court has made extensive use of legislative history in its post
Taft-Hartley Act cases, and has been attuned to the facets of
the legislative process that give rise to the legislation. One
of the clearest illustrations of this judicial awareness of the
facts of legislative life is the *Carpenters* case.[28] In admonishing
the NLRB against a construction of the Taft-Hartley Act that
would mechanically invalidate all "hot cargo" clauses, Justice
Frankfurter wrote:

It is relevant to recall that the Taft-Hartley Act was, to a marked
degree, the result of conflict and compromise between strong contending forces and deeply held views on the role of organized labor
in the free economic life of the Nation and the appropriate balance
to be struck between the uncontrolled power of management and
labor to further their respective interests. This is relevant in that it
counsels wariness in finding by construction a broad policy against
secondary boycotts as such when, from the words of the statute itself, it is clear that those interested in just such a condemnation
were unable to secure its embodiment in enacted law. The problem
raised by these cases affords a striking illustration of the importance
of the truism that it is the business of Congress to declare policy and
not this Court's. The judicial function is confined to applying what
Congress has enacted after ascertaining what it is that Congress has
enacted. But such ascertainment, that is, construing legislation, is
nothing like a mechanical endeavor. It could not be accomplished
by the subtlest of modern "brain" machines. Because of the infirmities
of language and the limited scope of science in legislative drafting,
inevitably there enters into the construction of statutes the play of
judicial judgment within the limits of the relevant legislative materials.

---

28. *Local 1976, Carpenters* v. *N.L.R.B.*, 357 U.S. 93 (1958).

THE MERGING OF UNION AND MANAGEMENT INTERESTS

One objective of the labor policy adopted in 1935 was to create a power unit in the union strong enough to counterbalance the power of the corporation over the employment relation. But once this relationship had developed, the underlying conditions tended to force these conflicting power units, union and employer, into ever broader areas of agreement. They found that, by acting together, they could accomplish mutually shared objectives at the expense of third parties. Law regulating such concerted action between union and employer is only beginning to unfold in this decade. For our purposes, the important point is that one of the first institutions to recognize the problems arising from such combined activities was the Supreme Court. The *Allen Bradley* case[29] in 1945 involved a union that, with a group of employers, had imposed a monopoly on the electrical industry in New York City. The union claimed immunity from the antitrust laws. The Supreme Court concluded that a union acting in concert with business was not entitled to immunity.

. . . we have two declared congressional policies which it is our responsibility to try to reconcile. The one seeks to preserve a competitive business economy; the other to preserve the rights of labor to organize to better its conditions through collective bargaining. We must determine here how far Congress intended activities under one of these policies to neutralize the results envisioned by the other. . . .

. . . . .

We know that Congress feared the concentrated power of business organizations to dominate markets and prices. It intended to outlaw business monopolies. A business monopoly is no less such because a union participates, and such participation is a violation of the [Sherman] Act.

---

29. *Allen Bradley Co.* v. *Electrical Workers Union*, 325 U.S. 797 (1945).

Thus the Supreme Court recognized the emerging phenomenon of union-management agreement and preserved the antitrust laws applicability toward them. This phenomenon of union-management agreement, which poses new and difficult problems for legal regulation, has not, as of 1961, been generally recognized because of a stereotype of union-management conflict. The Supreme Court in *Allen Bradley* showed that it was carefully attuned to changes in union-management relations that were reflected in cases brought before it.

Similarly, the Court has invalidated union-management agreements to discriminate against members of racial and other minority groups. The Court has held that employers may not take advantage of discriminatory agreements negotiated with unions, because the union may not, consistently with its duty of fair representation, enter into such an agreement.[30] The Court has subjected both union and employer to the duty of treating men fairly without regard to race under the regime of collective bargaining.

Conflicting Interests in Labor Law

Thus far we have examined the way in which law came to recognize and protect the labor union. We found that courts sometimes realized that their decisions were rooted in choices among values and that they occasionally showed acute awareness of the economic environment and institutional context in which they acted. Both of these conclusions are of considerable consequence to the sociologist who considers working with the law. For the values articulated and used by the legal system may be used for his own research purposes while his studies of institutional behavior may be useful in the unfolding of legal developments.

In this section we will examine another aspect of the legal system that might be of interest to sociologists: the manner in which law adjusts conflicting claims. Such adjustments take place

---

30. *Steele* v. *Louisville & Nashville R.R.*, 323 U.S. 192 (1944).

at many levels. One level we may roughly identify as involving the isolation and identification of the values to be applied in resolving the case: the level of articulation of legal policies.

Since Dean Roscoe Pound, the analysis of legal problems in terms of individual and social interests has become common. Dean Pound has described his system in the following manner:

> . . . we must start today from a theory of interests, that is, of the claims or demands or desires which human beings, either individually or in groups or associations or relations, seek to satisfy, of which, therefore, the adjustment of relations and ordering of conduct through the force of politically organized society must take account. . . . individual interests are claims or demands or desires involved immediately in the individual life and asserted in title of that life. . . . Social interests are claims or demands or desires involved in social life in civilized society and asserted in title of that life. It is not uncommon to treat them as the claims of the whole social group as such.[31]

Professor Cowan has recently suggested a further development of the interest analysis: the concept of group interests.

> Group interests are neither wholly individual nor wholly social. To be sure, a system of law heavily weighted in favor of individual interests is apt to treat all groups which demand recognition as though they were individuals. This was the way the nineteenth century treated associations. Corporations were individuals; unincorporated associations were merely aggregates of individuals. . . .
>
> . . . . .
>
> Groups make demands for themselves and resist the demands of individuals, other groups and the whole of society. To this extent they are analogous to legal individuals which act in the same way. . . . Their claims are collective; the members of the union, associa-

---

31. Roscoe Pound, "A Survey of Social Interests," 57 *Harvard Law Review* 1 (1943). For a detailed development of his system, see Roscoe Pound, *Jurisprudence* (St. Paul, Minn.: West Publishing Co., 1959), vol. III; Roscoe Pound, *Social Control through Law* (New Haven: Yale University Press, 1942); Julius Stone, *The Province and Function of Law* (Sydney, Associated General Publications Pty. Ltd., 1946), chaps. XX, XXI, XXII; Edwin L. Patterson, *Jurisprudence: Men and Ideas of the Law* (Brooklyn: Foundation Press, 1953), chap. 18.

tion, whatnot, make the demands in a collective capacity. To this extent the interests are analogous to those of the whole society, in other words, to social interests.[32]

These interests are not created by law, according to Pound. They are recognized by it.

Interests in this sense would exist even if there were no legal order and no body of authoritative guides to conduct or decision. Claims of human beings to have things and do things have existed wherever a number of human beings have come into contact. . . . Conflicts or competition between interests arise because of the competition of individuals with each other, the competition of groups or associations or societies of men with each other, and the competition of individuals with such groups or associations or societies in the endeavor to satisfy human claims and wants and desires.[33]

The development traced in the preceding section may be understood as culminating in the recognition by law of the group interest of employees acting in their collective capacity. Having recognized the group interest of employees, the legal system now had to adjust its demands in light of the claims of other recognized interests. This accommodation, on a policy level, can best be examined by using the framework of group, social, and individual interests.[34]

GROUP INTERESTS LIMITED BY THE SOCIAL INTEREST IN SECURITY OF POLITICAL INSTITUTIONS

In 1947 Congress was concerned lest Communists capture or retain control of the union movement. It therefore imposed a requirement that union officials sign a non-Communist oath before the National Labor Relations Board would protect the union against employer unfair labor practices. This was a limitation on the liberty of persons to seek union office and a

32. Thomas A. Cowan, "Group Interests," 44 *Virginia Law Review* 331 (1958). See "Symposium on Group Interests and the Law," 13 *Rutgers Law Review* 421 (1959).

33. Pound, *Jurisprudence*, vol. III, p. 17 (1959).

34. See Alfred W. Blumrosen, "Group Interests in Labor Law," 13 *Rutgers Law Review* 432 (1959).

limitation of the freedom of the employees to choose those who were to be spokesmen for the group interest. The limitation on the group interest was justified by the Supreme Court as a proper regulation of commerce against the evil of the "political strike" likely to be called by Communists, "when the dictates of political policy required such action."[35] The word "political" here must be taken, according to Justice Jackson, as connoting support for policy objectives of the Soviet Union. Thus the underlying justification for the limitation on the group interest lay in the social interest in maintenance of political institutions.

However, as Justice Jackson suggested in his concurring opinion, the task of balancing liberty and authority (undertaken in this instance in favor of authority) is never completed "because new conditions today upset the equilibriums of yesterday." And, since 1947, the scope and significance of the non-Communist oath provisions of the statute have been steadily limited in order to protect the group interests of employees.

The Court held in 1954 that although a union had refused to file the non-Communist affidavit, it was entitled to picket for recognition when it represented a majority of employees.[36] Although the union could not utilize the NLRB certification procedures, it could still apply economic pressure.

The Court in 1956 required the NLRB to process cases brought by unions whose officers filed *false* petitions.[37] The *only* sanction for such action was the criminal prosecution. The underlying reason for the course of decisions limiting the effect of the filing requirements was stated.

. . . [T]he rule written into § 9(h) is for the protection of unions as well as for the detection of Communists. It is not fair to read it only against the background of a case where the members knew their officer was a Communist. We are dealing with a requirement equally applicable to all unions, whether the members are innocent of such knowledge or guilty. . . . [W]e cannot find an additional sanction

---

35. *Communications Ass'n* v. *Douds*, 339 U.S. 382 (1950).
36. *Mine Workers* v. *Arkansas Flooring Co.*, 351 U.S. 62 (1956).
37. *Leedom* v. *International Union*, 352 U.S. 145 (1959).

which in practical effect would run against the members of the union, not their guilty officers.

With this set of premises, the Court held that the NLRB could not examine into the truth of the loyalty affidavit, and thus could not penalize the group of employees for a criminal act of a union official.

Thus, on the constitutional level, the social interest in the maintenance of political institutions prevailed, but the group interests of employees, which were potentially adversely affected by the decision, did receive protection by the same Court on the level of statutory construction. This course of decision sapped the statute of potential for interfering with the group interest of employees, and left it as limiting only individual wrongdoing.

Finally, in 1959, Congress confirmed the line of Supreme Court decisions by repealing the non-Communist oath requirement. The NLRB was now free to protect employee rights. Congressional concern for the security of political institutions took the new form of a direct prohibition on union officeholding by members of the Communist party.[38] Thus, Congress recognized the point made by the Court in 1956, that the employees should not be penalized because of the activities of union officers deemed to be inimical to the national security.

GROUP INTERESTS LIMITED BY THE SOCIAL INTEREST
IN PEACE AND ORDER

The elementary obligation of government to provide for the physical security of persons and property was clearly established as a limitation on the assertion of group interests in the *Fansteel* case in 1939.[39] There, a group of employees resisted serious employer anti-union practices (and thus themselves asserted a social interest, as well as the interest of the group in its own survival) by staging a sitdown strike. They resisted law-enforcement officers attempting to execute an injunction directing their

---

38. *The Labor Management Reporting and Disclosure Act of 1959*, 73 Stat. 519.

39. *Labor Board* v. *Fansteel Metallurgical Corp.*, 306 U.S. 240 (1939).

removal. Normally, employees striking against an employer
unfair labor practice have a right to reinstatement. The Supreme
Court, however, held that these men were not entitled to
reinstatement. Their action

. . . was a high-handed proceeding without shadow of legal
right. . . .

Here the strike was illegal in its inception and prosecution. As
the Board found, it was initiated by the decision of the Union committee "to take over and hold two of the respondent's 'key' buildings."
. . . This was not the exercise of "the right to strike" to which the
Act referred. It was not a mere quitting of work and statement of
grievances in the exercise of pressure recognized as lawful. It was
illegal seizure of the buildings in order to prevent their use by the
employer in a lawful manner and thus by acts of force and violence
to compel the employer to submit.

Similarly, violence on the picket line has been subject to
restraint by state authorities, despite doctrines that limit the
power of the state to regulate union activity both on the constitutional level and under the Taft-Hartley Act.[40] Even the
Norris-LaGuardia Act permits temporary restraining orders in
cases of violence. Mass picketing seems per se to be enjoinable
even though no violence is involved because of the risk of violence.[41] As indicating the strength of this policy, it should be
noted that a union striking for a perfectly legitimate object can
be shorn of the privilege of engaging in any picketing whatever,
if its picketing has engendered an "aura of violence" which has
the judicially determined consequence of making persons fear
rather than respect the subsequent picket lines.[42]

GROUP INTERESTS LIMITED
BY INDIVIDUAL INTERESTS

The group interests of employees as asserted through the

---

40. *Youngdahl* v. *Rainfair, Inc.,* 355 U.S. 131 (1957); *Auto Workers*
v. *Wisconsin Board,* 351 U.S. 266 (1956).

41. *Westinghouse Electric Corp.* v. *United Electrical Workers,* 139 N.J.
Eq. 97, 49 A.2d 896 (E. & A. 1946).

42. *Drivers' Union* v. *Medowmoor Co.,* 312 U.S. 287 (1941).

union may impinge on individual interests as well as social and other group interests.

The basic adjustment of these interests was made in *J. I. Case Co.* v. *Labor Board* (1944),[43] holding that the terms of the collective bargaining agreement override individual employment contracts, even those more favorable to the employee.

Individual contracts, no matter what the circumstances that justify their execution or what their terms, may not be availed of to defeat or delay the procedures prescribed in the National Labor Relations Act looking to collective bargaining, nor to exclude the contracting employee from a duly ascertained bargaining unit; nor may they be used to forestall bargaining or to limit or condition the terms of the collective argeement. . . .

. . . . .

But it is urged that some employees may lose by the collective agreement, that an individual workman may sometimes have, or be capable of getting, better terms than those obtainable by the group and that his freedom of contract must be respected on that account. . . . [W]e find the mere possibility that such agreements might be made no ground for holding generally that individual contracts may survive or surmount collective ones. . . . The workman is free, if he values his own bargaining position more than that of the group, to vote against representation; but the majority rules, and if it collectivizes the employment bargain, individual advantages or favors will generally in practice go in as a contribution to the collective result. We cannot exempt individual contracts generally from the operation of collective ones because some may be more individually advantageous.

The consequences of this legal relation between union and employee are many. The employee is bound by union decisions, but the union has a corresponding fiduciary duty of fair representation, both in negotiating contracts and in processing grievances.

In the case of *Steele* v. *Louisville & Nashville Railroad Co.,* (1944),[44] the Court wrote:

---

43. 321 U.S. 332 (1944).
44. 323 U.S. 192 (1944).

So long as a labor union assumes to act as the statutory representative of a craft, it cannot rightly refuse to perform the duty, which is inseparable from the power of representation conferred upon it, to represent the entire membership of the craft. While the statute does not deny to such a bargaining labor organization the right to determine eligibility to its membership, it does require the union, in collective bargaining and in making contracts with the carrier, to represent nonunion or minority union members of the craft without hostile discrimination, fairly, impartially, and in good faith.

The other side of this legal coin is the rule of *Ford Motor Co.* v. *Huffman,* noted earlier, that a union has a range of discretion sufficient to meet its needs for freedom in negotiating with the employer. The line between the *Steele* principle and the *Huffman* principle is a difficult one to draw, and poses one of the most difficult contemporary problems in labor law. One of the major factors in drawing this line may be the functional needs of the labor union for freedom in negotiating with the employer.

The Supreme Court has stated that the union must act fairly in processing the grievances of individual workers under collective bargaining agreements, but the law has not crystalized the elements of fair conduct. There are at least three discernible views on the extent to which an individual interest may limit union action in the collective interest. Archibald Cox takes the position that the union may not act in bad faith.[45] If the union acts unreasonably and for a wrong motive, in refusing to process an employee's grievance, it may be subject to liability. But beyond that, the union has freedom to engage in a process of adjustment of conflicting individual and subgroup claims. He characterizes the union as a resolver of these claims.

When the interests of several groups conflict, or future needs run contrary to present desires, or when the individual's claim endangers group interests, the union's function is to resolve the competition by reaching an accommodation or striking a balance. The process is political. It involves a melange of power, numerical strength, mutual aid, reason, prejudice, and emotion. . . .

45. Archibald Cox, "Rights under a Labor Agreement," 69 *Harvard Law Review* 601 (1956).

At the other extreme is the view of Arthur Lenhoff, who would give the employees some opportunity to process every claim that they had against the employer based on an alleged violation of the labor agreement, if the union refused to act.[46] His position is based on a philosophy protecting the individual claim against that of the group.

Between these positions is my view that an accommodation between the freedom of the union and the right of the individual can be reached by allowing the individual to compel the union to process *meritorious* grievances concerning *critical* job interests through the arbitration channels under the contract.[47] This gives some protection to the most important employee claims, but leaves much to the adjustment process within the union, and affords considerable freedom for adjustment between union and employer on the basis of overall policy considerations.

As the various jurisdictions adopt different views on this question, it may be possible for the sociologist to conduct studies to determine what effect, if any, the different legal requirements may have on the relation between individual employee, union, and employer. Information concerning this matter may be of utmost consequence to the courts when they meet this problem, because they are concerned with giving individual freedom without "unduly" affecting the collective bargaining rights of the union.[48] Studies of the effect of these various legal views on union bargaining behavior may be important in determining which will prevail.

---

46. Arthur Lenhoff, "The Effect of Labor Arbitration Clauses Upon the Individual," 9 *Arbitration Journal* (new series) 3 (1954). See also the 1954 Report of Proceedings, Section on Labor Relations Laws, American Bar Association, 50 *Northwestern University Law Review* 143 (1955).

47. Alfred W. Blumrosen, "Legal Protection for Critical Job Interests, Union-Management Authority versus Employee Autonomy," 13 *Rutgers Law Review* 631 (1959).

48. See Kurt Hanslowe, "Individual Rights in Collective Labor Relations," 45 *Cornell Law Quarterly* 25 (1959).

Some Implications for the Relationship between Law and Sociology

The discussion to this point suggests that the legal system is receptive to information regarding value and fact. Courts are aware that their decisions embody policy choices made when they are called upon to adjust conflicting values and interests. In making these decisions the courts seek an understanding of the characteristics and needs of the institutions being regulated adequate to the task of wise decision-making. The awareness of the importance of such understanding may lead them to defer to decisions made by those with greater familiarity with the institutions subject to regulation.

This pattern of thinking about legal problems is, of course, not confined to the courts. Lawyers trained to think in this mold fill many of the decision-making posts in the legal system as administrators or legislators. Furthermore, the nonlawyer in such capacity, by force of circumstances, must consider value choices and institutional consequences of his decisions. Thus our observations concerning judicial behavior hold, with differences depending on the role, for other participants in the decision-making process of the legal system. The receptivity of law to information about fact and value suggests general areas of law-sociology cooperation.

FROM LAW TO SOCIOLOGY: A SYSTEM OF VALUES

The sociologist may view the law as reflecting the value choices made in a particular context by an important institution of the society. This perspective may be useful to him because sociology, as a study, does not purport to make value judgments. It is within the range of his professional competence for the sociologist to investigate those values held by others. Thus the sociologist may wish to draw upon the legal system for evidence of those value choices which have been made. He may investigate the consequences of these choices to determine, for example, (a) the relation between the choice made by the legal system and the institution being studied; (b) the extent to which the behavior under study complies with the legal requirements; (c) the process of formulation and transmission of values; and (d) the probable consequences, in light of knowledge of institutional structure and function, of alternative choices that might be made by the legal system.

FROM SOCIOLOGY TO LAW:
ASSISTANCE IN REACHING WISE DECISIONS

What has gone before should not be taken as a defense of the legal system. Not all judges are aware of, or capable of using, policy and institutional analysis in making particular factual choices; not all legislators respond to the needs of public policy; and not all lawyers are conscious of the breadth of the role of counsellor. In fact, the dominant motivation that leads me to relate law and sociology is the desire for tools that will improve the quality of the legal system. And these tools sociology has, albeit they have not yet been extensively used. For sociological examination of human behavior, in light of the problems posed by the legal system, can yield information that would be of inestimable value in making legal choices.

In a simpler age, judges may have carried in their life experience sufficient material to deal adequately with the problems presented by the cases that came before them. The material in the preceding section indicates that this is no longer true. A judge faced with a request that a Negro be admitted to participation in union activities may have no personal experiences that bear on the consequence of his issuing an order one way or another in the case. If he refers to works such as Greer's *Last Man In*,[49] he can develop some conception of the possible consequences of admission of minority groups to union activities and hence is in a better position to make a judgment in the case before him.

Similarly, in an action to enforce an individual employment

49. New York: The Free Press, 1959.

contract, the judge may have no personal familiarity with the institutions that have developed concerning employment in the industry involved. Recourse to a work such as Vollmer's *Employee Rights in the Employment Relation*[50] may broaden his understanding of the institutional behavior he is called upon to regulate leading to a decision that is the wiser for having been made on the basis of fuller knowledge. We have already suggested that legal problems concerning the role of the individual in the collective bargaining context could be immeasurably illuminated by studies that indicated the effect of protecting the individual worker's expectations in either the negotiation or the administration of the collective contract. The issue here is the extent to which the law should protect the individual in the collective context. One of the factors that will shape the resolution of this issue is the effect of individual protection on the relations between the parties involved in the collective bargaining process.

THE LEGAL DIMENSION OF SOCIOLOGICAL PROBLEMS

The relationship suggested here is close to that identified by Selznick as Stage II in the relationship between law and sociology.[51] He says:

In sociology, the roughly defined area we call "social organization" remains a challenging frontier. In this field we attempt to identify the essential characteristics of different types of society, to locate the key human relationships that give a social order its distinctive qualities, to discover how major groups interact and what stable arrangements result. . . .

. . . . .

From the legal side, the important problems also suggest an emphasis on studies of social organization. . . . Thus an assessment of demands upon the legal system depends on what is going on within the major groups and in the relations among them. Whether modern

---

50. Berkeley, Calif.: University of California Press, 1960.
51. Philip Selznick, "The Sociology of Law," in Robert K. Merton, Leonard Broom, Leonard S. Cottrell, Jr., eds., *Sociology Today* (New York: Basic Books, Inc., 1959), pp. 118–124.

economic institutions can autonomously safeguard their members
against arbitrary treatment and undue loss of liberty depends on the
nature of participation and the dynamics of internal control. The
sociological answer to this question inevitably affects the role of the
courts. The potential achievements and vulnerabilities of both legal
and nonlegal institutions are a proper and even urgent subject for
sociological inquiry.

Selznick suggests that "sociology can contribute most to
law by tending its own garden." I would only suggest that
the sociologist may wish to define the boundaries of his garden by reference to the interest that the legal system has in
its fruits. Certain aspects of any problem under study might
disclose matters concerning organizational or institutional facts
or values that could be utilized in the process of legal decision
that we have examined. Sociologists may profitably decide to
study what we may call the "legal dimensions" of the activity
they are investigating, as well as those other characteristics
which they have chosen to examine.

But how is the sociologist to identify the legal dimensions
of such problems? He may seek this information by asking a
member of a law faculty who shares concern for value, policy,
and consequence, and who is interested in the legal problems
of the area being studied. This information would, in all likelihood, be forthcoming with a minimum of interpersonal difficulty.
It is not necessary to repeat the agonizing struggles of others to
achieve deep understandings between law professors and sociologists in order for the sociologist to elicit the relevant insights.
The sociologist needs the lawman to provide only enough
information about the legal system so that the sociologist can
identify the legal dimensions of his problem. Exit the lawman,
who will re-enter later to use the sociologist's results in the
nomal processes of legal decision.[52]

---

52. How such information will be filtered into the legal system is a
subject itself worthy of sociological investigation. One vehicle is the law
review. In "Legal Protection against Exclusion from Union Activities," 22
Ohio State Law Journal 21 (1961), I have made use of Scott Greer's
Last Man In in connection with a legal analysis of the problem of union
exclusionary practices.

The results of sociological inquiry that includes a study of the legal dimension would provide a fund of knowledge about human behavior and values, which apart from its possible contribution to sociological theory, would be of use to law because it was developed with those questions in mind which the legal system is likely to ask. This aspect of the relation between law and sociology seems likely to aid in the fashioning of wise legal decisions.

Index

227